The Dear Betty Chronicles

The Dear Betty Chronicles

A Memoir of 40 years in
Public Relations

Morris B. Rotman

This book was printed in the United States of America.

To order additional copies of this book, contact:
Xlibris Corporation
1-888-795-4274
www.Xlibris.com
Orders@Xlibris.com
15022-ROTM

Cover Design: Gary Wexler
Drummer Cartoon: Gloria Stein

DEDICATION

To my gang of four—Sylvia, Betty, Jesse and Richard

In Memoriam: To My Dear Sister Ricky 9/24/02

Forward

"Opportunities in Public Relations Careers"* by Robert W. Galvin, former Chairman of the Executive Committee, Motorola Inc.

(*Reprinted with permission)

Many people without training in the field consider themselves somewhat expert in public relations and advertising. When you stop to think of it, that is not totally irrational—after all, each of us is the public.

We are the target of the effort of those who seek to inform and shape public opinion. We know what we like and what we don't like. And we at least indirectly develop standards, expectations, and opinions as to what might have been done to have caused our reaction to be different, or what has caused our receptivity to have been favorable. Yet finding ourselves in this position may be one of the most dangerous of opinions to hold for we are at the greatest risk of not knowing what we do not know.

It has been my privilege to know a few of the leading public relations executives of the country. I consider Morris Rotman is a dean among his peers. A quality that each of us holds, and what Morris Rotman possesses in abundance, is the love of people and an understanding of them.

I presume there are some people successful in the PR business who do not necessarily have this genuine affection and empathy for people and who succeed at their level as a function of their expertise at the process. But if I were to advise someone entering the public relations field, I would ask them how deep is their interest in people. How able are they to put themselves in the shoes of those whom they wish to influence for good?

I have listened to and watched Morris Rotman work his way through a public issue and subject with consummate skill at the processes. But the distinguishing characteristic that added to the worth of what he is bringing to the issue was his intimate knowledge of what was on the mind of the public at that time. What could be realistically and reasonably accepted? At all times these well—rooted thoughts were always matched against a standard of integrity, for he, as well as any one I know, realizes that the public will accept only the truth.

This book encourages bright people to consider opportunities in public relations. Those with the most genuine interest in the public will serve those opportunities best.

Preface

First, the name "Dear Betty Chronicles." I never kept a diary and my career's history is lodged in file cabinets, a cluster of boxes, an assortment of plaques and testimonials on my office wall plus a couple of drawers overstuffed with nostalgic pictures.

There are some photos —Bert Given, Bob Galvin, Dave Hinson, and George Mitchell, all dear friends. A plaque from the Rehabilitation Institute of Chicago attesting to my Life Directorship. A framed Academy Awards program signed by Charlie Chaplin. A medal in a fancy box from the Prime Minister of Israel. I even have a plaque showing I am the only male member of the Mannequin's Guild, a professional models group I helped found in Chicago.

The plaque that gives me the most pride and/or sense of achievement is one given to me at a large farewell party in Puerto Rico when I graduated from the Young Presidents Organization. It says: "Certificate of Depreciation" and reads that it is presented "in recognition of his constant criticism of the principles and purpose of this organization." It is signed by Bo Calloway, president of YPO, and later Secretary of the Army. It was a none too gentle roast in good spirit.

Also a framed Peanuts cartoon given to me by the founders of Mattel, Elliot and Ruth Handler attesting to my contribution to their success.

Shortly after I was on my road to recovery from my encounter with the Stone Fish, which almost killed me, my daughter, Betty, asked a simple question, "Dad, why don't you write any more?"

An important activity of mine all my life has been writing news stories, letters, reports and other miscellany. She concluded that starting to use my mind again would assist in my recuperation.

Confined to sedentary activity at my computer keyboard, I could no longer travel and had to abandon golf and tennis. My outside adventures, in the initial days of my ailment, were conducted in a wheelchair with Sylvia pushing. Betty and Jesse did the same on occasional visits to our home. And I was no longer occupied with teaching at the College of the Desert. A wheelchair tour of the local mall was considered an outing.

I asked myself why I didn't offset the depressive effects of that nearly fatal infection by starting to assemble a track record of various events in my life, including strange and wonderful encounters with strange and wonderful clients and other people of the past. Cabbages and kings. At least a Prince: Prince Philip, at events of the Globe theater in London. A Princess from the Japanese Royal family. Industrialists. Heads of companies large and small. A couple of Presidential candidates. And some very interesting relations developed through my work for the Motion Picture Academy.

My wife and I also met many fascinating people through YPO and its tributary organizations. We acquired many friends in various parts of the world as we traveled on business or attended conferences of YPO and its subsequent graduate organizations.

I now had the time to get busy again at the keyboard, although I still kept up with my activities as King Rat of the Desert Rats organization, Young Presidents alumni group in the desert.

Betty gave me the impetus to pull myself out of my slump and tackle my computer keyboard again. This chronicle, based on weekly letters addressed, Dear Betty, was written between hospital visits, an hour here and an hour there. Sylvia was the first line of support and reaction, as well as providing instant proofreading with her keen eyes. She caught many a stumble and historical inaccuracy.

I looked to my two sons, Jesse and Richard, for additional reaction and suggestions. Finally, I sought the advice and editing assistance from Maureen McGivern Daly, former colleague at the City News Bureau of Chicago. My sister, Ricky, the unofficial family historian, supplied invaluable historical material, things I had never known about our family's early history.

I owe a lot to George Mitchell, former chairman of Mitchell Energy of Houston, and Marshall Wais, former chairman of Marwais Steel of San Francisco, who insisted I continue to serve their companies as outside counsel without necessitating frequent travel. Both felt I could accomplish service to a great extent by telephone and fax.

I couldn't have assembled this adventure in recreating the past without the guidance and assistance of my computer guru, Denise Welch, and her associate, Pam Maloof, who led me through the confusing labyrinth of the computer age. I salute Denise for her patience and optimism. She had more faith than I did that I could finish my book. I am especially grateful to Mary Rosner and Roseanne Welch, who edited my copy.

I dedicate this tome, written for historical purposes, to mom and pop, Etta and Louis, who came to the Promised Land in 1894 and 1899, respectively, and launched our family. It's hard to imagine what they went through and deprivations they suffered in getting here from Lithuania and Romania.

A special salute to Sylvia for being such a wonderful wife, helping me with my career, putting up with all my nonsense, nursing me through my ailment, supportive and loving all the way, and, most importantly, bringing into this world Betty, Jesse and Richard, all three decent, wonderful and devoted offspring.

There are of course the grandchildren who came out of this union and especially Jason, who earned his education at Princeton playing football for four years. Ettie and Louie would agree it was all worthwhile and it's a long way from steerage passage. It's also a long way for me from Wright Jr. College and Tuley High School.

Morry Rotman

Acknowledgement

I wish to express my thanks to the following:

Ettie and Louie, loving parents who made the voyage to the New World.

Oscar Olsen, Tuley teacher and mentor.

Isaac Gershman, City News Bureau managing editor and friend.

Bill Harshe, who gave me my big break.

Bill Stuart, client who believed in me.

Bruce Pascal, pal, friend in need and deed.

Carl Singer, who demonstrated his loyalty three times.

Lee Jennings, Charlie Davison, and Leonard Spacek, a team of champions.

Margaret Herrick, who saw my potential for the Motion Picture Academy account.

And sundry others who helped along life's byways, most especially:

Sylvia Rotman, friend, nurse, mother and wife extraordinaire.

Betty Rotman, daughter, who started me writing this book.

Jesse Rotman, son, who constantly encouraged me.

Richard Rotman, son, for his helpful editing and support.

Bert Given, who constantly affirmed his friendship by actions and deeds.

Maureen McGivern Daly, for her moral support and critical assistance.

Three wonderful secretaries, Marj Fries, Polly McCann (who

wrote all the college checks for our kids) and Laurel Goldberg, who transcribed some of my initial attempts in writing this book.

Patty Bonafede and John Levy, trainers, who got me back on my feet.

And Albert Matej, masseur, who kneaded me when I needed him.

MBR

Historical Footnotes

In 1899, my father walked across the face of Europe from Romania to England to board a boat to take him to America. My mother, Etta Harris, 11 at the time, accompanied by her brother, 13, made her way to Chicago from Lithuania in 1894. Her father, Grandpa Joe, fled Russia and came to the United States in 1890 after finishing his military service as an aide de camp to a Russian general. As he earned money he sent for small contingents of his family. My mother and father met and wed in Chicago, an event that ultimately made possible this account of my life in journalism and public relations.

Louis Rotman went to work for U.S. Steel as a tool and die maker, first in Gary, Ind., then at the South Chicago Works. At 13 Etta went to work as a cigar maker in a little shop on Chicago's Maxwell Street. She had a year's schooling and her father thought her big enough to earn money for the family. The cigar shop (famous for "LaPalina cigars") was owned by the Paley family, whose son, Bill, rose to fame as the founder of Columbia Broadcasting System.

During a severe recession in Chicago during the 30s, Louis couldn't find a job and he and Etta moved to Salida, Col., where he worked as a blacksmith helping to build the Denver & Rio Grande railroad.

I made my mark first as a journalist and later as a public relations counsel. After a year and a half at Wright Jr. College in Chicago, I started my professional newspaper career as a reporter and columnist on the *Lincoln-Belmont Booster*, a neighborhood weekly.

I lived a rich and rewarding life. My wife Sylvia and I are conversant with many of the treasures and experiences of most of the world. We attended more than 30 Academy Awards.

Most importantly Sylvia and I are the parents of three wonderful children, Betty, Jesse, and Richard.

There are four grandchildren: Jason, Betsy, Josh and Talia and two additional grandchildren through Richard's marriage to Gloria. Jesse and his wife Diana are the proud parents of a daughter, Betsy, and Jason.

My book relates my years as a reporter and editor in Chicago: Chasing fires, covering politics and the crime scene; witnessing the electrocution of a killer; having an experience with the Capone gang; digging for news and writing about scandals, murders, and other metropolitan mishaps.

In the following pages is an account of how for 30 years my firm handled public relations for the Academy of Motion Picture Arts and Sciences and how we helped make the Oscar an international object of interest.

How we were instrumental in making the Barbie Doll the darling of millions of kids world wide, and how we assisted Mattel, the manufacturer, grow into a colossus in toy manufacturing.

How we helped Hertz introduce the concept of car rental when it was not socially acceptable to do so. How one important editor turned me away saying "only kidnappers and philanderers rent cars."

How I became an advisor to the publisher of a major metropolitan newspaper, the *Chicago Sun-Times*.

How we were chosen to assist two Presidential candidates: Adlai Stevenson and Nelson Rockefeller. And how one of our political clients, Judge Saul Wachtler, went to jail while he was chief justice of New York because of an extra-marital affair.

There is an account of my years in Chicago weekly, suburban and daily journalism, particularly my adventures as a reporter, rewrite man and editor at the famed school of journalism hard knocks, the City News Bureau of Chicago.

I have also tried to write interesting profiles of some of famous men of industry who became clients and good friends as well. How I was selected to be the advisor to the chairman of the Securities & Exchange Commission. How he retained our services when he became president of the Getty Trust; and how we served as counsel to the founder of Midway Airlines, who went on to become administrator of the Federal Aviation Administration.

My latest activity: starting an access program for the handicapped in the Coachella Valley. My immediate objective is to launch a web site entitled *Disabled Digest* containing information about accessibility, laws affecting the handicapped and other pertinent information. My long-range plan is to launch an effort to build a facility similar to the one in Chicago called Access Living. Eisenhower Medical Center and Northern Trust Bank of Rancho Mirage have agreed to be the co-sponsors.

Before my accident, I taught communications as an adjunct professor at the College of the Desert in Palm Desert, Cal. I was elected to membership in the Young Presidents Organization and then, later, reaching the age 49, to membership in two YPO graduate organizations, The World Presidents Organization and the Chief Executives Organization. Presently I am emeritus " King Rat" of the Desert Rats, organization of graduate YPOers living in the Coachella Valley.

I Get the Oscar

I never really got an Oscar for anything, but I did, much to my elation and surprise, get the Oscar account in 1956, even though my home base was Chicago and our then modest little public relations firm only had a part-time representative in Los Angeles. There is a little story how I got the account.

It's a long way from Rochester, New York, to Hollywood, but that is where it all started, in 1954 in the office of Carl O. Hallauer, president of Bausch & Lomb Optical Company, one of our clients.

One day Carl summoned me to his office.

"You have an office out there, Morry," he said, displaying he didn't know our Los Angeles office at the time was really at half-staff, a part-time employee functioning out of a home study.

I nodded my head and did not disabuse him of his belief nor did I go on record with an exaggeration.

Bausch & Lomb had developed the wide-angle Cinemascope lens that was used for the first time in 20th Century Fox's production of "The Robe."

The company had tried by every means, including intercession by film tycoon Spyros Skouras, president of 20th Century Fox, to get a special citation from the Academy for the development of its optical system but to no avail. Bausch & Lomb had developed the lens system with considerable encouragement from Skouras.

"How about you working on an Oscar for us?" he asked.

I jumped at the chance even though I knew nothing about

the Academy and hadn't the slightest idea how one "gets" an award. I learned later, however, that sundry Bausch & Lomb representatives had tried to cultivate the Academy in pursuit of an award. All efforts, as I later discovered, inappropriate. Wrong. One doesn't get an Oscar by asking for it.

I knew the account was handled by another Chicago based public relations man, Howard Mayer. I told Mayer on the phone one day that I was seeking an appointment with the Academy to discuss Bausch & Lomb's development of Cinemascope.

Later, he was to regret his gracious introduction, although I was an innocent bystander to his misfortune. I didn't know at the time nor did I suspect, nor did he, that his hold on the Academy account was tenuous. My visit resulted in our getting the account without any direct solicitation on my part until after he lost the assignment.

Mayer arranged an appointment for me with Margaret Herrick, executive vice president of the Academy. "She can only see you for a half-hour," he said. The visit ultimately spanned two hours. I didn't realize she was intently looking me over for personal reasons. I didn't know her agenda included consideration of a change of PR counsel.

She quickly straightened me out. She informed me you don't ask for an award; you earn one by being recognized as innovative by your peers who do the voting. She also expressed surprise that Bausch & Lomb had gone through so many maneuvers to seek one without understanding the rules of the game. Now they had sent me, more innocent about the ways of the Awards than anyone at the optical company.

A description of Margaret Herrick could lend some dimension to this tale. She always reminded me of the actress Dame Judith Anderson. A slight woman with steel gray hair, ruddy complexion, a twinkle in her eye. A former secretary at the Academy, she had risen through the ranks to run the affairs of this Hollywood trade association with an iron and diplomatic hand. At the time I met her, she was in her early 40s and became a good friend and mentor through the years.

One secret of Margaret's longevity: She never competed for the limelight with her bosses, the board of governors, which included movie personages — actors, writers, directors, producers and others. Publicity of Margaret was taboo. She vetoed every attempt on our part to get her press coverage. She knew a low profile on her part made a great deal of sense in her job.

During my visit, Margaret Herrick brought forth the Bausch & Lomb file of entreaties. It was crammed with memos and letters of support from friends and allies, including Skouras and Farciot Edouart, head of the Scientific Awards committee.

There should be a way to start fresh, I thought. "May I see the file?" I asked. She handed it over. "Would you permit me to destroy it?" I asked. She nodded assent, a look of amused surprise on her face, and I tore it in half, discarding it into her wastebasket. "I hope we can now start with a clean slate," I suggested.

Margaret told me some manufacturers and service firms had been awarded honorary citations for exemplary service to the motion picture industry. She began, with some prodding from me, to relate typical projects needed by the Academy with no guarantees that, once accomplished, would reward the benefactor with recognition from the Academy. She encouraged me to carry back to Bausch & Lomb the message of public service for the general betterment of the industry.

I reported my findings to Carl Hallauer, describing the Academy's procedures in selecting recipients of honorary awards, and urged the company to participate in a public service project by making available special equipment for a Library of Congress film copying project the Academy wanted.

Within a year, the Academy chose the occasion of Bausch & Lomb's hundredth anniversary to mark that milestone with an honorary award for the company's many years of contribution to the industry. The company was cited for its development of special instruments such as reflectors and other devices used in filmmaking, including its development of the Cinemascope lens system.

Margaret Herrick later called to alert me that something was coming up. She asked me to have my client available at the next Awards presentation. Carl Hallauer got two tickets and the coveted recognition.

My reward was Margaret's invitation to come in for a definitive discussion about handling public relations for the Academy of Motion Picture Arts and Sciences.

Margaret Herrick had thrown a surprise at me at our initial visit. "How would you like to handle this account?" she had asked.

I asked a few questions about the present agency's relationship and was told they had not been informed of a possible change. I told her I would be happy to solicit the account if she should ever decide to make the change and notify the present agency.

She later informed me that the present agency had been notified and would be given an equal opportunity to solicit.

We made our presentation and were told we were chosen. Then all hell broke loose in Hollywood.

Every PR firm on the West Coast had a friend of influence who was a member of the Academy. Later Margaret showed me a leather folder of telegrams and wires from people like Sam Goldwyn and others protesting awarding of the account to an "outsider" to the Hollywood scene. The Academy felt constrained then to hear presentations from any firm that wanted to solicit. The committee heard over twenty-five presentations.

My turn came again. As I sat before the Academy governors, I came to the quick conclusion that the committee had now seen enough easels, slide films and dog and pony shows to fill a lifetime.

Before their eyes, I literally closed my easel (sure, I had one) and extemporaneously talked about our agency, about why we, as an outsider to the Hollywood scene, were an appropriate choice for the Academy.

I told them we had no other Hollywood interests and pledged

our agency would never take on a star or a film production so long as we represented the Academy.

How would it appear, I asked, if a public relations firm handled a star or a film, as well as the Academy, and the person or vehicle got an award? Would this not be suspect? My brief talk dealt mostly with what I considered the integrity of our agency.

We again emerged victorious in the final round. We lived up to the promise I made that day for nearly thirty years. We had many opportunities but never represented an actor or a film production company.

We had been reviewed many times by Academy PR committees. I felt our most insecure moment came the year Gregory Peck, former president of the Academy, assembled an all-star committee to explore enhancement of the film industry's image. Peck came to the conclusion that a new agency for the Academy could come up with a program designed to do this.

There were a few signals that possibly we might be on the way out, despite excellent support and recommendations from the Academy staff with whom we had worked for about twenty years at that point.

Our office manager in Los Angeles had trouble getting a date for my presentation. We heard rumors that big advertising agencies with PR departments were hot after the account. I smelled trouble.

Finally, a date was set. I arrived at the Beverly Hills Hotel on Tuesday for a Thursday meeting and found a message from my office that the meeting was canceled because a committee member had dropped out. The Academy wanted to know if I could come back next week. The aroma of trouble now was overwhelming.

I called our manager to see if there was any way the meeting could be reassembled that week. "Next week" meant canceling other appointments and I didn't look forward to two round-trips between Chicago and Los Angeles for what was beginning to seem like a hopeless cause.

I was told the Chairman of Warner Bros., Ted Ashley, a member of the committee, had to drop out and was only available the following week. I urged our manager to keep trying to schedule our interview that week and went to the pool to nurse my dejection and await word.

Steve Ross

As I slumped on a chaise lounge, I heard a voice: "Morry, what are you doing loafing around the pool in the middle of a weekday afternoon?", the person at my side asked. It was Steve Ross, an old friend. I told him my sad story. "Maybe I can help," he offered. "You know we're in the motion picture business." For the moment I had forgotten that Steve was chairman of Warner Communications. "You know we own Warner Bros.," he said. "Who dropped out of your meeting?"

I told him it was his CEO, Ted Ashley. He smiled and beckoned at a slim, slight man wearing a neat black goatee. The man approached.

Steve introduced us. "Ted Ashley, I want you to meet my

good friend Morry Rotman," he said. "You," he told Ted, "committed a carnal sin against Morry," (not exact reportage.)

He explained that Ted dropping out of the meeting represented a problem to me. Ted protested he canceled his Academy appointment because Ross called an unexpected executive meeting, held in a cabana at the Beverly Hills pool.

"How can you help Morry?" Steve asked. "Simple," Ted answered." "Let's continue our meeting tonight instead of going out for dinner, and I'll inform the Academy I'll be available on Thursday. We can finish up tomorrow."

Steve agreed and Ashley went to a phone and reset the meeting for Thursday.

Within fifteen minutes our LA office manager called to report a small miracle had occurred. "I was able to get them to reschedule the meeting for Thursday," he reported. I let him enjoy his victory.

Steve Ross and Ted Ashley turned the tide. When Gregory Peck introduced me to the committee, Ashley helped establish a friendly atmosphere and this helped me be less defensive and more positive about our firm's accomplishments for the Academy.

The committee had interviewed more than a dozen firms, but we held the account.

For a movie buff like myself, being associated with the Academy had been a fantasy come true. The Academy is the only film association made up of all the arts and crafts that go into making a film. Each industry has two governors on the board. And during nearly thirty years of work for the Academy, a lot of personal idols stepped out of film into my life.

We worked not just on the annual Awards but also handled Academy PR projects year round. In September, we started gearing up and expanding staff for the annual Oscar ritual.

Margaret Herrick was succeeded by Jim Roberts. Jim was responsible for recommending the Board of Governors elect me an associate member of the Academy, a rare honor for someone not fully involved with the industry.

At one time George Seaton, president of the Academy, and I toured various charitable foundations seeking financial support for the Academy. But we struck out because most of the philanthropies we visited felt the industry had sufficient wherewithal to fund its own Academy.

Once the movie industry itself, rather than outside sponsors, paid for the production and airing of the show. Mike Todd prompted the industry to come up with the money by voluntarily writing a check for $500,000 to assume complete sponsorship of the awards. The industry couldn't afford to permit any one individual to dominate the Academy Awards, especially a man known as a promoter.

Today the network buys the show from the Academy and negotiates commercial sponsorship.

One of our big responsibilities, working with the press committee, was to accredit literally hundreds of press people who wished to cover the Awards. Some were rejected for various reasons, mostly lack of room to accommodate everyone who wanted to come. Occasionally, someone would try to use an improvised credential, which we rejected. On Oscar night, we managed about 400 electronic and print press representatives in a teeming labyrinth. Our staff was aided by about 50 press people loaned by the studios.

Of all the highlights of the years of serving the Academy, Charlie Chaplin's return to Hollywood for the 44th annual Awards in 1972 was probably the highest. He brought with him a buzz of excitement that permeated the whole film industry.

The special Life Achievement award was given to Chaplin at the Awards by another great comedian, Jack Lemmon.

I was saddened to see he was now feeble and had difficulty navigating the rehearsal stairs, but Chaplin still had sparkle and wit. I had the good fortune to speak with him several times, both at the Awards rehearsal and at the Beverly Hills hotel.

Chaplin had very tight security arrangements at his hotel where he occupied a bungalow. One morning there was an alarm, and I was notified. A man had been found in the bushes outside of Chaplin's bungalow. He was almost thrown into the cooler, but identified himself as a well-known comic entertainer who idolized Charlie and wanted a picture and an autograph. He was invited in and given the picture and autograph he desired.

The memory capsule must record the streaker who ran across the stage and David Niven's aplomb in handling the interruption; the spectator who jumped on the stage and gave a miniature Oscar to Bob Hope, and Marlon Brando's sending Sacheen Littlefeather, an actress, to use his seats and misuse the Academy Awards for a political message.

There were tense moments and last minute frenzy when Martin Luther King was assassinated on April 4, 1968, and President Ronald Reagan was shot on March 30, 1981. The Awards were postponed from Monday to Wednesday evenings as a result of the Rev. King slaying.

When Reagan was shot, the Awards were held the next night, the decision having been made to go on twenty-four hours later once word was received of his condition. But try to imagine the work that went into rearranging network schedules, extending hotel reservations, notifying the press, and convincing the participants to rearrange their travel schedules. Only one presenter, Peter Ustinov, was unable to comply because of a commitment that called for him to fly on to India to start shooting a film.

During the Awards, I would remain in my seat briefly, hastening up to the press facilities to "check things out" although I was well aware our staff had everything under control. Occasionally an emergency arose, and I was consulted.

I looked forward mostly to the rehearsals the weekend before the Monday night festivities. The stars and other presenters showed up at various intervals dressed in their most casual California attire.

It was exciting to watch the participants in slacks and sweatshirts and what—have—you stepping up to the microphone to rehearse their parts, and summoning forth, almost instantly, professional skills required for the task.

I doubt I shall ever forget Maurice Chevalier coming to rehearsal almost directly from a plane trip from Paris and, tired as he was, enthralling the rehearsal audience with his rendition of "Thank Heaven for Little Girls."

There were many stops and starts in rehearsals for one reason or another. Unforgettable was the moment when Dudley Moore, the diminutive comic-musician, waiting to go on, sat at the piano and did an impromptu act worth any admission price.

Dean Martin at rehearsal was an adventure in hilarity. His performance one rehearsal was the funniest bit I had ever seen.

Debbie Reynolds also brought a touch of magic into the theater when she stood there, some months obviously pregnant, and rehearsed "Tammy." She really belted it out, and the audience rose to cheer her.

When we started our association with the Oscars, the event was held in the Pantages Theater on Hollywood Boulevard. The press was accommodated in a giant tent in a parking lot next to the theater.

In the early days, I was in the midst of everything. I would be stationed at the front of the theater as the guests and stars arrived, with the head of security at my side ready to handle any emergencies that might arise.

At my first Oscar night, I was put to a severe test. A limousine pulled up and out came a young lady in a gold lame' gown. Attached to her wrist was a long gold chain, a man dressed in a gorilla costume at the end. Obviously a press stunt was in the works.

"They can't go into the theater like that," I said to Jerry Moon, chief of security.

"They can if they've got legitimate tickets," he replied.

Nothing had prepared me for this decision, but I instructed him to bar them, assuring him I would take full responsibility.

The security chief and his men hustled beauty and the beast to the sidelines. She was told she could come into the theater alone. He could come back properly attired the "gorilla" was told, but not in costume. They protested vigorously, but to no avail.

What they had in mind, I figured, was a disruptive press stunt in the theater. Luckily, the Academy backed my decision even though a formal protest was filed the next day by the producers.

The crowds, assembled on Hollywood Boulevard from early morning until late evening, would cause serious, almost uncontrollable, security problems. Occasionally, a store window would be shattered as the fans pressed to get a closer look at arriving stars. The Academy ultimately came up with a solution: pay last year's gross revenues to all the stores adjacent to the Pantages and board up all the windows. It took some negotiating, but wisdom prevailed on both sides.

Later, the Awards were shifted to the Santa Monica Auditorium and then to the Dorothy Chandler Pavilion in East Los Angeles. There was an additional shift to the Shriner's Auditorium. The 2002 awards were presented in the new Kodak Theater on Hollywood Boulevard.

During the years our growing staff took over the vast detail work of the Awards, and my role became more and more ceremonial. My wife and I attended more than 30 Awards, missing only one in all the years when we couldn't get back in time from a trip to the Orient

Occasionally I was called in for consultation on emergencies such as threatened boycotts, picket lines and disruptions of the Awards itself.

One of my biggest problems was that the world of my personal relationships and business friends assumed I had Academy Awards tickets coming out of my ears. They did not understand we could not bend the Academy rules by handing out tickets promiscuously. One reason we kept the account all those years was that we did not attempt to manipulate ticket distribution to our agency's advantage. I can recall estranging a client who wouldn't believe I could not produce two tickets for him at the last moment.

Traditionally, the Academy Awards were staged either the last Monday in March or the first Monday in April, the evening selected on the basis of network time available and also because Monday was generally a slow night at the theaters. Latest word is that the Academy is considering the month of February for the Awards.

You would be hard put to miss the Oscars if you were most anywhere in Los Angeles the weekend before the Awards. Long, sleek limousines festooned with the flags of foreign countries scurry all over town; celebrities from all over the world fill the leading restaurants, and caterers have a field day with innumerable parties.

The swimming pool at the Beverly Hills hotel provided spectacular stargazing. In view were foreign stars, directors and producers from Czechoslovakia, Italy, Greece, Scandinavian countries, Japan, Israel and other countries whose entries were nominated for awards, and always a sprinkling of curvaceous, bikini clad starlets hoping to catch the eye of a producer or director.

In the Polo Lounge of the Beverly Hills hotel at night, the mixture of show business folk and the cacophony of foreign tongues could be overwhelming. At the Lounge one night, one of my close friends, the late Barry Levinson, a former agent and a successful international television and motion picture producer, met a person with a "property"; met another person with foreign money to invest in a film; got an option on the "property", and made a deal for a production — all in about an hour's time. For my benefit, he gave a spectacular display of charm, opportunism and deal making

One late evening Sylvia and I returned to the Beverly Hills hotel after the Academy Awards and dropped in to the Polo Lounge where we saw John Huston holding forth with friends. He recognized me and insisted we join his party, where he was generously pouring champagne. He was repeatedly ordering fresh bottles. He kept shouting to the waiter," more blanc de blancs!" It was several hours before we managed to find our way to our lodgings. It was also one of our more delightful experiences. Huston was a raconteur unsurpassed, full of laughter and vitality.

Art Carney wondered what was on my hair.

The barber and beauty shops at the Beverly Hills hotel had a special relationship with the Awards because many of the hotel guests with a part in the ceremony made advance arrangements to have themselves "done" at the shop. Over the years, I had fallen into the habit of doing likewise and fell prey to the blandishments of one of the barbers, who turned my sparse crop of graying hair into a towering achievement the day of the Awards.

The barbershop employees constantly referred to the number of awards they "won" last year and how many they expected to "win" this year — meaning awards that went to their clients. One year, I sat in my barber chair getting anointed, polished, rinsed and what have you, while Art Carney sat in the next chair getting his particular treatment. We exchanged pleasantries and talked a moment about the upcoming Awards. That evening at the post Oscar party, Art and I ran into each other, and I congratulated him on the Oscars he had won. He recalled our talking in the barbershop and told me he asked his barber, "What's that' s— they are putting on his hair?" The barber told him about all the processes of beautification I was having. That was the last year I went through that treatment.

I gave up my personal involvement with the Academy when we merged with Ruder & Finn. The firm lost the account after several years, when I was no longer associated with the agency and the Academy set up its own internal public relations operation under the supervision of John Pavlik.

The Academy built a large cinema library at the corner of LaCienega and Pico and named it after Margaret Herrick, who died in the Motion Picture and Television Hospital.

Escorting Rhonda Fleming at Awards.

Sylvester Stallone Gives Sylvia vigorous embrace.

With Jacqueline Bisset and Alexander Godunov.

Press room at the Awards.

Barbie

Carson Roberts, a west coast advertising agency with a number of joint client relationships with our firm, had done an outstanding job of helping Mattel to become the world's largest toy manufacturing company.

The company was created by Ruth Handler and her husband, Elliott. They invested $20,000, the entire capitalization of their small toy company, advertising the Barbie doll on all Saturday morning children's programs at the recommendation of Carson Roberts, then a small advertising agency. The company grew to a multi-billion dollar enterprise.

Ralph Carson, one of the partners, called me and asked if we would be interested in the Mattel account. Kal Druck and I visited the Handlers in their display room on lower Manhattan in a building devoted to toy merchandising.

Ruth Handler, who did most of the talking, was a gray-haired, forceful woman, who apparently ran the company. In later relationships, we found her to be a warm person, a kind grandmother and mother. The Handlers had two children, Ken and Barbara, after whom their dolls were named.

Elliot, a balding genial man, headed the design and manufacturing for the company, letting his wife run the show. He and his wife ran the company as a team and Elliot always knew what was going on.

Ruth talked volubly about her creation, the Barbie doll, and her plans for expansion of the company. I was identified as the responsible principal on the account with Kal heading up New York activities.

We came to terms quickly. I was so impressed with their plans that I immediately called my broker to place an order for some stock. I first asked Ruth's permission to do so. She was apparently pleased I was going to invest in her dreams. In the long run, it was a marvelous investment.

Meanwhile, our California office began an upward climb in billings. We started with Mattel with a budget of $50,000 a year and billed more than $350,000 in fees annually in our final relationship. We added the California Avocado Board and others and I was spending a lot of time commuting.

One of my friends, Emmett McGeoughy, became chairman of the Los Angeles Police Advisory Board and invited me to make an address on public relations before the police department's officers' club.

Whenever I talked, the police department arranged for me to be picked up by two detectives in an unmarked car and then returned to my hotel. On one occasion they came in a standard police car. The doorman said to me when I returned, "I hope you're not having a serious problem." He apparently thought I had been nabbed for some infraction.

Our people did very effective work for Mattel. At one time we distributed a matrix service to hundreds of small newspapers with a column bylined by Barbie. It was printed widely. We produced tons of newsprint about Ken and Barbie and the subsequent dolls. The women's pages regularly printed stories and photographs about Barbie and her fashionable attire. Later we added the assignment of promoting the company's new development in miniature racing automobiles and other products.

Our work soon spread into internal employee communications, international marketing and Washington public affairs. Our international associate, Joe Hazan, a management consultant based in Paris, was retained to locate manufacturers where Mattel products could be made abroad.

Ruth talked to me about the concern she had about parent backlash due to their enormous advertising ("'wall-to-wall!"') on children's shows. She was looking for a way to curry favor with parents forced into purchases by children's demands.

Working with Carson Roberts, our people developed the concept of the Barbie Fan Club. Membership blanks were distributed on store counters and in each boxed Barbie doll. We proposed and wrote a four-color magazine, which was available for $1.50 a year. Membership in the club was free of charge.

The entire theme of our campaign was good grooming and good manners for children on the assumption we would be teaching something constructive to the kids and earn good will with parents.

I came to our Los Angeles office a short while after the club was launched. The office was cluttered with mailbags. Each letter contained stamps, coins or checks with membership cards for the club and I instructed our manager to make an immediate arrangement with the bank on the main floor of the Tishman building where our offices were situated.

In the land of enormous movie star fan clubs, we could find no mail house willing to or capable of handling the enormous number of pieces of mail we were getting. The Fan Club grew to more than one million members, more, we were told, than the Girl Scouts of America. Mattel ultimately took over the direct mail through their own facilities in their plant.

Ruth became preoccupied with the price of their company's stock. She once told me she was going to become expert in communicating with analysts, stockbrokers, financial institutions, and financial writers. She brought Seymour Rosenberg into the company as an executive vice president. Seymour had a reputation as the man behind the scene in all of Litton Industry's many mergers. Seymour was a dwarf-like little man with a perennial scowl on his face, reminding me of Oscar Levant. He and Ruth went after acquisitions and acquired controlling interests in companies that made children's dollhouses and other products. They also subsidized the making of motion pictures. There seemed to be no end to the company's growth.

On one of my visits to their offices I saw something new outside Ruth's office, a glass box containing information about the movement of Mattel's stock on the New York Stock Exchange. It told how many shares were purchased each day and the current price per share.

When I went into our meeting, I shocked Ruth and Elliott when I said I regretted the presence of that box on the outside wall, stating that I was fearful this could change the culture of the company from a highly creative one to a firm that gave its major attention to elevating its P/E ratio.

Luckily I was in good stead with Ruth at that time or she might have tossed me out of her office. She pointed out their executives all had stock options and the company was making acquisitions with securities. Appropriate indeed for other companies, I thought, but not Mattel or Ruth Handler.

What I had feared came to pass. Mattel went through a spate of earning problems—a stevedore strike that limited shipments and a crippling fire in its Mexico operations. Seymour and Ruth were both indicted for allegedly "cooking the books"—misrepresenting earnings. They pleaded guilty and were given probation. Ruth was fined $57,000 and sentenced to 2500 hours of community service. Seymour spent his time thereafter studying the Hebraic scriptures.

Ruth's humiliation called for her to report to a probation officer. Her active brain couldn't rest during that period and she developed the idea of utilizing white collar criminals behind bars to teach young offenders useful trades. In effect she started a remarkable trade school with a faculty of people behind bars. She ultimately acquired a run down hotel in Los Angeles and converted it into her school.

Before all this happened, Seymour ordered us to place an announcement on the broad tape at an exact moment to affect the market. The story was something we had released previously.

We told him we were unwilling to try to do so and he fired us from the portion of the account that had to do with financial relations. I complained to Ruth and she merely said, "Just continue with other parts of the program. Be happy you don't have to work with him. I hate the son of a bitch myself."

What had been a very large account started to dwindle down in size as our former employee, Spencer Boyce, head of our LA office who had come to us from Procter & Gamble, began to build his own internal capabilities. He had been hired away by Ruth.

At that time an opportunity opened for us to handle PR for the National Toy Manufacturer's Association and we resigned what remained of the Mattel public relations account to do so.

After being forced out of Mattel, Ruth put her marketing skills at work by starting a new company, Ruthton Corp., utilizing her own experience with her own mastectomy and her understanding of malleable plastics. She developed the Nearly Me prosthetic breasts for women who had had mastectomies. Sales passed one million and she sold the company to Kimberly-Clark.

I would see Ruth in later years primarily at lunch at the Hillcrest Country Club and she would embrace me each time. She told me that during her legal troubles she was too embarrassed to ride the front elevator in the Century City building where they lived.

During our business relationship, Ruth and Elliott were very kind to our family. She would enjoy having our children and us for dinner. She was a wonderful hostess. But in the office she could be as ruthless (Ruth less) as any tough businessman.

About the time we lost Mattel we had replaced all that billing with other business so the loss of Mattel revenue wasn't devastating.

Ruth Handler died of colon cancer April 27th, 2002. Her son Ken, after whom the doll was named, died of a brain tumor in 1994.

She was a remarkable woman, an outstanding marketing genius.

POSTSCRIPT: While I was involved with Mattel, I never fully comprehended how enormous a social phenomenon the Barbie doll became with collectors worldwide, virtually a cult. I later was amazed to learn that there were conventions of Barbie doll collectors that attracted enormous number of attendees. The dolls were traded or sold like commodities.

Mattel owners thank me for my contribution

The Chicago Sun-Times

Once upon a time, long long ago, I worked briefly as a reporter for The *Chicago Sun*. More than twenty five years later I was back as public relations advisor to its successor, *The Chicago Sun-Times*.

The paper had been acquired by Rupert Murdoch, known for his flagrant approach to newspaper publishing. The purchase brought enormous public relations problems to *The Chicago Sun-Times*. Murdoch's reputation was well known and unpopular in Chicago. Leading advertisers abandoned it as well as many readers, especially those in the affluent northern and northwest suburbs.

Simone Nathan was promotional head of the newspaper. She told her boss, General Manager Don Piazza, that the paper needed my services, and set up a meeting between us.

(I had met Simone, a former nun, when she was public relations director of the Rehabilitation Institute of Chicago. For many years I had been chairman of the hospital's public relations committee, serving as advisor to Simone before she moved on to the *Sun-Times*.)

Based on my outsider's opinion of the circumstances and my understanding of the Chicago psyche, I prepared a memorandum on what I thought to be their problems in the community. A number of my points seemed to hit hot buttons with Piazza and he quickly arranged a meeting with Bob Page, the publisher, who was a handsome, tall man, well dressed, apparently committed to Turnball & Asser kind of shirts with white collars.

I learned later he was a former wire services editor with a background in Boston newspaper publishing.

The Sun-Times account became my personal responsibility. Initially, I set out to conduct interviews of the top staff, including the executive editor, Frank Devine; Ken Tower, the managing editor; heads of the news departments, and Irv Kupcinet, star columnist, an old friend. I also spent time with Sydney J. Harris, a predecessor editor of my high school newspaper. Syd was now a popular editorial page syndicated columnist.

I found Devine to be a delight, a Murdoch disciple with a sharp wit, given to literary phrases and frequent friendly digs. As we got to know one another, we became occasional social friends, having dinner with our wives, although once, in presenting me to his executive staff, he referred to me as "the devil's own disciple," referring to my relationship with Page.

The three executives were at constant loggerheads and I emerged as the only acceptable bridge between the constant warriors with Page and Piazza, on one side, and Devine on the other.

Devine invited me to a meeting of the executive editorial staff and I listened intently as the editors discussed the layout of the next edition and planned the feature stories on the front page. I made one small contribution. I asked the group what was the official name of the paper. Why, they answered *The Chicago Sun-Times* (as though I had asked a foolish question.) Then I asked why Chicago was not on the front page. They had neglected to include the name of the city in designing a new masthead.

Page was a marvelous public relations representative for the paper, but impatient with details. He rarely attended meetings of the research committee set up to solve the paper's problems with the community and advertisers. He also spent money lavishly on entertainment and promotions but he had unique qualities of community outreach. In a brief period of time, he knew most everybody important in town. Had he not been betrayed by a palace revolution, he might have brought the paper to success and greatness.

He instructed me to charter a special plane to take a group of advertisers and bigwigs to the Super Bowl in New Orleans. It was first class all the way—special buses, dinner at Antoine's etc. Midway Airlines was my client and its chairman, David Hinson, was pleased to charter a plane to the paper. I went along, accompanied by my son, Richard.

Devine was committed to the Murdoch method. When he ran blatant headlines, reminiscent of the days of Hearst, departing advertisers felt the paper was being published for an audience that did not spend money in the Michigan Avenue specialty shops. He would not listen to my pleadings that Chicagoans did not find Rupert's style palatable.

Working with Joe Rueben, research director of the paper, our staff conducted a series of focus groups in various parts of the city. Marlene Bellis, an outside consultant, served as head of our research activities.

Our findings showed why circulation was down in key areas, why many advertisers now took more business to the *Chicago Tribune*.

I presented our report to Devine and the editorial board. I discussed the report in limited detail and read some of the interviews from our focus groups. When I finished, Devine smiled and said that all that was very well and good but no changes were contemplated. Dead end.

Our efforts to resuscitate the paper's position were not limited to the Devine faction. Other avenues were being explored and I was consulting with Bob Page and others on the staff.

One day, discussing the leadership loss with Page, I told him many of my friends no longer read the paper. They felt there was nothing for them to read in the *Sun-Times*. To bring readers back, I suggested a visit to the University of Chicago to see if I could develop a connection with the paper. I was looking for what I termed an "upward cultural tilt" for the paper.

Page told me I had carte blanche to conduct any activities I wished and encouraged me to visit the U. of C. This led me to a luncheon date with my old army buddy, Professor Dick Thain, head of placement activities, who started me on a chain of introductions at the university.

Robert Rosenthal, Director of the Special Collections library, was intrigued with my mission and introduced me in turn to both Wayne Booth, of the literature department, and Richard Stern, a writer himself of some prominence and one of Saul Bellow's best friends. He was the author of "A Father's World", "Sistermony", and other fiction.

I learned that Bellow had deposited his collected papers at the library and was planning to sell them. The U. of C. library desperately wanted to own the papers held in its care but didn't have the funds for the purchase. He had already sold part of the collection to a university in the south.

I suggested to Page that the paper sponsor a Saul Bellow Foundation to honor him, to hold Bellow symposia, organize his papers, and to raise funds to buy his papers.

Page was enthusiastic and told me he would have the paper pledge $150,000, on a basis of fifty thousand a year, and agreed to talk to the president of the U. of C., Dr. Hannah Gray, to get official university sanction. He went out to the campus to see her and got her approval.

Now I had to face the literary lion. An appointment was arranged.

Rosenthal cautioned that Saul could be testy and to approach him with caution. However, Saul and I spent several wonderful hours together, mostly talking about the good old days at Tuley. I asked him whether he was still in touch with some of his old friends, Sydney Harris, Sam Friefeld, Dave Peltz and a few others. He said he didn't see Harris much because he was "too noisy." He was guarded about the breakup of the relationship with Sam, and said he no longer saw Peltz.

At the end of our talk, he gave his approval of my plan. My next step was to get a contract drawn, which was done by Newton Minow, former chairman of the Federal Communications Commission, *The Sun-Times* legal counsel.

Rosenthal advised me that Bellow was short of money, having depleted his finances in his recent divorce. He told me Saul's divorce had cost him his Nobel Peace Prize money. Based on my knowledge of Bellow's alleged need for funds, the lawyers wrote a contract that avoided taxation for Saul and passed the funds through to his children. I think that later became a big obstacle in our negotiations.

In our discussion, Bellow agreed to contribute regularly to the *Sun-Times*. This news was greeted enthusiastically by Matt Storin, editor, who was excited about having Bellow in the paper. By then Saul had won all the great literary prizes, including the National Book Award, the Pulitzer and the Nobel Prize for Literature. I won some points with the editorial staff by that proposed arrangement.

When I met with Saul again he had made a negative turn. He didn't want to seem to be begging for money, he exclaimed. He killed the deal in a letter to me in which he wrote:

> *"These philanthropists of yours are also weirdos specializing in baseless suspicions of people who describe themselves as artists. I am not about to be, to use an old word, beholden to such a..........."*

Some time later Murdoch placed the paper up for sale. Page assembled a group to buy it, including financier Leonard Shaikin, a U. of C. graduate in literature. Page's brother-in—law, a New York financier, headed the search for investment capital. Page emerged as a stockholder as did Don Piazza.

Page swore me to secrecy about the proposed acquisition. With a couple of my associates, we stayed up most of the night to deliver news of the acquisition to the press. Later that morning, I walked into Page's office and handed him an editorial I had written, knowing he wouldn't have time to do so himself. He made a few corrections and it appeared under his signature on the front page entitled "A Pledge. "

After the sale, Devine left the paper and went on to become an editor of several Murdoch papers. I visited him when he was managing editor of the *New York Daily News* and we had a friendly get together. He still had some caustic comments to make about his former colleagues, Page and Piazza.

Meanwhile, I had attended a Young Presidents convention in Montreal and heard a Canadian researcher talk about local demographics in a way I found fascinating. Her name was Kristin Shannon. On my return, I suggested to Page we hire her to conduct a one-day symposium for staff and advertisers to examine the changing demographics of Chicago. He agreed and I made arrangements for her to come to Chicago.

I had proposed a one-day seminar but hadn't counted on Page's enthusiasm for a new toy. He committed a lot of money for continuing discussions with the outside researchers, who soon realized I was reluctant about the cost and continuity of the project.

Kristin transmogrified into a female Svengali to Page and ultimately convinced him I no longer needed to attend the meetings, eliminating my anticipated interference. Page talked to me about not attending. His deal with Kristin Shannon was to lead to his departure from the paper.

Some staffers blamed me (or credited me) for his demise as publisher. Don Piazza led the charge to decapitate Page and Kristin Shannon testified against him in detail to the bankers. He was deposed. And we lost the account. It was all in all an interesting adventure, but an unhappy ending to one of my most challenging and rewarding assignments.

Page moved to Orange County and purchased a string of small papers. Initially bitter about my early introduction of the Canadian researcher, he was a gentleman and realized I had acted in the best interests of the paper. We had a pleasant re-union one day at the Balboa Beach Yacht Club in Newport, Ca. He rode up in style in a brand new Jaguar convertible.

POSTSCRIPT: One of my early interviews with the *Sun-Times* staff was with Syd Harris. He and I were somewhat competitive in high school. Now I found myself in a position where I might be helpful to him and the paper. I listened as he told me of his unhappiness with his situation. He said he had submitted his employment contract months before, with no response. He was considering taking his popular column, "Sharps and Flats", elsewhere.

I reported back to Page and Devine, and his contract was handled with all speed.

Sydney was a brilliant, erudite writer, a boyhood friend of Saul Bellow. It was my sad duty to manage the paper's memorial tribute when he died a couple of years later. Bellow gave a very touching speech about Sydney during the paper's memorial, held in the paper's auditorium. (I still have the tape.)

Bellow talked of their early days together as teens, spending days at the dining table in Syd's home, writing, writing—essays, poems and what-have-you. Syd's mother once berated them, exclaiming, "Why don't you kids go out and play?!"

The future columnist and the Nobel Prize laureate!

In later years Syd avoided mentioning his early Chicago educational background. He talked about his studies at the University of Chicago. Actually he never graduated from Tuley due to a fracas with a teacher the students called "Crazy Morford."

Syd stood up in class and denounced the occasionally inebriated teacher for "kneeing" girls as they passed him in the doorway of the classroom. This was an act of bravery on Syd's part. When he was sent to the vice principal for reprimand, he shouted," You and your dubious assets can go to hell!" He was expelled and continued his education at Central YMCA College.

Front Page Pledge.

The City News Bureau of

Chicago

The memory doesn't fade easily when you have a vivid fox-hole experience working at the City News Bureau of Chicago, famed training ground for some of journalism's brightest and most successful luminaries.

Among those who at one time or another worked there were columnist O.O.McIntyre; Walter Howey, legendary managing editor portrayed by Cary Grant in "Front Page"; Seymour Hirsh, the Pulitzer prize winner; Hal Bruno, of American Broadcasting Co; Mike Royko, *Chicago Tribune* columnist; *Karin Walsh, city* editor of *The Chicago Sun-Times; Clayton Kirkpatrick*, editor of *The Chicago Tribune*, and Charles MacArthur of Hecht—MacArthur fame, co—author of "Front Page" who was married to Helen Hayes for over 25 years.

Even a movie star, the late Melvyn Douglas, once got his training there only to achieve later fame in the movies. The list goes on. There are more than 1,000 alumni.

I feel especially fortunate to have been trained and survived a stint at City Press, as it is frequently referred to. A former staffer, Chet Opal, calls it the "country of our youth." It was a noble legion, the basic training program of journalism. It taught you how to get to the bottom of things quickly; how to synthesize, and how to do magic tricks on the telephone in a search for information. Sylvia says I think in "headlines" even today.

I realize the Bureau doesn't exist any more (see announcement of closing 10/29/98), but what I recollect includes editors sitting at large paper—strewn desks barking staccato orders; rewrite men and women wearing headphones persisting in demands for information; the switchboard lady phoning in assignments to the reporters on the various beats around the city, and the copy boys and girls scurrying about carrying wax sheets back and forth.

In those days the stories were typed on wax sheets on ribbonless typewriters and edited with a steel stylus. The sheet then went on to a duplicating device, which produced multiples of purple paper sheets. The stories were sent down to the media by pneumatic tubes like those in antiquated department stores. The tubes ran through tunnels under Chicago streets. Once we sent down a live mouse; frequently a Coke bottle to the man below, who for years manned the tubes.

There was a noise and tattoo drumbeat to the everyday operations of the news bureau, which 24 hours a day searched out the city for its drama and vital statistics to be transmitted (then by tube and later by Teletype) to all the news organizations who were subscribers to the service. There was a sense of excitement in that room. Now I am bothered by minor distractions; then I could function and concentrate in that boiler room, handling a half dozen fast breaking stories at one time. Your ears were assaulted by the constant clanging of the fire bells, and the uninterrupted din of the police radio. Veterans could "read" the fire alarms while concentrating on other duties.

There was a crackle and din to the place, no sanctuary for concentration or hearing well for that matter. The place smelled of smoke and coffee all the time. In the center of the room was the big double desk where the editors cleared copy for transmission to the various news outlets.

There was an employee in the bowels of the building, whose assignment it was to accept copy from upstairs and redirect it to City Press clients— then *The Chicago Tribune, The Sun Times, The Herald Examiner, The Chicago Daily News, The Chicago*

American, the AP wire and later the TV and radio outlets that bought the service. In my day, two major papers owned shares in CNB, *The Chicago Tribune* and *The Sun-Times*.

No question it was a pressure chamber. You had to be durable to survive. Once, when I was manning the editor's desk, I phoned our beat reporter, Terry Colangelo, three times in 10 minutes with requests for bulletins on fast—breaking stories. First a murder; then a 4-11 fire, and then a mysterious death. When she didn't respond quickly enough I called back. "We have to send out bulletins!" I shouted. I demanded action on all three stories because they were in her beat. I heard a thump as I was talking to her.

The desk sergeant got on the phone and demanded," What did you say to her?" He said she was lying in a faint on the floor. She was apparently unable to handle the pressure so I told him to send her home in a taxi. We got our bulletins via other reporters in the field.

As you entered the City Press office, there was my benefactor, Gladys Ruby Ryan Wherity, who intercepted you at the swinging gate barrier, working at an old plug—in switchboard with white wires like extruded intestines that connected via the old wooden switchboard to the reporters in the field. You only called her Ruby if she granted you familiarity.

Ruby retired after she had worked there for nearly 50 years. She had a gruff exterior with a gentle heart for those she liked. She had a ruddy complexion and her hair seems to have made occasional excursions to the henna patch. She seemed to have ears all over her head. In a busy newsroom, she could hear everything anyone said and still work her switchboard while cocking her ear for the police and fire alarms.

Over the years, she became a good friend. Later a friend to son Richard, too, when he became a reporter. Sylvia and I called her Ruby, remembering her with flowers long after I "graduated " from the bureau in tribute for her many acts of kindness, including opening the door for me initially.

When she first saw Sylvia she advised me, "Don't let her get away!

It was a stroke of fate one morning that Gladys Wherity sat next to me at the W&R delicatessen in the Ashland Block building where City News was then situated, across from the Sherman hotel at Randolph and Clark. The Ashland Block was replaced by a Greyhound station and later by a hi-rise office building.

Gladys greeted me warmly over my bagel and coffee. "I remember you," she said. "You're the young man who has been trying to get an appointment with Gersh."

That lucky morning, when I enjoyed my breakfast with her, she volunteered that she would get me in to see her boss if I came that afternoon when his schedule was light.

I came back and Isaac Gershman agreed to take me on as a beginning reporter at a salary of $30 a week. But he did tell me I was an exception because of my lack of academic credentials. He was impressed with my previous professional training on weekly papers. I had been covering police stations for years; now I could do my job carrying a City Press credential. That certified press pass seemed like a magic wand to me.

Gershman was the managing editor, a soft-spoken, kindly, chain—smoking, sallow—faced newsman who ran the place. He later became a key person in my life. I was one of the few people he ever hired without a degree from a university and without being on the dean's list at a journalism school. He must have counted my years of service on the community papers as equivalent of a college education. Anyway, he took a chance on me.

He was among the first to advance the idea of not identifying anyone by their color in news stories and convinced editors on Chicago papers to go along. Gersh also worked out election coverage in Chicago with Joe Notaro of Statistical Tabulating. The papers got up—to—the—minute election returns from CNB.

He later became a surrogate father to me. He found the first house Sylvia and I bought in Glencoe. When I first met Sylvia, I took her to meet him before she met my folks.

Gersh and I would occasionally lunch together, an exceptional treat considering the fact he fraternized with few staff members. This continued when I left the Bureau. We used to dine at the Bamboo Cafe, a Chinese restaurant below ground at

Washington and Clark. Most often on Chinese chop suey "with extra meat." One of the veterans at the office called me Gersh's "lap boy," an envious and derogatory term. Gersh must have seen something in me worth nurturing.

Our families visited. When Jesse, our first son, was born, Gersh promised a job for him at City Press. But Richard was the son who went to work there. Jesse, interested in architecture at the time, passed it up. Jesse would have done well at the bureau. In later years he proved to be an excellent writer. He switched from architecture to journalism at University of Ohio and became editor of his college paper. One of his journalism instructors turned out to be Joe DelPorto, who used to work at City Press with me.

It was a strange feeling , some 25 years later , seeing my son, Richard, then still in high school, standing in front of the desk sergeant at the Chicago avenue police station, inquiring about some news story he was following. I was filled with trepidation and pride.

Richard was trained to be a reporter when, according to law, he was too young to do that kind of work. The late Larry Mulay, city editor of CNB, decided to turn him into a professional newsman because he felt Rich was mature, big and smart enough to do the job despite his young age. He was told to tell everybody he was in college, not high school.

One of my favorite stories deals with the time Richard was doing rewrite in the office. He was rubbing a sore neck muscle acquired while skiing. One of the female reporters inquired about his discomfort. He explained his skiing ailment. She said," Rich, why don't you come up to my apartment after work for a martini and a neck rub?" He called me. "She doesn't know how young I am, dad, " he said. "What should I do?" I urged him, "Send your father! Send your father!" I also told him she probably knew his age anyway. She did, as he later found out.

When I started at City Press, I was assigned to cover a police beat, making my first rounds with another reporter, Ernie Leiser, who later in life became a CBS producer. Later, my over-zealous-ness almost got me bounced. I discovered an interesting missing child case (the second in the same family) on the police Teletype and rushed to the Hyde Park police station to get the story. But I didn't tell the Desk I was on the move. I broke a pretty big story and all the major media followed up on my early reports.

When I signed out at the office at night, editor Joe Levander said to me, "You're not a f— detective. You're a reporter. Don't ever leave your post again!" Here I thought I'd be praised. But he was right.

Working at City Press was drudgery; hard, grubby work all the way. Resentment from police personnel who thought you were in their way. Also desk sergeants had their favorites for news tips, most often *The Tribune* reporter, not necessarily someone of the Jewish faith.

I soon discovered newspapering was a cynical business, not for the weak or emotional. Columnist Mike Royko once said that the difference between Sir Walter Raleigh and a newspaperman was that Sir Walter, seeing a puddle, spread his cloak while a reporter, seeing something similar, would spit in the puddle and call the sewer department to demand why it wasn't draining.

There was constant pressure from the Desk to follow up on stories. But quickly! In many cases it was difficult to get facts out of victims, policemen, fire captains, hospital personnel —a whole array of people to whom we had to go for facts. And frequently we were sent scurrying for an additional fact for an obscure story angle. And cursed out if we didn't meet the challenge.

Some of the editors and rewrite people felt they had to act surly to train reporters and were frequently insufferable. Maureen Daly says I was considered a kind editor. I never felt it necessary to browbeat to get the job done.

When it came to obituaries, we were given only a name and address of a person who had died and we had to find out if the person was worth a story. Occasionally we used what was then a cross index (a book of registered voters) to call neighbors of the deceased person. I understand the cross index is no longer used because many considered it an invasion of privacy.

One editor, Arnold (Dorny) Dornfeld, a legendary, crusty guy, who always smelled of manure because he worked his farm when he wasn't a newsman, insisted I find out the kind of tree into which several drivers had crashed into on a curving road in suburban Glencoe. He wanted to write a feature about a "death oak." I had to call several people I knew in Glencoe in the middle of the night to find that actually it was an elm.

The mandate at City Press was for reporters to check and re-check their facts. Dorny, in pushing reporters to exactitude, allegedly first used the phrase, "If your mother says she loves you, check it out." The phrase was also claimed by another editor, Ed Eulenberg.

I was considered part of Dorny's young crowd and occasionally was invited to his Palos Heights farm. The friendship ended when I went into PR. After that, he had no use for me because I had abandoned journalism.

Eulenberg was an avuncular, rotund man with an academic air. He used to stage an annual dinner in Chinatown of reporters who had covered the Chinatown beat. He wore traditional Chinese garb at these dinners. The assemblage was called "The Mandarin Dinner." Eulie delighted in awakening reporters who had worked the night beat with demands for additional miniscule facts.

In Chet Opal's words, Eulie's "verbal ministrations over the phone to the awakened reporter were ornate and orotund and right out of a hymn book" as though the reporter had committed a mortal sin by not getting the facts right in the first instance.

Another desk editor, Art Kozelka, allegedly was booted out of City Press by Gersh when the latter discovered Art had a social relationship with Gersh's no. 1 secretary, the keeper of the secrets like staff payroll.

Kozelka went over to the *Tribune* as a garden editor although generally there was some doubt he knew much about gardening. He was quite bitter about his banishment from City News Bureau.

Once I went door to door in the rain at 3 am in the Wicker

Park neighborhood to locate a family involved in some peculiar happenstance. I was dressed very lightly and only had a book of matches with which to examine mailboxes. I soon exhausted my supply but found the family. My editor wanted me to get a quote out of them. The rule was that any reaction became part of the story—anger, hysteria, refusal to talk. On another occasion a woman fainted when I tried to question her on the phone. I told my editor. "That's the story," he said. "Just report that she fainted," he advised.

I can't quite attest that reporting was an exalted experience for me. I didn't like awakening people to wring facts out of them especially under moments of family distress. I didn't particularly like hanging around police stations. I did smoke a lot of cigarettes but I wasn't very good at pretending I liked beer and booze. I had a few close friends in the police department. Among them was a detective named Sgt. Pete Harlib of the Town Hall police station, who became a pal of mine, even taking me to the Medinah Club once in a while for a swim.

There was a desk sergeant, Sgt. Ralph Petacque, at the Maxwell Street Station, who used me to do his paperwork behind the desk and gave me free reign of his post, including using his phone extensively to follow up on the other police stations on my beat. Petacque used to talk to me about his son, Art, at the University of Illinois, who later became an ace crime reporter on *The Chicago Sun—Times* and won a Pulitzer.

I covered all the beats during my shoe leather days—City Hall, the Federal building, the Criminal Court building , the so-called "dog watch" at Detective Bureau (midnight to 8 am). I liked Criminal Court because there was continuity to the stories. Also doing that assignment seemed a higher calling as a newsman. At least you weren't hanging around police stations.

The Desk assigned me to cover the electrocution of a criminal who used to wander the elevated Illinois Central tracks on the south side at night and watch for people parking their cars behind their homes. The garage light was a signal for robbery. He would pounce on them in the darkness and rob them. He killed one victim. I saw him burn. Not a pleasant experience. Somewhere I still have a copy of his last meal.

Working at the Detective Bureau at 11th and State meant hanging around from midnight to 8 am with a bunch of hard-hitting newsmen, a couple of them rough men out of the circulation department of their respective papers. They used to browbeat people for news, frequently pretending to be from the coroner's office or acting as "Sgt. Frank Murphy of the police department."

Buddy McHugh of United Press; Frank Winge from *The Sun—Times*, John Pastor from *The Chicago Tribune* and Adolph Wagner from *The Herald Examiner*, were among the men I worked with. The press office was a scene out of "Front Page." As the youngest reporter, I did a lot of phone checking for them and also hustled coffee.

There is a newspaper legend, perhaps apocryphal, that *Tribune* reporter Joe Morang, imitating "Commander Keating", called a police station and started to berate a cop for screwing up a report. The cop finally said, " Is this Keating?" "Yeah, what the — do you care?" shouted the reporter. "Hold on," said the cop, while he put the real Keating on the phone. "Who is this? " demanded Keating. The reporter asked him if he knew who was calling. "No, I don't, God damnit," shouted an irate Keating. "You really don't know who this is?" asked the reporter. "Well, then — you!" he shouted. Whereupon he slammed down the phone, much relieved.

At the police building one night, I heard the announcement of a stickup in a jewelry store on North Avenue near Kedzie. I knew the operator of the store, Morris Trachtenberg, and called him to get some facts. He lived next door to our family in the Humboldt Park neighborhood. I explained I was a reporter and heard the alarm on the police radio. He later told his family he didn't believe me and thought I was involved in the robbery. "How did he find out so quickly?" he asked.

When Richard started covering the central police building, he introduced himself to the newsmen in the pressroom. One reporter exclaimed," What, another Rotman!" My friend Pat Leeds, who worked that beat, was very kind to Richard and showed him around the police building. She introduced him to her contacts in the detective bureau. Pat died at an early age of cancer. She had been an occasional girl friend of mine. I recall her particularly because, returning from a horseback riding date, we heard the news of Pearl Harbor on my car radio.

Richard later was assigned to the Criminal Court Building and went into the court of Judge Saul Epton, who was famed for his activities with youth offenders. The judge inquired who the disheveled young man was, wandering about the court and asking questions. "Oh, that's the new City Press kid," the bailiff answered. The judge called Richard into his chambers and advised him that he had to be neat—appearing while in his court. He let him wash his face and comb his hair in his private facilities. He and Richard became great friends and through that Sylvia and me likewise.

Frequently, when Richard brought a sandwich for lunch, the judge would, too, and they would dine together in chambers. Epton often said, "I didn't realize I was keeping company with a kid." He said they talked about all kinds of mature things. He finally got Richard to confess he was still in high school. "You can't lie to a judge," he threatened. Through the years when he saw us, Judge Epton would inquire, "How is my son?" Richard had a wonderful friend there.

I was assigned to rewrite when I came back from service after short employment at the *Chicago Sun*. I was promoted to assistant city editor, which essentially meant I got a few more bucks in my paycheck, and was in command of the reporters in the field at various intervals, mostly Sundays and late afternoon hours. The rest of the time I was first—string rewrite.

When Marshall Field III started *The Chicago Sun* he hired a bunch of men who came off the Hearst paper strike. The publisher, Silliman Evans, came from Memphis and the managing editor from Philadelphia. They didn't know their way around Chicago. They didn't understand Chicago. I worked there briefly until Gersh wooed me back to CNB.

When I got back, I was assigned the same rewrite desk I had before I was drafted. My notes and my address book were still in the same drawer I used. No one ever cleaned drawers at the bureau.

I enjoyed the challenge of the rewrite assignment and also the company of a good group of stellar writers, Clarence Jensen, Bud Hubka, and Opal. The latter became a close friend and we are in touch even as this is written.

The city editor at the center desk was Mulay, an excitable, short and dark man, who became a good friend to me and later an admirer of Richard. He was a topnotch newsman with intimate contacts in the city. He would come to work each morning and carefully wipe off his desk and spray the telephone mouthpiece with disinfectant before facing the world.

I am also in touch with Maureen Daly, one of the gifted women reporters who came to work in journalism when the war opened opportunities for them. Maureen wrote the best seller," Seventeen Summers." She still writes books and does restaurant reviews for Palm Spring's *Desert Sun*. Sylvia and I dine with her frequently. She has become a dear friend to both of us and serves as a great sounding board for me.

Opal was and is a gifted writer. I used to envy his skill at batting out a slick phrase in record time. On his 26th birthday, Chet went to work at the University of Chicago, where he served as President Robert Hutchins' press aide. He then went to the State Department, where he was a foreign affairs troubleshooter. We still correspond and I save all his wonderfully—written letters.

One day I got the opportunity to become a minor legend in journalism quite by accident. The Desk had sent a reporter, Walter Ganz, to the Woodlawn police station to get the word on a bandit who had been caught by the police after a holdup shooting. Walter had a thick Russian accent and was frequently lampooned but was a good if excitable reporter.

While Walter was giving his story to me from the police station phone booth, a companion of the man held walked into the station brandishing a gun, demanded the release of his buddy and fired a shot at the desk sergeant, who wasn't wearing his gun. It was in a drawer. He blew off a button on the sergeant's uniform. Luckily he was sitting sideways.

The invader then demanded release of his friend and began to herd people into the back room of the station. As he passed Walter in the phone booth, he shoved his gun into his back and herded him into the back room along with the rest of the personnel. Walter blurted to me something about a gun in his back and facetiously I announced to the staff "someone finally shot Ganz". Everybody began to applaud. One editor shouted "About time!"

The man with the gun was finally subdued and Walter, who had cowered away from the others lined up along the wall in case there was any shooting, finally returned to the phone and said to me, "As I was saying . . . ." He then went on to give me the rest of the story. That story of the police station invasion, mentioning my part in it, ended up in a lot of journalism anthologies. Another excitable reporter, who thought and talked fast, was Earl Busch, who became the first Mayor Daley's press aide. He achieved fame during the so-called "police riot" during the Democratic convention.

The morning of the so-called "riot" he called to tell me of his plans for handling the press. Bunching them all in front of the Hilton hotel turned out to be disastrous. The press didn't have to go very far for their story. That was an unfortunate mistake by Earl. In later years he got himself into a legal jam over his organization of a company to provide billboards at O'Hare airport and almost went to jail. Mayor Daley told him he could set up the company, but also warned him he would deny it if Earl had any problems.

Being on rewrite gave us some moments for fun when the news was light. We used a chart developed over the years showing the location of rooms in The Sherman hotel across the way. Once we called in a fire in one of the rooms but most of the time we were involved in playful activities. It is alleged one editor interrupted a swain in the midst of amour with a telephone call announcing," This is God. Aren't you ashamed?"

We would assemble in the back room of the bureau for our occasional adventures in voyeurism. The room was dimly lit. We used a pair of binoculars that had only one lens; otherwise the binoculars would have been purloined in previous years.

I was manning the desk one late night when I saw a group of girls in a double suite across the way in the Sherman in various states of undress, preparing for bed. Phil Weisman, our sports editor, a pal of mine, and I connected to the room through the switchboard without telling the girls where we were but, because they were a couple floors below us, across the street, they had no idea how we could see them.

We finally confessed where we were and began a relationship on the phone. The young girls were in the cast of "Call Me Mister," then playing in the loop. The next night I called again and a man answered. He berated me unmercifully, threatened he would tell my boss about my peeping tomism. It turned out it was Phil on the phone, who had worked out a deal with the young ladies to be on hand when he anticipated I would call.

Phil and I dated two of the girls while they were in Chicago, sisters. We even traveled to Milwaukee to see them when the show moved on.

My desk sat near a series of green lockers. Behind me, Joe Levander, the ancient assistant city editor, short in stature but long in experience, went through the same ritual each day before reporting to the Desk. First, he took out his old aluminum coffee pot and prepared his brew. Then he donned sleeve garters and a green eyeshade, which covered a visible hole in his forehead. No one ever knew how he got that hole. Joe was famous at City Press for one thing. Whenever staff members had a romantic rendezvous at the tiny hotel across the street, they used Joe's name in signing the register. We found Joe signed in 26 times one year. He had a love life he never suspected.

I had just met Sylvia when I was assigned to follow a fast breaking story. Dr. Raymond McNealy, the eminent and hand

Joe Levander with reporter at City News.

some head of surgery at Wesley Hospital, was keeping a mistress secretary, Marjorie Tyler, 28, in an apartment across from the hospital. She sensed things were coming to an end between them and decided to end it all by putting her head into a gas oven while he was away.

She was discovered in time by her mother and a young physician, Dr G.L. Lands, assistant to Dr. McNealy, who decided to protect his boss from scandal. He spirited her all the way across town to County hospital and registered her under an assumed name with a fictitious ailment. He could have taken her across street to Wesley hospital. We got a tip and broke the story when she died. He allegedly improperly listed her ailment on the hospital's records as a respiratory disease without adding the suicide attempt.

Our tipsters at County hospital were reliable and extraordinary. Mulay had a close relationship with Warden Ole Olsen of the hospital. Someone once called Larry to inform him there was a would-be suicide standing on an outside ledge of a window. Larry called the warden to inquire, "I hear you have a leaper. " As they were talking, a body came by the warden's window. "How did you know?" he demanded.

In connection with the McNealy case, we encouraged Dr. Al.Brodie, the coroner, to call a blue ribbon jury to investigate the matter. It was much ado about nothing but the people involved in the incident were prominent. We got Dr. Brodie out of his Sunday Turkish bath to assemble a blue ribbon jury. Ruby always knew where all officials could be reached, even on Sunday. What I didn't know was that McNealy was a friend of Sylvia's father, Sam. Between jobs, she had agreed to serve as McNealy's interim secretary. I used to call McNealy's office every day to follow up on the story and the polite voice on the phone gave me courtesy but no information.

Meanwhile Sylvia and I were starting to see each other regularly. It wasn't until later that Sylvia confessed she had worked in McNealy's office for a while. And she answered the phone when I called. "Why?" I asked. "Why didn't you give me a tip? And why didn't you identify yourself?" She explained she didn't know if we were going to continue to see one another but McNealy was an old family friend.

McNealy came to sister—in—law Ruth's wedding. He looked at me and said," Haven't I seen you somewhere?" I never told him I used to see him every day while he was testifying. I even remember badgering him for information.

My rewrite career almost ended on a disastrous note but, through the kindness of Gersh, I survived. It taught me a bitter journalistic lesson. One morning I came down to work and started to do all the things required to start the job. I skimmed the dailies, read the first news accounts and clamped on my headphones, ready for action.

Larry Mulay advised me we had a hot story about a confessed murderer and urged me to start writing the story in time for the early afternoon papers. It seems a former football hero from Drake University had married an heiress. They were checked into a small apartment hotel in Chicago while he looked for a job in journalism. We found later we had his resume in our own office.

The previous evening they had a tiff and he shook her vigorously with his hands around her neck. She apparently went to sleep on a couch, not in bed with him. When he awakened in the morning he found her dead on the couch. He called the police and declared he had strangled his bride. I started to write the story.

By the time I finished, the *Chicago Daily News*, using my account, was starting to print a front page story about a Drake football hero who had confessed strangling his bride. The headline, "Football Hero Slays Heiress Bride." There was even a picture on page one where the body was found.

I suddenly realized I couldn't find a coroner's pathology report. That was the first thing I should have sought when I started my story. I called our county building reporter and demanded, "What does the pathology report say about how she died?"

The reporter came back with the report that she was not strangled but had died of a heart attack. A lot of corrections broke loose when I told the Desk. Later Gersh called me in and told me I was almost fired for that colossal mistake.

The young man involved in this story was quite bitter about his experience, feeling he had been accused unfairly by the press. The police decided to book him for disorderly conduct in an act of self-preservation for letting out the story that he had "confessed." There was some talk about his suing City News.

Don Reuben told me that the Kirkland law firm, where he was a partner, and which represented City News Bureau, was prepared to defend the case should he have sued.

Closing reflection: I was lucky to work at the City News Bureau at a very robust time. Some of the things I remember are no longer there. Wax sheets aren't used any more. The E-mail and the computer replaced the ancient means of communication we had. The tubes are gone and for all I know the tunnels under Chicago streets may serve as an aviary for bats. In fact, City News is now gone, replaced by a similar enterprise.

Today we would be fired and maybe even hauled into court for posing as police officers or coroners in a search for news. The female reporters would certainly charge us with sexual harassment if they witnessed our adventures with the Sherman chart. The din is gone and there is no clack clack of typewriters.

I feel sorry that today's young journalists will never live through the romantic days of the undisciplined City News Bureau I knew.

POSTSCRIPT: The *New York Times* reported Oct. 29, 1998, that venerable City News Bureau, after more than 100 years of service, would close its doors some time in "the first quarter of next year." The Bureau's general manager, Joe Reilly, called the staff together and made a laconic announcement. The story was that CNB, owned jointly by *The Chicago Tribune* and *The Chicago Sun Times,* was losing money and had in fact lost one million dollars in 1997. I'm glad I got these thoughts down on paper while there was still life in the old girl. R.I.P.

"They'll Never Take You"

Everybody except the draft board felt I would never be called to military service in World War 11 because of my eyesight.

My boss at *City News*, Larry Mulay, gave me my Monday assignment one weekend when I told him my number had come up and I was scheduled to report to the draft board the following day.

"Oh, they'll never take you," he said.

I called him from Camp Grant Monday afternoon and told him to take me off the assignment sheet, that I had been drafted, and I had already been inducted at Camp Grant, near Rockford, Ill.

I have to admit that I was not a happy draftee. There was no question it was my responsibility to serve in a war I felt was just, but the realization in my bunk the first night left me with despair and uncertainty over my future and the nature of my potential military duty.

The next day my civilian clothes were packed away in the little cardboard suitcase I had brought along and I was outfitted in ill-fitting khaki and GI shoes.

My next post was Jefferson Barracks, outside of St. Louis, Mo., an outpost dreaded by most of my fellow soldiers because of the inadequate sleeping facilities and lousy grub.

Jefferson Barracks was infamous for its cluster of sleeping tents dubbed "TB (tuberculosis) Gulch" by most of the soldiers because the tents sat in a virtual low-level swamp.

I had gone through a battery of tests during which it was

discovered I had an affinity for music because I could detect the tones of the musical notes in one test.

My guess was I was going to join a band somewhere, although I could not play an instrument, but I was shipped to Scott Field, near Belleville, Ill., an Air Force base, formerly the home of lighter than air dirigibles, but now an Air Force cadet training center and a radio school.

My being able to detect tones meant I was to be assigned to the radio school to learn how to operate a sending key on a B-17 bomber using Morse code.

Learning how to "read" Morse code by listening to a constant flow of dots and dashes through headsets was a headachy ordeal. To me it was auditory Chinese torture as the sounds relentlessly kept pouring into my ear hour after hour.

One day when I was called in for another of those infernal medical checkups. It was decided radio operators were to be sent to gunnery school at Harlingen, Texas, to learn how to operate bomber machine guns in moments of combat.

The Air Force seemed to be uncertain about my competency for combat service because of my eyesight. Here was a case where the military and I were in total agreement. I had visions of myself downing one of our own planes in combat if I lost my eyeglasses.

When I finished the various tests, the medical officer asked me, "how did you ever get into the service?" This was also a question I had asked myself. He told me I was not qualified for Harlingen and I was taken out of the radio school and assigned to squadron duty, which essentially called for adeptness at picking up debris, cleaning latrines or other janitorial duties.

This time I was housed in a wooden barracks and there seemed to be an upgrade in the quality of food. Somewhere along the line I learned that pork chops were a frequent staple of military diet and I went off the non-pork diet which was mine most of my life in a somewhat kosher home.

My buddy in the barracks was a psychologist from New York, also busted out of radio school, and he and I realized we could escape janitorial assignments by falling in line in the morning in our "class A" khakis, rather than fatigues, indicating we had an office job somewhere. While Master Sgt. O'Neill, an Irish gnome with a raspy voice, assigned our barracks mates to various menial duties, my buddy and I and I marched off for a day at the library, or an afternoon movie, lolling around the PX or just sunning ourselves. We would only march back for lunch and dinner.

One day I saw a bulletin board notice seeking a correspondent from the base for a St. Louis weekly. I got on that one real quick, and in short order found myself a job as a columnist, writing essentially about activities at Scott Field. Not content with ordinary reporting, I indulged in an occasional editorial fancy. I don't recall the issue but soon all kinds of letters swarmed in, some argumentative and angry, a few supportive.

Eventually I was summoned to the office of the post public relations officer, who was outraged I was writing for the public without permission of his office. He was steamy. "What right do you have to write for a St. Louis paper?" shouted Lt. Cliff Jaffe. I meekly answered I had no idea I needed approval. "Do you have any professional experience?" he demanded. I explained I was a former assistant city editor of the City News Bureau of Chicago.

Suddenly his demeanor changed and he became very cordial. "How would you like to work for the post paper, the *Scott Field Broadcaster*? He asked. He saw a live one before him. In short order I was transferred to a brick barracks with better facilities and found myself with a desk in the office of the paper. Within a few weeks, a dramatic event occurred in Air Force Public Relations that was to have an effect on my future at Scott Field.

The officer in charge of all Air Force public relations, Lynne Farnol, a veteran New York PR executive, released a photograph purportedly showing farmer's fields in the US furrowed in the form of arrows giving directions to enemy planes. *Life Magazine* as well as others printed the story. It was discovered it was all a hoax. Shock waves went through the Air Force and personnel were shifted from various PR offices including the one at Scott

Field. PR offices were henceforth limited to two enlisted personnel.

Sgt. Ronald Lorenzen, editor of the *Broadcaster*, chose to stay in public relations. The paper was the responsibility of Special Services, where I was assigned, and the officer in charge, Capt. Bram Rose, had to find another editor. The staff voted me in as managing editor. Now I was in charge, wearing only private first class stripes, heading a staff of about 25 with few capable of the editorial duties.

Capt. Rose, who soon advanced to major, was a former advertising executive from Cleveland. Divorced, he had been married to a Uhlein daughter, owners of Schlitz brewery. Bram and I became close friends even though he had officer status. Occasionally he would sneak me out of the base hidden in the back seat of his car so we could have some fun in St. Louis.

(After the war, when I was running our public relations agency, he joined our company as my executive assistant. Unhappily, he succumbed to cancer after a few years of invaluable service to our firm.)

There were two photographers assigned to our staff, Pvt. Johnnie Pagoria, and a Sgt. Hardin Walsh, whom we called "Smokepot, " because he frequently used smoke pots to dramatize military pictures. The military used pots which, when lit, emitted clouds of smoke.

Pagoria was always getting into scrapes from which Bram had to extricate him because he neglected to salute, took pictures when he was ordered not to, and continued to function in uniform as though he was still a Chicago newspaper photographer.

My stalwarts were Dick Thain, former *Chicago Daily News* reporter and former advertising man, and Harold Asen, who had written college musicals and became a proficient news writer. The three of us really put out the paper. We hung around together mostly on the post. After the war Dick became a professor at the University of Chicago in charge of placement activities. Harold returned home to his contracting business.

The rest of the staff was an odd group, a mishmash of talent not necessarily appropriate to the publishing of a newspaper. The base would assign anyone to Special Services who didn't fit in anywhere else. One was a professional crossword puzzle maker. Another, an opera singer. Another, Pete Badrich, a ventriloquist. Peter and his wooden counterpart, Oscar, would accompany me on circulation day as I passed out the paper to the top brass in the headquarters building. This gave me an opportunity to insult the brass through Pete and Oscar without guilt, blame or punishment.

We even worked over Gen. Wolcott P. Hayes, our commandant, and he took it with a smile. Otherwise we'd be hanging by our thumbs.

Another man on the staff was Sgt. Don Hesse. I was never quite sure what he did but he rose rapidly to become a staff sergeant because he was put to work drawing identification and fancy designs on officer footlockers. With that kind of talent I reasoned he could do cartoons for the paper. He along with Cpl. Bob Faner garnered awards from the military newspaper network.

Our unit had the responsibility of organizing USO and other entertainment for the post. One of the men involved, Faner, was a former professor of English at Southern Illinois University in Carbondale, Ill. I convinced him he could write editorials and our paper won several awards as a result. I learned later there is a building named after Bob at his alma mater.

Bob had a unique backstage experience one evening. As he stood in the wings, Ada Leonard, the shapely brunette Chicago stripteaser, did her act on the stage and then returned to the wings for a costume change. She took off her outfit, handed it to Faner, and donned another while he helped. This may have been the highlight of his military experience. We gave the shy professor the nickname, "Muggsy" Faner, after the great jazz pianist, Muggsy Spanier.

I earned my corporal stripes and headed a staff which included a couple of staff sergeants and a warrant officer but Bram

Rose told them that, even though I was outranked, I was the boss and my authority should not be questioned.

Our small group put out a paper that went on to win first prize as the best letterpress newspaper in the Air Force command.

Cliff Jaffe, a former sports writer from Chicago, was the officer in charge of the public relations office. His aide, Sgt. Ronald Lorenzen, previous editor of the paper, was a former Des Moines newspapermen.

Cliff, who came to see me in Chicago after the war about possibly joining our agency, became a problem to me when he discovered we were turning out original news for our paper which the soldiers read before the news hit the St. Louis papers. He told us we were required to give him our fresh news material first so he could release it to the press, which meant it would be stale before our soldiers read about occurrences at their own base in our paper. We decided to outwit him by churning out feature stories not of particular interest to the St. Louis press, like a photographic feature of a sweetheart visiting her beau at the base or a story and photograph about an interesting soldier.

Lorenzen had to go to work on news stories and we got the benefit of his output. Dick, Harold and I came to the conclusion that Lorenzen was a spook and frequented cemeteries at night. It was obvious to us because of his sickly greenish complexion and the fact no one knew where he went at night.

My career at Scott Field came to a crisis when I was visited by Col. Jerry Johnson, head of the whole section, who displayed a story he had written allegedly showing how he had run the new obstacle course at the field. He demanded major coverage.

Col. Johnson, who in civilian life ran a service station in nearby Belleville, was a pudgy little guy with an ever-present pipe in his mouth. I felt he couldn't do the obstacle course without a coronary. I also knew my paper would get major hee-haws if I printed that story.

I was polite and gave him a vigorous "yes, sir" and consulted Bram Rose. I told him I wasn't going to run the story as written. He understood but he warned me Johnson would ship me off the field if I didn't comply. But he backed my decision and went over the colonel's head for approval.

I ran a watered down story and immediately applied for Officers' Candidate School. I wanted to get into the war anyway and was tired of the constant hassle by Jaffe and Lorenzen. I also realized the colonel would be after my scalp. In a few weeks I was accepted and sent to OCS at Miami Beach. I dreamt of getting an overseas assignment in an officer's uniform.

I was shipped with several hundred men, a two-day trip in a train with no sleeping facilities or air conditioning. In Miami Beach I was assigned to a barracks in what was formerly a hotel at 19th and Collins, the Abbey, across the park from a library.

I thought, this is the life. A library and Wolfie's deli on the corner. I was to visit neither during my stay.

We were four soldiers to a room, bunk bed style, and got a rude awakening the first morning when we were herded into an assemblage on the sidewalk at 6:30 am. There were loud, unpleasant upper classmen there to remind us of our lowly antecedents with instructions that we were to stand at attention with our chins screwed down into our chests.

The West Point style hazing became a terrible ordeal all the time at OCS, morning, noon and night. We learned Donald Budge, the tennis star, ended up in a hospital as a result of hazing. Clark Gable was in a previous class and became an object of repeated upper classmen bracing. We were forced to eat "square" meals at mess, which meant bringing food to your mouth in a square arm movement.

Frequently we were given assignments to memorize stuff and be ready to recite the next morning. These assignments often were given just before "lights out. " I can recall studying a silly poem one evening by flashlight in the bathtub. We were penalized if we were caught with lights on after "lights out!".

In the early morning, as you stood at attention with your chin screwed down to your chest, you were asked to recite the lengthy

OCS code or such things like "soldier, what is the whifflebird?" Your response had to be:

"Sir, the whifflebird is a bird that flies in equally concentric circles until he flies up his own —."

We were then marched off en masse to breakfast at what was formerly the Hickory House restaurant while we were admonished to sing popular war songs along the way. Any lack of enthusiasm was punished by extra marching.

There were 5,000 of us in the corps. Each morning we ran to the LaGourse Country Club, a "restricted" establishment, to do the obstacle course. It was sadly ironic that I could train at LaGourse but not play golf there.

I lost 15 pounds in a few weeks and felt like a fighting machine. They taught me how to fire an M-1 rifle, how to shoot a .45 and how to dismantle and reassemble a machine gun with my eyes blindfolded. I figured this might be useful when I returned to Chicago.

I was beginning to have dreams of myself with gold bars on my shoulder (the bars Bram Rose had given me when I left Scott Field) when I was summoned to the medical office for another going over. In its infinite wisdom, the Air Force came to the conclusion it had a redundancy of limited service officer candidates and wanted to cut down manpower.

Again the question: "How did you ever get into the service with that kind of eyesight?"

I must have been overcome with idiocy. When informed I would probably be given a Certified Disability Discharge and sent home, I pleaded to be sent back to my old job at Scott Field. The examining officer countered with a sad tale that he was a psychiatrist with a healthy New York practice and here he was giving physical examinations in a military outpost. "Consider yourself lucky," he said as he dismissed me.

The situation in those days at Miami Beach, almost totally occupied by the military, was that you were either a soldier or a patient. There were no facilities for transitory lodging. Accordingly several thousand men in OCS found themselves lodged in hospital facilities, stripped of uniforms and privileges and given pajamas, robes and slippers for all day wear.

Some of the men who went into mothballs were former warrant officers, physical training instructors and others in fine physical condition. No matter, we were now patients with hospital confinement. We marched to chow in our bathrobes and even marched to a nearby movie one evening in the same attire military police fore and aft. At night, a pretty nurse came around and offered cathartics to any one who wanted one. Our frustration was so intense the nurses soon demanded guards for their nightly visits among the hard up GIs.

We were next shipped to the King Cole hotel, a former lush spa, where our daily recreation was confined to knocking down coconuts from the trees with garden implements. Most of the time neither the tools or coconuts came down.

We were then shipped to a nearby new facility where all of us, regardless of rank, were assigned to KP duty and other maintenance chores.

One day another soldier and I, a lawyer from Cleveland, decided we had to have a chocolate ice cream soda and the hell with potential punishment for the infraction. In our bathrobes we set out along the streets of Miami Beach to find our soda. We got to a drug store on Collins avenue and had just finished our treat when the officer in charge of our group stormed in.

Someone had snitched and he tracked us down like prison escapees. Angrily, he pushed us into an MP sedan and exclaimed," It's full time KP for you guys!" You would have thought we stole military secrets.

When I got back to my bunk, there was an envelope there for me, notification that I had been granted a Certified Disability Discharge and I was no longer a ward of Uncle Sam.

When the officer stormed in the next morning demanding to know why I hadn't reported for kitchen duties, I waved my CDD under his nose and walked away.

I wandered around Miami Beach for several days, breaking all the rules, eating openly in places previously off limits to me.

Several times I was challenged by MP's and had to produce my discharge papers. I then headed back home to Chicago to resume my career. On the way I stopped off at Scott Field to see my old buddies. Bram Rose assembled a party in my honor at Don Hesse's house in Belleville.

I ran into Sgt. O'Neill, my former master sergeant, who looked at my trim figure, my tailored outfit, my new OCS trained military bearing, and exclaimed," They finally made a soldier out of you, Rotman!"

I wandered around Chicago for several weeks wearing my OCS uniform, a plain khaki outfit with only an OCS patch on my sleeve. After a while, when my money ran out, I decided to see if I could get an executive training job in industry, feeling I was tired of the journalism rat race and its limited future. But industry didn't want an ex-GI with no academic or business credentials.

I thought it would be worthwhile to apply at the *Chicago Sun,* started by Marshall Field, and I was hired as a reporter, but I found the paper was staffed by out of towners and ex-Hearstlings. They were slow to respond to fast breaking news and I felt totally underutilized. Then one day Isaac Gershman called me to come back to City News Bureau. The rest is history.

Hertz Rent a Car

In the early days, shortly after I had taken over the business, the big break I needed was a national account whose name would be recognized by everyone. I realized this could pave the way for other prominent firms to consider us. The lucky break came along in the way of the Hertz Corporation.

One day I got a call from David Cox, one of Bill Harshe's previous partners, who told me that a fellow bridge player, Joseph J. Stedem, executive vice president of Hertz, knowing David had been in the public relations business, told him that he was considering hiring public relations counsel. David recommended I call him right away.

I readily got an appointment with Joe Stedem, and we seemed to hit it off pretty well. He was a short, dynamic, feisty guy with piercing, bright eyes and a tight smile. We settled on the characteristics of the program and fee, and he asked me to go in and present myself to Walter L. Jacobs, president of the company.

Coincidentally, both Jacobs and Stedem were bridge masters and played in tournaments all over the country. I should have suspected that their skill at the card table would place me in an unequal position in a business negotiation with them. In addition, while working effectively with one another, they were fierce competitors.

Walter, a genial gentleman with a face like a smiling owl, finally told me I could have the account, but he said Hertz couldn't afford what Stedem and I had agreed to. I saw this great opportunity of mine slipping away, and I agreed to take the account for less. He agreed we should start work immediately.

What I didn't understand was that Jacobs was outfoxing his colleague and certainly me. From then on, even though we worked with one another for perhaps fifteen years, Stedem would cut me off and refer me to Jacobs whenever I brought up the subject of budgets for public relations. It was a convenient device for him. We nonetheless did all right, but Stedem never ceased reminding me that I had crossed him in my initial negotiation.

Working for Hertz in the early days was an exciting experience. At the time, Hertz was an obscure subsidiary of General Motors Corporation, and it didn't hurt our various presentations when we were able to point out that we were retained at that time by General Motors.

GM was somewhat schizoid about its ownership of Hertz. It acquired the company when it bought John Hertz's truck interests and, as part of the deal, inherited the Hertz car rental business. But GM didn't promote its ownership of Hertz because it felt it was in effect competing with its own dealers by urging people to rent rather than buy automobiles. This uncertainty about its own position ultimately caused GM to dispose of the Hertz Company.

Historically, Walter Jacobs was regarded by many as the father of the car rental business. He had a used car lot in Chicago and, in 1931, decided to rent some of his unused vehicles, which proved to be a better business than unsold used cars. John Hertz tried the same idea about the same time but made a basic marketing mistake. He offered rental vehicles all of which were painted similarly, marking them as rented cars. The public resisted the idea of driving a car everyone knew they didn't own. Lou Browne of Denver, another car rental veteran, was also considered one of the originators of the renting idea.

I was invited by the company to sit in on the deliberations of the advertising committee, which decided on the disposition of all advertising and promotional funds. Early members included pioneers in the field like Richard Robie, who had a vehicle rent-

Joe Stedem gives me the knife while Walter Jacobs looks on.

ing and leasing empire in New England; Tony Grandolph of Florida; Lou Browne of Denver, and Paul and Art Goldstein of Omaha. Campbell-Ewald was the advertising agency.

The early Hertz concept was a per car contribution for advertising by each licensee. The advertising fund grew large when it was initially subsidized by General Motors after the latter had sold off its interests in return for exclusive focus on GM cars in all Hertz advertising. Later, a similar arrangement was switched to Ford.

The heart of Hertz' growth was the acceptance by licensees of the philosophical position that you enhanced your long-range interests by serving other licensee's referrals even though at the moment there was limited profit potential. For example, the Chicago licensee handled hundreds of calls for car rentals elsewhere in the country. So did licensees elsewhere for him.

Most licensee reservation services are now done by the 800 number system, but, in the early days, cross service by licensees was the key to the system's growth.

The other key was the massive advertising program abetted by a rapidly expanding public relations program.

The public relations program we undertook was to supplement advertising coverage with exposure of Hertz services in the media.

We placed hundreds of stories illustrating how one could take a fly-drive vacation. We researched unique usages of rental vehicles and wrote a story about every one of them. We took economic facts about leasing trucks and turned them into articles in business magazines.

I encountered an unusual resistance in one discussion about a possible major story in a leading consumer magazine. An editor at the *Saturday Evening Post* told me that renting cars was not necessarily socially acceptable. "Only stickup men, kidnappers and philanderers rent cars," he insisted at the time.

We persisted and ultimately were able to arrange for major articles in *The Post* and *Reader's Digest,* and most every other major publication.

When Hertz sold its stock to the public, we now had another challenge — to report the financial news. At that time, we worked under the direction of Donald Petrie, executive vice president, a young former house counsel to Hertz. Don left Hertz when he didn't ascend to the presidency and became a prime mover behind the development of the Avis system. At one juncture, he became a partner in the New York banking firm of Lazard Freres.

When Hertz moved to New York City, we were given an opportunity to handle public relations out of our New York office, and we held the business for a number of years. We lost the account in a policy dispute with the internal public relations director, but we had about sixteen good years of service.

One incident persists among many vivid experiences. Wherever I traveled, I rented Hertz cars. After a Los Angeles visit, during which I made a speech at its national convention, and during which I rented a car for a week before returning to Chicago, I received a letter from the Hertz station manager in Los Angeles berating me for committing some traffic violation at the airport, receiving a ticket from the police officer, and insisting the Hertz clerk take care of the violation.

The hapless station manager included a copy of the summons with his letter, only the ticket had been written literally hours after I had arrived home in Chicago. Obviously, I was not involved in the transaction whatsoever. Unfortunately for him, Hertz had a policy at the time that any letters written by station managers had to be sent in carbon to Jacobs and Stedem. Stedem was on the phone the minute the letter hit his desk.

I explained the circumstances and read the issuance time on the summons.

Joe let lose a string of profanity dealing with the intelligence and antecedents of his station manager and vowed to fire him immediately.

"Wait," I said. "I've got to work with those guys. Let me write to him, advise him as to the error involved and suggest a more sensitive approach to customers."

I wrote to the station manager, pointing out what my connection with Hertz was; that he may have heard me talk at their national convention; that the summons had been written after I departed; that I never talked to the clerk about the matter, and that, were I an ordinary Hertz customer, I would be offended by the tone of his letter. "Dear Mr. Rotman," he wrote back, copies to Jacobs and Stedem. "I don't care who you are. You probably walked off with the keys and caused the ticket incident."

Stedem received his copy and was on the phone again.

"Okay wise guy," he said, "What bright ideas do you have now? I'm going to fire the s.o.b. whatever you say."

"Hold on," I said. "You do whatever you want about him, but we would like to study all the letters written by station managers in the last six months to see whether we ought to be doing something about letter writing."

We collected a huge batch of letters and found there was indeed room for improvement. What came out of the experience was a manual containing typical letters and a series of training sessions conducted by our staff. At the various licensee conventions, we would take forty or fifty licensees at a time and go over situations and correspondence.

I remember one stunt we helped Stedem pull off at a national convention. He had a loud speaker set up connected to a tele-phone, and, while the licensees listened, he called various stations around the country to make a reservation. In many cases, it went well, much to his surprise. There really were some dumb ones, much to the chagrin of some of the operators present in the audi-ence.

One day I convinced Joe Stedem that Hertz would have a major public service obligation were there to be a national emer-gency and that it would be wise to go to Washington and talk to the Department of Transportation to explore how the company would be affected in such an eventuality and how it could be of service. We traveled to Washington together and reached an ac-cord with the Department of Transportation that Hertz would make available vehicles in a national emergency.

There were plans made to announce the accord at a Wash-ington press conference.

Stedem was very pleased and looked forward to reporting the arrangement to Walter Jacobs. The latter listened intently and then turned down the proposition, stating, "we don't want to turn over our cars unless we have to."

We continued to serve Hertz for several years when head-quarters was moved to New York City. We reported to a new Hertz executive, Milton Kramer, an abrasive, unpleasant man who seemed to relish pushing around our people, but was surface pleasant to me. He would constantly make outlandish demands. There were times I prayed for the return of feisty Joe Stedem. At one time Kramer insisted we place a full time executive in the Hertz office. Our designee was Les Waller, a published author and a former associate at the City News Bureau of Chicago. The relationship with our firm was terminated several years later.

Bob Galvin. With a Song In

His Heart

Robert Galvin is the former chairman of the executive committee of Motorola, Inc., one of the world's great corporations. Taking over as chief executive after his father, Paul, the company's founder, died, Bob built it into the industrial and technical powerhouse it is today. He is one of America's greatest business executives; he was even described as "legendary" by the *Wall Street Journal*. But I know him in another context—as a dear friend. There are many Bob Galvin stories—and here are mine.

As this was written, Bob announced his resignation from the board, declaring more than 50 years of service on the board was enough.

I recall the day Bob called to tell me I was to be interviewed by the FBI.

"Why," I asked. "What did I do?" He said he was being appointed by President Nixon to the Foreign Intelligence Advisory Board and he was obliged to get security clearance. The Board, he explained, reviews U.S. military agreements with foreign countries.

I told Bob he had many highly prestigious relationships and wondered why he offered me for this dubious honor. "You're one of my friends," he replied, "and they are going to run into your name in connection with me. They will want to interview you."

My secretary, Laurel Goldberg, had already had a call from

Mary and Bob Galvin.

the FBI and she was abuzz with excitement. "The FBI wants to interview you!" she exclaimed. I told her to go ahead and book the appointment.

The quintessential FBI agent showed up. Shoes polished and hair neatly combed. A somber look and a Brooks Brothers suit. J. Edgar Hoover would have approved.

Before I would permit questions, I asked for a display of credentials. I think Humphrey Bogart did this in one of his films. He pulled out a pad and I did likewise. I wasn't a former reporter for nothing. For every question he asked, I asked one. Before long, I had as much information about him as he had about me. He plunged on gamely.

He finally got to the question I anticipated he would ask. "What is your relationship with Bob Galvin?" he asked. "Does your company work for Motorola?" I explained we sometimes got business from the company but Bob had nothing to do with these arrangements. "Why did he give you as a reference?" He had sprung the trap!

I said, "We're just friends. I'm his token Jew. Every Gentile has to have one. I'm his."

He was writing furiously up until that point and stopped in mid stroke of his pen. He didn't believe what he had heard but took down everything I said. His report probably caused some consternation among his superiors.

After the interview, I dispatched an account of the interview and Bob later told me he circulated it to some friends. From then on, he would occasionally introduce me as his "token Jew." Likewise, he is occasionally identified as my "token Gentile."

This bit of opportunistic irreverence tells little about my more than 40-year relationship with Bob. At opposite ends of the political and economic pendulum, nonetheless our friendship has survived. We just enjoy being with one another.

Bob and I met when we were both involved in activities of the Chicago chapter of the Young Presidents Organization.

The chapter was planning to honor one of its members, Seth Atwood of Rockford, who was recently elected National President of YPO. It was customary for each chapter to stage a bit of hoopla at the national meeting when one of its members was anointed.

Bob and I decided to put our energies into creating something special for Atwood. We came up with the idea of a musical review called "Seth Pacific" and Bob and I set up a schedule of meeting together at each other's homes for the creative process.

He would show up at our home in Glencoe and roll up his creative sleeves to do some lyric writing. I would occasionally go out to his place in Barrington. We used the lyrics of "South Pacific" and wrote parodies. Bob proved to be an excellent craftsman of lyrics. My main contribution was some creativity and coffee.

When we were done, we had a nifty review. We enlisted the involvement of nearly 25 YPO members, who came to the Motorola plant in the dead of winter to rehearse the songs and learn four-part harmony with the assistance of a choral director supplied by Bob. Each member bought a similar blue formal jacket to wear at our appearance at the convention. We also enlisted the services of Jana Wacker, former professional chanteuse, the wife of Freddie Wacker, to sing "I'm Gonna Wash That Man Outa My Hair." We knocked them dead.

Bob and I didn't have much in common at the start, but we seemed to enjoy each other's company. Bob never tried to convince me to like Richard Nixon or Ronald Reagan and I kept my thoughts mostly to myself on political matters, although his wife, Mary, has taken a whack at me several times about some of my beliefs.

Mary and Sylvia get along very well. Otherwise, I suspect there would be few private dinners at the Galvin farm in Barrington and Bob and Mary would not venture into the city to dine with us.

The problem of dining with Bob is that, with some help from me, he has become an amateur oenophile, a devotee of fine Bordeaux wines, and it's expensive to entertain him. I amortize the cost against our occasional trips together on his Grumman 11 and that he sends his limo for us. I may have accidentally started Bob on the road to becoming a wine expert. Another good friend, Bob Svendsen, joined in this educational process. The truth of the matter is that Bob and Mary had simple tastes when it came to food served at their home. Excellent sliced beef or lamb; a fine salad, and a lovely dessert. But never a glass of wine.

The wine education of Bob began on a trip to Vail when he and Mary entertained us and another couple, Betty and Frank Major, also YPOers, at their condo. Bob had arranged for a ski instructor to be with us on all ski runs—another indication of his class.

As we took our evening walk after a day on the ski slopes, Bob posed a question: "Morry, why do you have such interest in food and wine?" At first, I thought he was joking, making some kind of snide commentary about my appetite, but he was dead serious. "Why do know so much about wine?" he went on.

I replied that I felt it was important to try new foods; that I felt one should know which wine complimented which food, and that I felt it was a host's duty to have excellent vintage when entertaining business and political leaders. Bob listened to me intently. I knew Bob and Mary frequently had bigwigs at their home for dinner.

That was the same trip when Frank, a beefy leprechaun with an outlandish sense of humor, almost killed me by imitating the voice of the Swiss ski instructor, urging me to "point your skis straight down." When I started down the slope I suddenly realized how foolish I was but by then I was traveling at a high speed. Snow plowing didn't help much and I just sat down, my skis and poles flying off in all directions. Luckily I wasn't hurt.

On a trip to London with Mary, Bob made his first exploration of Harrod's while Mary shopped and he fell into the hands of one of their wine experts. The result was a planeload of superb wines for Bob's new cellar.

Bob and Morry improvise costumes out of bed sheets at YPO party while Mary looks on.

One of Bob's stories about me, which I feel is not terribly humorous, deals with the time Svendsen brought along a rare vintage, a '53 La Tache, as a gift when he flew to Phoenix on Bob's plane to attend a YPO convention. We were all there to attend the same convention. As Bob was about to uncork the wine at dinner, Mary said, "Why don't we invite the Rotmans?" Bob scorned the suggestion, asserting the bottle was not sufficient for six people.

The next day, however, Bob brought along a trophy, the cork from the La Tache. Big deal. This has been Bob's best wine story for years, told ad nauseum.

My relationship with Mary weathered a minor crisis of which I was unaware. My cigars. I didn't know Mary abhorred my cigar smoking in her spacious home. Occasionally Bob joined in. She confined our smoking together to a far off study. When I came to my senses about the matter, I no longer smoked in her home. Nor, to that matter, anywhere else today except at an occasional reunion with son Richard.

One year Bob and Mary were the guests of the British government at a round of receptions. Wherever they dined, the tradition of passing cigars was followed. Mary collected all the handout stogies, saved them in a shoebox and forwarded it to me on return with a note, "But don't smoke them in my house."

Through the years Bob has gotten me involved in a number of projects. One was a special fund-raising dinner for then Sen. Chuck Percy, one of his friends. Henry Kissinger was the guest of honor. Bob Pritzker, another good friend of Bob's, was co-chairman. The honorary vice chairmen of the dinner was a who's who of Chicago commerce and industry.

Knowing that most political dinners are an evening of ennui, I decided to develop a Roman New Year's theme, although it wasn't the first of the year anywhere. That year the movie "Animal House" was popular and it featured a toga party. I prevailed upon Percy to circumvent Dr. Kissinger's press people and ask his participation. I anticipated being turned down by his PR people since I wanted to print an invitation showing a drawing of Percy and Kissinger in Roman togas.

The evening of the event, Dr. Kissinger started out by saying that he was born in Bavaria, how the King had been mad and that he suspected I was equally insane for celebrating New Year's eve at this time. But he said he was willing to go along for Chuck Percy and that I had talked to him about inventing some Roman New Year historical items.

Henry Kissinger made a very funny speech. He told how he had gone to our press party, went to the bar, and ordered a "martinus" in the spirit of the party's theme. The bartender said, "You must mean a martini." Kissinger related that he had told the bartender, "When I want two, I'll order another."

He also said, "When Chuck talks, I listen. But when I talk, he turns off his hearing aid. "

On another occasion, Bob called and told me he wanted me to be the co-chairman of a dinner along with Bob Pritzker during which he was to receive the Bnai Brith's prestigious Americanism Award. I would do anything for Bob but give a dull speech about him in public. The dinner presented a great opportunity to work over my friend.

I spoke for 16 minutes how, among other things, Mary cut Bob's hair (which she did at one time); how she collected all the fallen hair to make pillows so that Motorola employees could sleep better at night, knowing they were sleeping on Bob's hair. I related how his favorite song was "If I Were a Rich Man, " and how inappropriate I thought the song was for him especially. I sang a few bars of the song while Sylvia walked onstage carrying a barber pole made of red and white carnations. I told one yarn about Bob skiing at Vail, how he learned everything by the book including skiing, and, how, absorbed in his book, he accidentally skied through the kitchen and came out with a brisket in his hands.

True it was a lot of nonsense. The audience found it amusing except for Motorola's public relations officer, Allen Center, who said it was the longest 16 minutes of his life. He spent his time polishing Bob's apple and thought I had done some damage to his boss's image.

While it took a lot of time, I was flattered Bob would ask me to be involved in public events where he was being honored. All these years I have been waiting for someone to honor me so I could ask him to head up the event!

He called one day and asked if I would plan the event when he was being publicly honored as the new board chairman of the Illinois Institute of Technology. This is generally a very formal ceremony full of pomp and circumstance but Bob told me he didn't want that.

I assembled my YPO chorus and went through the process of preparing for the baccalaureate event. I wrote some lyrics to the tune of "How Are Things in Glocca Mora." The idea for a costume occurred to me when Sylvia and I dined in a deli, Kaplan's, near our office in New York. The waiters all wore heavy red suspenders. I got the name of the supplier and purchased enough braces for my chorus.

The president of ITT initially was opposed to my plan for the evening but now he was horrified when he learned what I really had in mind and asked that I clear everything with Bob. When Bob read my lyrics, he came to the conclusion that he could do better and proceeded to write parodies about himself, including one that declared "How Are Things at Motorola. We Don't Really Care."

Attendees at the event were confounded when Bob joined the chorus and seemed to know all the lyrics without referring to the sheet music we all carried. Many later commented on the effectiveness of our costume—white shirts and red suspenders.

Most people don't know the real Galvin, a clown at heart. We play a little game of exchanging semi humorous letters with each other. There is only one time I can recall that Bob bested me, when I asked him to write a letter of recommendation for a club in Palm Springs. Bob decided to write a fake letter, sending a carbon to me, but also wrote a legitimate endorsement to the club. His phony letter told how I had a "dainty backhand", how I had a weird sense of humor and how my social blemishes were balanced by a lovely wife

I called Bob and complained furiously. "I wanted to get into that club," I exclaimed. He then told me the truth about his little joke. Mark one up for him.

Bob and I continue to see one another sporadically despite his constant travels and in spite of our living in California. He has come out on his flying carpet and he and Mary spend a weekend with us. When we are in Chicago, Bob will send his limo to bring us out, knowing I can't do the heavy driving entailed with going to his place in Barrington since my Stone Fish encounter. We go out for a cruise on his pontoon barge and have wine and hors d'oeuvres before dinner. He steers the boat with a small battery operated gadget.

This boy at heart occasionally operates the movement of several tiny boats on the water. I note he has two bottles of fine white on board and later we sit down to dinner with a bottle of superb red.

All in all, he's not a bad guy. And I am pleased he thinks likewise about me.

A Texas Mensch* George

Mitchell

* A person having admirable characteristics.

Sylvia and I were on our way to Athens to attend a YPO convention. Sitting next to us was George Mitchell, a quiet man traveling alone to the same conference. We learned later he and his wife traveled separately because they had 10 children and never flew together out of concern for their brood.

As we talked we learned George was also making a trip to his father's birthplace in the Peloponnesus to do a film of the village to present to his father, who was at home in Galveston confined to a wheelchair because of a broken hip. While he was there, he planned to establish educational scholarships and a permanent dowry fund for young women of Nestani, the town where his father had been a goatherd.

George was a balding man who talked very rapidly in a way you wouldn't guess he was Texan but that was where he was born and raised by his mother and father. His father, he told us, ran a dry cleaning shop and later a shoeshine parlor and managed to send George, his two brothers, Johnny and Christie, and a sister, Maria, through college.

During the course of the trip, he said he was in the energy business and, upon learning what I did professionally, said he would some day need public relations service and would call me. Some months later, he did call and invited me to come to Houston to make a presentation to his people. Other agencies were considered, but we were retained.

George Mitchell turned out to be an extraordinary man and our relationship flourished both personally and professionally. He and his wife, Cynthia, became close friends. We made many foreign trips together to attend Young President and later Chief Executives Organization functions.

George did not like to travel and leave his business but he felt comfortable making a trip if Sylvia and I were going . Occasionally, Cynthia would use this argument as a means of getting George to make a trip she wanted to go on.

When we traveled, George referred to me as his "restaurant grazer" because I would select the places we dined. Through the years he would also introduced me as his "PR guru."

We made various trips together to China, Yugoslavia, Italy, Sicily, Great Britain, and France and spent time together at their homes in Galveston, Houston and Aspen. George and Cynthia made a one-day turnaround trip to Palm Springs to help celebrate my birthday.

We had many memorable adventures, including a rental car that broke a gear as we traveled up the mountain to visit the village of Mostar in Yugoslavia. We picked up a car at the airport in Palermo and, after traveling about 25 miles, learned the auto had no reverse gear, obliging me to run up an inclined road, back out and return for a new car.

Of all the people I have worked with through the years, George was the most creative and profound, generating ideas at a staccato pace and attending to a multitude of affairs all at once. No detail escaped his attention. The principal problem with George was that his voice couldn't keep up with his brain. But he tried. Often it was hard to hear him, he talked so rapidly. Through the years I developed a special GPM auditory system.

George worked his way through college, mostly on scholarships at Texas A&M, where he was captain of the tennis team. George and I won many a doubles matches mostly because he

Cynthia and George Mitchell.

covered his side of the court as well as mine. During his business career he managed to play tennis every day, late afternoons
with his cronies even when his knees began to give him trouble.

After college, he went to work for Amoco as an exploration
geologist. Later he decided to strike out on his own and prevailed upon his brother, Johnny, and small group of men from
Galveston and Houston to subsidize him so he could become a
wildcatter .He made them all very rich.

He launched Oil Drilling, Inc., the predecessor to Mitchell
Energy, with his brother, Johnny and a partner, H. Merlyn
Christie. It became the largest independent producer of natural
gas and other related products. He went into the pipeline business and supplied the City of Chicago with 25 percent of its
natural gas. He added refractors and storage tanks. At one time
Mitchell was grossing close to a billion dollars in revenue.

Realizing there were limits ahead for the supply of energy, George decided to expand his company's role in land development. In nearly 800 separate transactions through intermediaries he purchased nearly 27,000 acres of contiguous land about 30 miles north of central Houston. I came into the picture at the time he was launching The Woodlands, his new town, on 37 acres of his newly acquired land.

George decided to establish the most perfect new town in the United States. He hired the best architects, land planners, lawyers and other professionals to build a town that retained the natural elements of flora and fauna.

He wanted a town where people could live in arboreal splendor, where they lived and shopped and worshiped in beautiful surroundings, and where their kids could go to school without crossing dangerous highways. Ultimately hospitals, schools, a hotel and a meeting center, three championship golf courses, professional tennis and swimming facilities, shopping centers and all the necessary amenities of good living were provided in The Woodlands.

George determined there would be no manufacturing in his town but he did establish a commercial zone for laboratories and other light industries.

He reasoned there could be a great market for Houston employees to make an easy commute to a nearby suburban living environment. Before long, a throughway was built from Houston past the main entrance of The Woodlands.

His pride was the establishment of the Houston Area Research Center for which he donated land and was an important benefactor. Its function was to be a miniature university where scientists could work on projects that would provide new ideas and breakthroughs for industry. George announced he would leave a substantial part of his fortune to HARC.

As this was written, George and Cynthia announced a thirty million dollar gift to the MD Anderson hospital in Houston for a research center.

George did not forget his native hearth, Galveston, and became the city's largest benefactor and taxpayer. He established several developments along Galveston Bay, on one of which he built a lovely modern home.

On our visits to his home on Galveston Bay, George and I would jump into his powerboat and proceed to seed the bay with wire cages to snare white crabs for dinner. One dusk time, George and I went back for our catch only to find that our motor sputtered and died about a half-hour out. Incidentally, the craft had only one paddle.

Luckily the water was only about four feet deep at that point. Despite my protests that I share the burden, George jumped into the water and proceeded to pull the boat ashore, rope around his neck, while I paddled and sang what songs of the sea that I knew.

After we collected our crabs, George would clean them carefully and break them into small pieces after which they were deposited in the refrigerator. He then barbecued the sea feast on a grill with only salt and butter for flavor. One of the great meals of all time.

George was determined to eradicate the city boy in me and exposed me to fishing and hunting. We did night fishing off his dock and occasionally went after doves in a nearby field. When we fished, George baited the hook until I got the hang of it, but most often he did the casting. He would permit me to bring in our catch.

George had sequestered 6,000 acres of his land for his family use. He brought in exotic game in cooperation with the state. There were a number of streams and the ranch, called Cook's Branch, abounded in deer and wild turkey. Sylvia would accompany me while I waited in a blind at 5 am for a deer. George called me "the great white hunter" because instinctively I turned into a sure shot.

George, Sylvia and I once went after white geese in a marsh not far from Houston. We were all garbed in white smocks and lay in wait for our prey while guides festooned the field with white diapers to lead the geese to be believe others had already landed. At about 5 am several of the guides began to quack like geese and you soon heard an enormous din as thousands of birds rose into the air. Sylvia pointed her gun straight into the air, closed her eyes and pulled the trigger once. She was quite sure she brought one down.

Before long, George and Cynthia proceeded with their plans to restore The Strand area near the docks to its previous glory. It was now a rundown area of warehouses and neglected buildings. It never went back to its former usefulness after the devastating Great Storm that wiped out Galveston and killed thousands. They invested 65 million of their own money to buy and restore 17 buildings.

They felt The Strand needed a quality hotel if visitors were to be lured back to Galveston. They hired fine decorators and architects and what emerged was the Tremont, rejuvenated from an old warehouse and now a modern hotel with fin de siecle interior design.

Cynthia spearheaded the emergence of a fine restaurant near the hotel, called the Wentletrap after a seashell prevalent in that area. Other dining spots soon followed, all owned or sponsored by the Mitchells.

George decided to bring back the Mardi Gras to Galveston. It was also a casualty of the Great Storm and subsequent bad times. He went to New Orleans, bought floats for his Mardi Gras and sent them to Galveston by barge. Before long, 600,000 people were coming to see the Mardi Gras and watch a mile of floats and parades. Sylvia and I were always invited by George and Cynthia to be their guests at the Mardi Gras.

At one time George asked me to spend some of my time in Galveston to see if I could develop a hospitality program for the city. Galvenstonians were friendly but laconic and imparted little about their city to visitors.

I met a number of times with key leaders to try to stimulate enthusiasm for a city-wide hospitality program. There were enthusiasms but no pledge of financial support. Our meetings always ended with suggestions I get the money from George.

The program was really going nowhere when George decided to divest his real estate holdings. He sold The Woodlands Development Company for $543 million dollars in 1997 but retained Mitchell Energy as purely an energy company, later selling that, too, to Devon Energy for a reported more than three billion dollars. George and Cynthia retained substantial real estate holdings in Galveston. And George became one of the largest shareholders of Devon.

After the sale, when Mitchell became entirely an energy company with a capable internal public relations staff, there was no longer any need for my professional counsel and we ended our long business relationship.

A word about Cynthia Mitchell. She's now a gray-haired beauty with a penchant for unusual, colorful clothes.

She seemed to raise her family with gentle discipline, always interested in what they were doing and, in later years, as her family married and moved off, she spent a great deal of time traveling around the country to see them. Her relationship with George was also stern but loving. She would take no guff from him. She was probably the only person in the world who could straighten out her husband's frequent absent mindedness, functioning with total devotion to his business matters. And yet, we noticed, many warm conversations between George Mitchell and his gang of ten. He kept a careful eye on his kids.

Besides being appreciative of his reliance on our firm, and on me, I am most grateful for his long friendship. I feel specially rewarded for that chance encounter with him on a plane trip to Greece.

He is in my mind most memorably for his conduct when his executives came to him and informed him the company needed an internal public relations coordinator and had their eye on Joe Kutchin, one of our vice-presidents, who was in charge of their account. George called to tell me what was happening. I always had a policy of never resisting such a move by clients if we were to continue as counsel even though we had employment contracts with members of our staff.

I asked George whether his company planned to continue with us and whether Joe would be financially advantaged by the move. He answered in the affirmative on both points. He then asked about our contractual agreement with his company. When he learned we had an agreement calling for 90 day advance notice of termination, George said, "we'll extend your contract a couple of years. As soon as they get Joe, they'll want to throw out the agency."

Bert Given.

The Garbage Man

Bert Given received a telephone call from a friend one day who told him GE could not service her garbage disposer and she wondered if he could be helpful. Bert was then in the used machinery business with his father Sam and brother Howard. He took her disposer to their shop, took it apart and discovered a fundamental design error. When he reassembled it, she had a working disposer and he had an idea for a future business.

At the time, he and the company's engineering head, Hans Jordan, sketched some ideas, which they filed away until after the war when Bert was looking for consumer products for their company, Given Manufacturing, to manufacture and he remembered the early sketches of the disposer. In March of 1947 their company produced the first Given Disposer, later called Waste King. He was frequently asked about his business and he would joke he was in the garbage business.

When the company went public 51 percent of the stock was equally owned by the family with his father as president. Bert later succeeded to the presidency.

In seeking public relations counsel for his fast-growing company, Bert conducted a most unusual search, something I had never seen done before by any prospective client. He interviewed the important editors of shelter magazines to determine which agencies do the best job of servicing their needs. He came up with a list of three and our firm was on all three lists.

I received a call from Bert asking if I could meet with him in Milwaukee where he would be attending a convention of appliance manufacturers. We met in his hotel suite for several hours and I went through a verbal Rorschach test. Bert didn't want to see any examples of work we had done for other clients nor was he particularly interested in any of the sales stuff I brought along.

He wanted to know what I read; what my outside interests were; what my career was like before I got into public relations; what was my educational background, and something about my family life. Freud couldn't have done any better. During that interrogation we each got to know each other pretty well.

We were retained after that meeting. Thus began a wonderful business and personal relationship that has lasted more than 46 years, many years beyond the original business alliance. He is a concerned, nurturing person and always looks out for the best interests of friends and family. He doesn't just look; he acts.

Waste King was a personal responsibility for me and I would participate in the affairs of the company often as my travels to Los Angeles permitted. It was a rewarding relationship because I had a client who trusted me and seemed to regard my counsel highly.

Our staff enjoyed working on the Waste King account. Working closely with Bert was a group of top notch executives. One, Elm Weingarten, a Harvard Business School graduate, became a friend.

Bert would go along with most of our creative ideas and back us to the hilt. At one conference, I told him I thought his internal engineering department lacked comprehension about the marketplace and wasn't designing with an eye on consumer interests.

I felt they were designing for maximum utility without considering what would sell competitively. Bert assembled the engineering and design departments and invited me to make a speech on the subject. Bert later told me his engineering people responded favorably to my talk. After that, he reported there

Buff and Bert Given

was more talk in the engineering department about marketing.

When Waste King acquired Universal Stove of Chicago, there was intensive debate about the name of the merged company, with a view to preserving the identities of both. By then Waste King had a high recognition factor in the marketplace. Bert brought together his executive staff and outside advisors for a roundtable discussion. He invited me along with Henry Dreyfuss, their designer; the president of the Jorgenson advertising agency, and Dr. Ernest Dichter, the social scientist. Unfortunately the latter became ill and had to leave the discussion.

(Incidentally, we worked with Dr. Dichter on the Mosler Safe account. He told Mosler that safes were masculine in characteristic and they should address their safe advertising at secretaries and office managers. Their advertising agency committed a colossal blunder with a campaign in *Life Magazine* urging secretaries to throw away their old safes, a colloquialism in the east for condoms. The ads were quickly canceled.)

During our conference some held out for retaining the name Waste King for the combined enterprise. Howard Given suggested the company go back to its original roots and take the name Given Enterprises. I did not endear myself to him by stating that, at this point, after so much brand name identification, it would be easier for the family to take the name Waste King. The decision was made to call the company Waste King Universal.

Howard was always uncomfortable with my personal relationship with Bert, feeling it was based on personal outside interests. At one time when Bert was on sick leave and Howard was running the company, he threatened me with cancellation of our services, if, in his opinion, we weren't adequately serving Waste King.

Family businesses encounter special difficulties. My involvement with the Given family's business/personal problems taught me a lot about the obstacles facing family business members who attempt business relationships. Later, when I organized seminars on family businesses for the Chief Executives Organization, I was able to draw upon the understanding I gained through my observations at that time.

Bert merged his company with Norris Industries and joined that company as a key executive for a brief period of time. Later he bought several industries with partners. He sold his last venture, Califone, manufacturers of audiovisual products for educational institutions.

Bert lost two wives to death. The first, Nan, welcomed Sylvia and me into her home very warmly. My family felt a closeness to her and were grief-stricken when she died. Bert's second marriage was to Kayla, a psychologist, with whom we were less close.

When Bert married a third time, he found Buffy, an architect, writer and social activist. She is a delightful person, a bundle of energy and a perfect helpmate for Bert at this time of his life.

From his union with Nan, came three children, Judy, Bob and Johnny. We cherish a familial relationship. When Nan died,

Bert decided to sell his lovely home to his daughter, who married a brilliant young attorney, Howard Smith, who became a friend. Unfortunately, he died in the same house where Judy's mother had succumbed. She is happily remarried.

Bert and Buff are active theatergoers, attend musical events often, and are extremely involved in the affairs of the American Jewish Committee. Buff has just written a romantic novel, which was recently published.

When Bert and I first met, I told him I had a modest collection of paintings and sculpture, including several by an American artist working in Rome, Robert Cook. By coincidence, Bert had seen a piece by Cook in New York and was buying it. It's called "Leapfrog."

Bert may have saved my life by his intercession when I was suffering the ravages of my Stone Fish infection. At the time I was being treated at the Eisenhower Hospital in Rancho Mirage, but Bert wasn't satisfied with my progress and made repeated calls to inquire about me. He kept insisting I consult with a tropical disease specialist in Los Angeles, Dr. Clare Panosian. It was she who made the diagnosis of my ailment and recommended appropriate treatment.

I have had three wonderful brothers and Bert became my fourth, perhaps my closest confidant, a foster uncle to our kids and a loving friend to Sylvia. Over the years our families grew close and exchanged visits in each other's homes. Our offspring, Betty, Jesse and Richard, have high regard for Bert and think of him as part of our extended family.

Bert Given. A better friend you couldn't have.

Dan Rather. His Chicago

Dilemma

Yelling and gesticulating wildly, the man hanging out the rear window of a Yellow Cab speeding south on Chicago's Lake Shore drive clearly needed help.

He got it from a passing police squad car. This is his story: he was being kidnapped by the driver.

Dan Rather, CBS Evening News anchorman, had gone to Chicago to interview a Chicago celebrity, Studs Terkel, homespun journalist, author and radio personality. His taxi driver couldn't find Studs' address on the near north side.

He insisted Dan get out of the cab and continue his search afoot. Dan refused, and the driver sped off in the midst of their argument with his passenger still in the back seat, probably heading for the central police headquarters south of the loop.

There was a big hullabaloo about the incident in the Chicago media. *Tribune* columnist Mike Royko severely lampooned Dan; there were front-page stories implying Dan's behavior had been erratic and foolish. I don't know if the interview with Studs ever happened.

Sylvia and I heard the story from Dan when we dined together with his wife a couple months later at the 21 Club in New York. We had the table in the corner in the downstairs bar area of the Club, favorite spot for celebrities. At one time our firm represented 21 Brands, owned by the family that started 21.

Dan told us that Chicago was one of his favorite cities, but he was reluctant to go back. "Maybe the cab drivers will picket me and the press will turn unfriendly again," he said. I told Dan I couldn't permit his romance with Chicago to be broken. "Leave it to me," I told him, and Dan agreed to come back if I found the climate had improved for him.

When I got back home, I called Dr. Rolf Weil, then president of Roosevelt University, where I was on the Board. I recommended Dan be invited to make a commencement speech and given an honorary degree. Rolf said he would be happy to present Rather with a Medal of Freedom but would not award him the honorary degree.

Surprised and disappointed, I called Jerry Stone, chairman of the university, (then chairman of Stone Container Corp.). Jerry immediately saw the advantage to the University of Rather receiving an honorary degree and speaking at commencement and arranged it.

Next I contacted someone I knew at Chicago's Television Academy. Would they like to have Dan Rather as a luncheon speaker? It would have to be on a Saturday, I said. They leaped at the chance.

Finally I called Jerry Feldman, president of Yellow Cab. "Jerry, can you assure me of no unfriendly protests by your drivers when Rather comes to town?" He promised the drivers would cooperate and offered to send 150 cabs to the airport to escort Dan into town. Dan refused that kind offer, as he had refused the company's offer to fire the driver who "kidnapped" him.

Dan and Jean came to town and stayed at our lakefront apartment.

Dan did a beautiful and impressive job of talking to his colleagues at the Television Academy. He spoke extemporaneously and with a great deal of erudition at the pre—commencement luncheon at Roosevelt. His commencement talk was warmly received. When he did his radio broadcast that weekend, and talked about Roosevelt, one listener, Col. Henry Crown, sent in a $25,000 contribution.

Dan has expressed his gratitude for my intervention many times, once sending us a lovely apple in Steuben glass, an apple from the Big Apple. Recently he sent me a prized CBS News golf cap and a T-shirt with the CBS insignia on it along with his embroidered signature. That hat gets a lot of attention, especially when I travel and line up at the ticket counter.

On our first morning together Sylvia stayed home recovering from surgery while Jean, Dan and I spent several hours touring the art galleries on the near north side

When Dan decided to go back to our apartment to work on his speech, Jean continued her round of art galleries.

We were close to the Outer Drive, so I suggested to Dan that we take a short cut across busy Lake Shore drive, at the bridge where Pres. Roosevelt had made his famous "day of infamy" speech.

Dodging the traffic, we discovered a concrete barrier in the middle of the drive, too high for us to climb over. This was something I hadn't anticipated.

Beside us a recreational vehicle was momentarily stopped by the traffic, going our way. "Hey mister, " I shouted, " How about giving us a lift to the corner?" The driver may have recognized Dan; he told us to hop in and we clambered into the vehicle with Dan spilling into the rear seat where a lady sat contemplating the scenery.

She looked up in surprise as the new passengers came on board. "Dan Rather!" she exclaimed. "Only in Chicago! Only in Chicago!"

They took us right up to our front door at 400 East Randolph Street.

Recently, while writing this book, I wrote to Dan and asked if he would send me a message for inclusion in this book. His nice salute adorns my back cover.

Bob Dickerman. My Cowboy Buddy

I suffered an acute sense of loss when Bob Dickerman died.
I was fortunate to have had him as a thoughtful friend for more
than 25 years and had a profound feeling of sorrow when I learned
he suffered a fatal heart attack one day in his Century City office.

Bob was a YPO buddy, who became a close confidant over
the years and a friend with whom Sylvia and I shared many adventures and common interests.

He was an attorney with many real estate holdings, who started
out as house counsel to Microdot Corp., a publicly held company, and eventually became its president. He built Microdot
into a sizable company.

There were many tennis and golf games and frequent dinners together when Sylvia and I came to Los Angeles. He was a
source of information on the latest dining spots and insisted that,
in his town, he was always the host.

In our occasional telephone conversations he would always
inquire solicitously what was doing with me, how Sylvia was and
what new projects were occupying my attention.

We saw each other frequently in Palm Springs because Bob
and his wife Madeline had a hobby of finding condos, decorat-
ing them and selling them at a profit. For a while he had a home
at the Lakes Country Club and others in Beverly Hills and Newport Beach.

Bob Dickerman.

He was very interested in boating and had several boats at Newport, including a motor launch he designed. The soul of generosity, he invited us and a group of his friends to travel on his boat to Catalina Island and stay for a weekend at his expense in the former Wrigley Estate.

Bob and I both loved western clothes. On various trips together, we searched for bolos, western belt buckles, cowboy hats and shirts with ornamentation, most of which I hardly wear these days. Bob must have had a half dozen western hats. I can recall the two of us walking jauntily down the Champs Elysee in Paris wearing our western duds, unperturbed that we were attracting a lot of stares.

When I was asked to arrange one of the national conclaves of the Chief Executives Organization, I induced Bob to be the educational chairman and he did a great job of collecting a star assemblage of communications experts to participate in our seminar, called "Strange Encounters with the Fourth Estate."

Bob called one day and asked if Sylvia and I were interested in joining a group of his California friends in a cruise from Venice to Dubrovnik and back. We met him and Madeline in Paris for a few days, then traveled to Venice for another couple days for a stay at the Gritti Palace before boarding our chartered yacht, "The Columbaio." We traveled in luxurious splendor along the coastline, occasionally hearing the noise of gunfire farther inland as a war was being waged. The coast cities were tranquil but we saw evidence of shelling when we arrived in Dubrovnik.

One year we decided to take a Tauk tour together and traveled to the Canadian Rockies by bus and then rented a car to see the American Rockies.

Among his virtues, Bob had a good eye for art. His homes reflected his and Madeline's good taste. Sylvia and I have a modest collection of paintings by Jean Charlot, the Frenchman who went to Mexico to join Diego Rivera during the revolution. He became known as the father of the muralist school. I discovered Bob was also a fan of Charlot's and had some of his work.

An exhibit of his generosity was when he and my friend Marshall Wais paid for a huge party on my 78th birthday at Chasen's in Los Angeles.

A lot more could be said about the many wonderful characteristics of my friend Bob. After he died, a huge memorial service attended by hundreds was held at Hillcrest Country Club. I was among the many speakers. The size of the audience was testimony to the way so many people felt about him. We keep in touch with Madeline and have lunch with her when we are in Los Angeles. There's something missing.

Sam LeFrak. No Small Plans

A stranger loomed beside my chaise lounge as I read at poolside during a YPO convention in Puerto Rico. I looked up and saw an imposing figure. He introduced himself as Sam LeFrak and said he had major interests in the movie business.

I was somewhat startled by his declaration and I quickly realized he thought I too had "substantial movie business interests." He apparently read my fact sheet in the "Who's Who" booklet circulated at the convention and assumed my PR representation of the Academy of Motion Picture Arts & Sciences indicated I had financial clout in the industry, a very mistaken assumption.

He plopped down beside me and we began a conversation that has lasted for more than 40 years. Sam enveloped Sylvia and me to the extent we were constantly together at the convention; at dinners, and when he met with his friends. At least one of them, Norman Alexander, now chairman of Sequa Industries, remains a friend to this day. Another crony was Steve Ross, who later in life formed the Warner Communications

Sam is a stocky man with a ruddy complexion and red blonde hair. Many people, I learned over the years, are repelled by Sam's forthrightness and his unabashed account of his successes, but I always found him fascinating—an American original with more creativity and daring than almost anyone I ever met.

When Sam said he was a landlord with ownership of 85,000 apartments in New York, he was. (He later told me he sold 15,000 and was down to about 70,000.)

Ethel and Sam LeFrak.

When Sam said he was in the billionaire class, he was.

When he related he is going to build a city on the west side of the Hudson, he did. ("Newport City.")

He talked about building affordable apartments for middle-class New Yorkers. He did. ("LeFrak City" in the Queens.)

Sam is Dr. LeFrak now. Also, "Sir." He has honorary degrees from more than a dozen universities and countries. He spread the word for low cost housing throughout Europe and Scandinavia. He called and said he was coming to Palm Springs in his plane. He had been invited to see the Walter Annenberg art collection. (Sam himself has an enormous collection of valuable paintings and sculpture). When he arrived, he said he only wanted to see two people in the desert, Walter Annenberg and me. I wondered if the latter was impressed to be included in my company.

Sam bought a magnificent 85-foot yacht from Sam Bloom, "The Jonathan", a world-class boat featured in yacht anthologies. Sam calls it a "floating furniture store." Priceless paintings, Chinese antiques, comfortable guest staterooms. Bloom, of Jim

Beam fame, used the yacht for pinochle games with friends in Chicago's Belmont Harbor.

Sam would occasionally call and invite Sylvia and me to weekend on "The Jonathan" when it was moored in Miami Beach or Freeport. We would play tennis ashore and do some fancy eating.

On one cruise Sam announced he was going to buy a larger yacht and invited me to go along to inspect some in Miami.

One was owned by Augie Busch; another by Sam Rosensteil. Both were magnificent yachts, larger than Sam's. To me it was like inspecting multi-million dollar homes I could never afford. My recollection is that Busch's boat was about 125 feet long and had all kinds of amenities like walk-in freezers and a dining room that could seat 25 guests.

Rosensteil, who was confined to a wheelchair, had an elevator installed so he could get to the deck. (We were told he wanted to keep it out of his wife's hands in an impending divorce.)

When we got back to the yacht and were dressing for dinner, Sam pounded on our stateroom door. He had to see me right away. I tried to get him to wait until dinner a half hour later but he was adamant and, in my bathrobe, I stepped into the hallway.

He said he was going to make an offer for the Busch boat and wanted my opinion, as an alleged expert in "images." I asked why he needed a larger boat. Sam explained his family was growing; he needed more staterooms, and wanted to cross the ocean. Besides, he said, others in New York had larger yachts and "The Jonathan " was not consistent with the image he wanted to maintain. I dismissed his concern.

Sam and his wonderful wife, Ethel, are always gracious to us when we come to New York city. On a recent visit he proudly showed us through the metropolis he built, "Newport City", a new town of office buildings, homes, schools and other metropolitan amenities. When it came time for lunch, the large restaurant he owns opened just to serve the four of us an excellent meal

Sam's son, Richard, now runs the company. Richard is a

refinement of the species, a well-educated soft-spoken man. Sam has three daughters, Jackie, the youngest; Francine and Denise. Francine has made a career for herself in the production of movies. There are also vigorous, well-educated grandsons coming along.

I first got an appreciation of Sam's opportunistic creativity at one YPO convention when Walter Reuther was a guest speaker. The organization looked around for someone to host the labor leader for an afternoon. Most at the conventioneers were not eager to entertain him. Knowing Sam had his yacht in the harbor, they asked him.

He readily agreed and they set out for an afternoon cruise, during which Sam inquired how the automotive union invests its money. Reuther talked about treasuries and other conservative investments. Sam gave him a lesson in mortgages. He described in great detail the investment returns from mortgages. Later when Sam needed some big money for one of his developments, the United Auto Workers became a principal investor.

Recently, I heard a story about Sam's yacht from Everett Kovler, who was Bloom's son in law. After Sam bought the yacht, he invited Bloom aboard to celebrate the purchase of the yacht. During their dinner, Bloom mentioned he was removing a recent purchase of steaks from the boat's freezer. Sam replied he had purchased everything on the boat. Besides, he pointed out that Bloom had promised to make certain repairs, which he hadn't done. The dinner ended on a low note.

Kovler told me LeFrak sued for the repairs. The suit tied up Bloom's estate in probate and he had to settle for nearly $40,000. Bloom should have bought new steaks.

Marshall Wais.

Twenty Bucks Richer

Marshall Wais is possibly the only industrialist in history to have been kidnapped and made a modest profit from the experience. Twenty bucks.

He was asleep one morning in his San Francisco home in Sea Cliff when he was awakened with a gun at his head. Two kidnappers had waited for the housekeeper, Yung Wong, to bring out the refuse at 7:15 am, apparently knowing her habits. Handcuffed, she was ordered to show the way to the master bedroom on the second floor where Marshall was asleep. Wong offered to make coffee for the intruders and they removed her cuffs, after which she summoned Marshall's stepson, Tom, asleep in a lower bedroom of the mansion.

Barely able to speak English, Wong excitedly thrust her arms at him as though holding two guns and indicated there were two armed men upstairs. Tom climbed out of his bedroom window, a precarious activity since the house rested on a ravine, and quickly hurried to a neighbor's house to summon the police after which he called his mother, Lonna, who was visiting in New York.

The invaders permitted Marshall to pull some clothes on, tied him up, blindfolded him and forced him into a white mini van, driving away at rapid speed, telling him they wanted a million dollars in cash.

A cool customer, Marsh made a classic remark: "I don't have

Lonna and Marshall Wais.

that much on me but I can probably get it." Marshall then talked them down to a half million.

The police arrived almost immediately but by then the van was on its way. The kidnappers permitted Marsh to call his treasurer, Bill Griffin, to tell him to assemble the cash. By then the FBI and the San Francisco police were involved. While the kidnappers drove around Golden Gate Park for almost eight hours, Griffin hastily assembled the cash from various bank accounts and delivered it as instructed to an empty car.

The two men then pushed Marsh out of their van and gave him twenty dollars for cab fare to return home.

Meanwhile, the cops, knowing where the mini van was, formed a road block, surrounded the vehicle and hauled the men off to jail. They were later sentenced to prison. One was an older man, a three-time loser, and other a younger man. Both were criminals with records. The older man was sentenced to life in prison. The younger man got eight years and eight months.

Marshall had always tried to keep a low profile in San Francisco but the newspaper stories and the television coverage of

Lonna when she returned to San Francisco propelled both into the limelight they had sought to avoid up until then.

Sylvia and I dine with the Waists frequently whenever they come to roost in Rancho Mirage, most often at his favorite restaurant, Lord Fletcher.

He is a generous host when Sylvia and I have the good fortune to vacation in his spacious Eze villa with its infinti pool. Lonna and Marsh and their friends entertain each other with large dinner parties at the posh restaurants of the Riviera and always include Sylvia and me.

Most of their friends are quite special. It apparently takes special qualities to winter on the Riviera. One, a nephew of comedian George Burns, was a wonderful raconteur and told hilarious stories about his uncle

I met Marsh before we were both in YPO and when he lived near us in Glencoe. In later years, I ran into him again in connection with YPO conventions and we began to pal around together. He was between marriages and most often had a chauffeured car, which made our various adventures most convenient. He was a bon vivant with class and generally with a luscious babe at his side.

In those days it was nothing, when we were at a convention in Monte Carlo, to take a trip several hours away to dine on bouillabaisse at Menton or three—star cooking at the Moulin des Mougins restaurant in Mougin.

Marshall had a special allure to women. He could be likened to the actor Yul Brenner with his shiny dome. He looks tough but he is actually a benevolent softy with a lot of acumen going for him. Without good business sense he couldn't have built what was probably the West Coast's leading specialty steel processing plants. When he married Lonna, he decided to cash in his chips in order to spend more time with her at their various residences and travel wherever they wished to go.

Marshall impressed me and a lot of other people one day at a NATO conference in Brussels sponsored by the YPO. He took the microphone when the speaker didn't show up and delivered an absorbing speech about the importance of NATO.

Many of Marshall's friends are military leaders. One recently told me Marsh was a hero to the Air Force because his company produced the steel shelters that protected U.S. planes from enemy shelling.

Marshall knew of my involvement with the building the Globe Theater in London. When Sam Wanamaker was in town, I arranged for the two of them to meet, expecting a modest but generous contribution. Marshall pledged a quarter of a million dollars and later donated steel needed for a proscenium in the Globe. Marshall is honored with a special etching on the wall of the theater.

His leadership activities in the Young Presidents Organization earned him the presidency of the World Business Organization, one of the successor groups for YPO graduates.

David Hinson. "Roger, 10-4"

I asked David Hinson why he gave up the lucrative field of corporate counseling to take on the assignment of administrator of the Federal Aviation Administration at a drastic reduction in income. "Because I want to be regarded as America's top aviator," he replied. Dave is not given to braggadocio.

He had been a Navy flyer. A test pilot for Northwest Airlines. He operated an airplane service business in the northwest, and founded Midway Airlines. When the U.S. got him to head the FAA, he may have been the most savvy aviation man in history to manage the authority Until Dave, heads of the FAA were always retired admirals or generals or political figures who knew little about the airplane business.

Before he divested himself of his businesses in the northwest, he got special permission from the governor of Oregon to fly one of the Air Guard's new McDonald Douglas F4 Phantom fighter planes.

Sylvia and I can testify personally to his prowess. He flew from Sun Valley, Idaho, to Palm Springs to pick us up in his own plane and then brought us to Sun Valley to stay in his lovely home. He and Ursula made arrangements for us to see the magnificent jazz festival there.

Ursula is a living doll, a Swiss miss who was formerly an airline flight attendant. One of their sons, Eric, is also a former Navy crack pilot whom I regard as an adopted son.

Dave was a Republican in the Democratic Clinton administration. He had told the President he would serve only one term.

Ursula Hinson.

Dave Hinson.

There was tremendous pressure from people in Congress to convince him to stay on when George W.Bush won. As Dave would say—negative.

Dave told me had made a recent trip to Saudi Arabia with just one aide on a large Air Force jet. I inquired why he hadn't flown commercial.

"When I arrive, " he said, " I want the Saudis to know I am representing the President of the United States."

He is a very serious guy with a streak of pixie in him. He is given to military terms like "Roger " and "10-4" and all that lingo but I love him nevertheless. We play golf occasionally in Sun Valley and in Rancho Mirage at Tamarisk.

Dave was doing a magnificent job of building Midway into a significant factor in the airline business when his resources were strained by the oil shortage shortly after he had invested millions in opening a hub in Philadelphia. Unable to continue, he closed down Midway and accepted corporate counseling assignments. One, for Raytheon, caused him to travel the world in its interests.

He became a consultant for McDonald Douglas and sold one

of the largest military contracts in history, a two billion dollar contract to the Saudis. He was also elected to the board of trustees of the Smithsonian Air and Space Exploration Museum in Washington.

John D. MacArthur

I had a misadventure trying to handle public relations for
John D. MacArthur, president of Banker's Life Insurance.
MacArthur was an intense, short guy. He talked fast, explicitly.
"I want a lot of publicity, " he declared. I interviewed him as
much as his short span of attention would permit. MacArthur
was an irascible, impatient character. Once on the way to a meeting in his car he was offended by traffic and stoplights. He just
drove onto the sidewalk whenever it suited his fancy.

I soon discovered John loved to gallivant around the country
in his own twin engine plane. I did some research and discovered how many Chicago companies owned planes at the time.

I suggested to John we organize a "Mercy Fleet" comprised
of corporate planes that would fly missions of mercy on call. I got
the Red Cross to cooperate by placing me on 24—hour notice
for emergencies of that nature. They were delighted with the
scheme. Then I approached Lou Shainmark, managing editor of
Chicago's *Herald American* newspaper. Would the paper like to
co-sponsor the "Mercy Fleet?" I asked. Lou felt it was a pretty
good promotional idea.

Then I reported to MacArthur. He agreed to the terms I set
forth, including serving as Commander of the "Mercy Fleet."

The *Herald American* ran a big picture of John on the front
page, announcing its sponsorship of the "Mercy Fleet." And then
I just waited for the first emergency. I wanted to launch the program with a mission by a MacArthur flight. I could imagine the

Air Fleet to Aid Sufferers

READY TO FLY HELP to sufferers, Chicago business firms owning planes have pooled them into the Chicago Herald-American Mercy Air Fleet. Organization will use facilities of this newspaper. John D. MacArthur (right, above), is fleet commander. He sits with Pilot Frank Porter in the plane of Bankers Life & Casualty Co., which he heads. BELOW, nurses from Mercy and Michael Reese Hospital line up on wing of International Harvester Co., B-23, ready for mercy missions. (Herald - American photos)

John MacArthur in his plane.

front-page headline: "Commander MacArthur on First Herald American Mercy Mission."

I waited for the first emergency call on the services of our "Mercy Fleet." It finally came. A call from the Red Cross during the night. A need for plasma in flooded Mississippi. I called MacArthur's office. He wasn't available and no one was talking. MacArthur had a habit of disappearing, I later learned, with an errant female. His staff was tight-lipped about his whereabouts. I was frantic! I finally reached his pilot, who told me he could not fly without MacArthur's OK. Excitedly I told him MacArthur would approve if he did the mission. He, too, could not reach his boss. I told him I would take full responsibility for the ordering the

Herald American

Mercy Fleet was front page news.

flight. Off he went and the headlines in the *Herald American* told the story, as though John were aboard.

MacArthur came back from wherever he was. He apparently read about his heroics in the paper. I explained I had urged his pilot to fly. "This was what we were waiting for," I exclaimed, feeling proud of my achievement.

"I never intended to fly," he said. "You're fired!" Harshe later told John he couldn't fire us because we quit. Years later, after John's death, we were again hired by Banker's when Bob Ewing was president. When I told him the story, he said that was

McArthur making deals at hotel coffee shop.

one he had never heard before but didn't doubt its veracity, knowing his old colleague.

John MacArthur used to sit in the coffee shop of a hotel he owned in Florida making deals while chain-smoking cigarettes and drinking endless cups of coffee, a telephone at his elbow. He died a billionaire.

Ewing once showed me the inventory of companies Banker's owned as a result of those coffee shop deals. The list covered two pages of closely spaced printing on eight by 10 paper. He even owned an advertising agency, which Ewing didn't know about.

After MacArthur died, his son, Rod, led the move on the board to commemorate John by establishing the now—famous Catherine and John D. MacArthur Scholarship Awards.

The Jokers Wild Club

Isn't there room any more for peaceful discourse? I asked myself one evening after I had spent a couple of hours at a dinner party listening to an uninformed idiot carry on about a variety of issues—Bush, Enron, Israel, terrorism, etc. etc. ad nauseum. No exchange of ideas, no opportunity for calm conversation. He wasn't willing to listen what I had to say. My voice was drowned in the torrent of his words.

Where are the good conversations of yesteryear? Most annoying was that my accidental dinner companion acted like he was a country club field general, safe from harm's way, advising Sharon how to conduct the war, berating Israel policies. He was not only wrong and stupid, but in a loud voice.

As a personal antidote to this kind of experience, I started a new venture in February of '02—a luncheon club where nothing of a serious nature could be discussed. I tried out the idea on a few friends and we have held two meetings at Marie Callendar's, a nearby restaurant affording a private facility. I seem to have a hit on my hands and most of my fellow celebrants have asked if they could bring guests. I told them they could if they subscribed to club rules:

You can only attend if hitherto you have exhibited a sense of humor.

No interruption of storytellers and no rolling of the eyes or the slightest indication you have heard the joke or tale before.

For the time being, no women to avoid exclamations of horror when a member uses a word they pretend never to have heard before.

Violators of rules are subject to expulsion or fines. Most egregious violation would be the introduction of serious conversation.

No dues because I don't want to do any bookkeeping. Enough that I do meeting announcements. Fines are given to the waitress.

In my initial announcement, I urged members to read an article in the *New Yorker* magazine, where the writer, Adam Gopnick, seeking his Jewish roots, began to examine Jewish humor. He wondered why Jewish humor is so offhand and self-deprecating and gave several examples, which I passed on in my first notice:

Customer in a restaurant: "Waiter, what's the fly doing in my soup?"

Waiter: "A back stroke."

Another customer: "Waiter, what's that fly doing in my soup"

Waiter: "There wasn't room for him in the potato salad."

I almost bent our male chauvinist rules by inviting Myra MacPherson, former *Washington Post* reporter and nominee for the Pulitzer Prize for her book on Vietnam. I suspected Myra knew how to shut up and not express indignation over words she's heard before. Unfortunately, being on a book tour, she couldn't attend and left me with this story:

A priest is assigned by the Vatican to spend solitary days examining all the literature of the church to bring matters up to date and make corrections needed. The Bishop in full ecclesiastical dress returned a week later and found the priest sobbing.

"My son, " he asked. "Why are you weeping?"

The priest stood up, his eyes filled with tears, and exclaimed, "It said celebrate. Not celibacy!"

My initial contribution was a recount of an experience I had at the International Art Show in Palm Springs. I wandered into a Danish exhibit of wood work and began a conversation with the exhibitor. I told him I had been to Copenhagen. In leaving I tried to think of the only Scandinavian words I had heard in Denmark, a salute over a drink. I pride myself on knowing a variety of ethnic drink salutes.

As I departed, I extended my hand and said, "Dinna Skoal, Flikka Skoal."

His reply:" How do you do. I'm Sven Jensen."

It reminded me of the time I prepared for my first business visit to Japan by signing up for 10 lessons in Japanese at Berlitz. My teacher, a Japanese lady, asked the purpose of my visit. I explained my business purpose and told her I was going to make a speech at Dentsu Advertising agency and asked her for the words in Japanese for public relations, which I wanted to use in my speech.

"Oh, Mr. Rotman," she exclaimed. "All through Japan it's called PR."

One of our Jokesters, Bill Pattis, comes to our sessions brimming with jokes to tell. Bill is a rather large individual, weighing *well* over 250 pounds, and treats his corpulence with self-mockery. He told of the time he stood on a scale in a drug store, inserted a coin, and received a paper message that read: "Come back when you're alone."

Bill's latest: Patrons in Kabul were watching a striptease where the dancers were clad only in veils. According to Bill, the men kept shouting, "Take it off! Take it off! Show your face! Show your face!"

Mel Goldberg, retired physician, golf nut and practicing amateur comedian, always has a few morsels for the Jokesters. His latest:

Son comes home with good news. "Mom I found the girl of my dreams!" "That's wonderful. When can I meet her? Is she Jewish?"

Son: "Yes, she is. You'll like her"."What's her name?" " Monica Lewinsky." Mom: "What happened to that nice Catholic girl you were going with?"

Don Wexler, architect par excellence, told the story of the man lying in bed, dying, in the last moments of his life, suddenly began to awaken and sniff at a familiar aroma coming from the kitchen. "She's making honey cake!" he exclaimed to his visitor. "Go to the kitchen and tell her I'd like a slice." The visitor returned a few minutes later, empty handed. "She turned me down," he reported. "She said the cake was for later."

Norman Mark, TV personality and writer, told of the rich guy who bought a new Lexus and, as he opened the door, a SUV slams into it, knocking it off its hinges and severing his arm. The unlucky guy is lying on the ground crying "Oh, My Lexus. My Lexus" A passerby who rushed over to help cried out, "why are you crying about your car not your arm?" The man on the ground then cried out, "My Rolex. Oh, My Rolex!"

Bob Berkoff, former dress manufacturer, told of the IRS agent who called the rabbi of a New York synagogue and inquired whether one of his congregants, Jacob Cohn, had contributed $50,000 to the synagogue. "Yes, he will," answered the rabbi.

A recent article in the *Jewish Forward* newspaper, May 3, 2002, ran a lengthy article by Abraham Genauer, examining the special qualities of Jewish humor. He wrote that much current Jewish humor had a launching pad in the Borscht belt, the tryout stage for many leading comics like Milton Berle, Danny Kaye and Mel Brooks, who once was booed off the stage and yelled to the Jewish crowd "You're anti-Semitic!"

Genauer wrote about comic Mickey Freeman, who once said he had worked in so many sloppy Catskills hotels, their "postcards had unmade beds on them."

In my youth, when I was sentenced to four years in Hebrew school by my mother, I read Sholom Aleichem in Hebrew. "Fiddler on the Roof" is attributed to his writings. I recall one of his stories told of the man taking a train ride from one Russian town to the next, on his way to visit a friend, the president of a synagogue. Everywhere he went he got insulting remarks about his friend. When he arrived, he inquired why his friend served as president of the congregation if people sullied his reputation. "Oh, for the honor," he replied. "For the honor." For the "kovid". It's funnier in Yiddish.

A contribution to Jokers Club by Marlene Bellis, Chicago

honorary member:

It was a sweltering August day when the Cohen brothers entered the posh Dearborn, Mich. offices of Henry Ford. "Mr. Ford," announced Norman Cohen, the eldest of the three. "We have a remarkable invention that will revolutionize the automobile industry. Ford looked skeptical, but their threat to offer it to the competition kept his interest piqued. "We would like to demonstrate it to you in person."

After a little cajoling, they brought Mr. Ford outside and asked him to enter a black automobile parked in front of the building. Hyman Cohen, the middle brother, opened the door of the car. "Please step inside, Mr. Ford."

"What!" shouted the tycoon, "Are you crazy? It must be two hundred degrees in there." "It is," smiled the youngest brother, Max, "but sit down Mr. Ford, and push the white button." Intrigued, Ford pushed the button. All of a sudden a whoosh of freezing air started blowing from vents all around the car, and within seconds the automobile was not only comfortable, it was quite cool.

"This is amazing!" exclaimed Ford. "How much do you want for the patent?" Norman spoke up, "The price is one million dollars." Then he paused. "And there is something else. The name 'Cohen Brothers Air Conditioning' must be stamped right next to the Ford logo!"

"Money is no problem,"retorted Ford, "but no way will I have a Jewish name next to my logo on my cars!" They haggled back and forth for a while and finally they settled. Five million dollars, but the Cohens' name would be left off. However, the first names of the Cohen brothers would be forever emblazoned upon the console of every Ford air conditioning system. And that is why, even today, whenever you enter a Ford vehicle, you will see those three names clearly printed on the air conditioning control panel: NORM, HI and MAX

.

Spencer Stuart, a friend of long standing, is an honorary member of the Jokers Club because he contributes E-mail humor on a sporadic basis. Spence, who founded a consulting firm bearing his name, is a desert expatriate building a new home in Arizona. His most recent:

A couple had been married for 40 years and also celebrated their 60th birthday together. During the celebration, a fairy godmother appeared and said,"Because you have been a loving couple all these years, I will give each of you one wish." The wife requested a romantic vacation with her husband, and the fairy godmother with a poof! placed in her hand two tickets for a voyage around the world. Next it was the husband's turn. He paused for a moment and said," Well, honestly I would love to have a woman 30 years younger than me. Boom! this time. The fairy godmother waved her wand and he was 90 years old.

The Enigmatic Joe Bolker

Joe Bolker was a tall, handsome man with prematurely gray hair, reminding me of the late actor Jeff Chandler. He was well built and lean and swam about six miles every morning. He dressed beautifully, his shoes always carefully polished and he maintained a fashionable apartment in a Beverly Hills high rise. My wife likened him to the Peter Sellers role as Chauncey Gardiner in the film, "Being There", whose solemn mien was mistaken for wisdom. By coincidence, Chauncey and Joe were both landscape experts.

.

Joe was married four times, three to daughters of some very rich men. The first spouse was a lovely redhead, Janice, the daughter of Mark Taper, the savings and loan king of Los Angeles, who donated lots of money to artists in Los Angeles. The second was the daughter of Judge Samuel Huffines, who built the Astrodome in Houston. His fourth marriage was to Victoria Leonova, of Russian descent, with whom he had a child.

His most celebrated marriage, his third, was to the daughter of Aristotle Onnasis, the billionaire Greek shipping magnet, who ultimately threatened his daughter with disinheritance unless she permitted annulment essentially because he was opposed to her marriage to someone of another faith.

Joe met Christine Onassis at pool side in Monte Carlo where she was serving as a volunteer hostess at the YPO convention. She flipped for his good looks and masculinity and literally followed him when he returned to Los Angeles. Joe hadn't encouraged her to do so, but they were married and she moved into his apartment in Century City. People still talk about how she rewarded elevator operators, beauticians, manicurists and grocery clerks and others with hundred dollar tips. For the first time in her life, she went shopping in a supermarket and wandered the city alone. Before, she lived like a princess, a sheltered, protected life. Here was Mrs. Bolker, housewife at large.

It was not a marriage made in heaven but she was in heaven until papa forced her to come back home. The marriage was annulled and she and Joe remained friends thereafter. She later died allegedly of an overdose although it was publicly described as heart failure.

I met Joe at a YPO convention in Puerto Rico when I noticed him across the swimming pool one afternoon and saw he was wearing the little beanie worn in those days by freshmen members. I walked across the pool to introduce myself and see whether I could offer advice or introductions to a new member. He was sitting with his lovely looking wife to whom he introduced me.

I inquired where he lived and what he did for a living, and, when he told me he built homes in Los Angeles, I mentioned there were many builders among our members. My eyes caught sight of Sam LeFrak sitting across the pool and I mentioned to Joe that Sam was one of the largest builders in the United States. Sam was known then as New York City's largest landlord and No.1 builder.

I asked Joe if he would like to meet Sam and he agreed to go across the pool where Sam was talking energetically with several friends. I caught Sam's eye and made the introduction. "What do you do?" asked Sam. Joe answered he built homes in Los Angeles and Sam said he was in a number of projects there with several partners. When Joe asked him who the partners were, he replied when he heard the names, "They're both crooks". I could see the icicles quickly forming in Sam's eyes and he turned away from Joe.

Later Joe apparently checked on Sam and, realizing his significance, asked me how he could recover from that that gaffe. I suggested he approach Sam that evening at the dinner when Sylvia and I would be seated at the same table with him and try to apologize.

It was interesting to watch. Sam was in the midst of an energetic conversation when Joe interrupted him and said he wanted to apologize for his remark.

Sam didn't look up and continued with his conversation, leaving Joe standing there. I was on the dance floor with Joe's wife and he rushed out to retrieve her, muttering, "You and your lousy advice!"

Later when I was next in Los Angeles and ran into Joe, he insisted I come to his home in Truesdale Estates for a swim. I wasn't looking for a swim nor was I anxious to visit, but for some strange reason Joe was insistent. It was a lovely large home overlooking Los Angeles. His father in law, Mark Taper, was visiting and I was introduced to him. I had a brief conversation with him and I noticed Joe and he didn't speak to each other. Apparently they had a frigid relationship.

One day, while I was finishing my work in our Los Angeles office, preparing to rush to the airport for my flight home, the phone rang. It was Joe. He apparently called Chicago and learned where I was.

He exclaimed, "Morry, it's urgent I see you." I explained I was rushing to the airport but he insisted it was of extreme urgency that I briefly delay my departure for a visit with him.

When we got together, I immediately inquired about the emergency that required a change in my travel plans. He answered with a question:

"Have you been in London recently?" I began to suspect I'd been had. "Yes, I get there about every month now."

"Have you ever seen the American Embassy there?" was his next question. Now I knew I'd been had and he was wasting my time.

Next question: "What do you think of the landscaping at the Embassy?" I suddenly recalled Joe had studied landscaping at college.

"What's this all about Joe?" I asked, regretting I had stayed over for this. "I want you to start a campaign to have the landscaping improved, " he said. I decided to play along.

"Who is my client?" I asked. "And who is going to pay the fee and expenses?" "I'm your client but I don't want to be identified with the project. You be the client but I'll pay, " he replied.

I quickly pointed out that it would be unprofessional, unethical and a conflict of interest to carry on a campaign like that without an appropriate client. Besides, I told him, I thought it was a lousy idea. I left his office wondering why I didn't kick him in the ass.

Joe died at 69 of leukemia. Our mutual friend, Hank Hendler, probably Joe's best friend, serves as the trustee of his estate. I always felt it was more of a father/son relationship than a deep friendship. Hank was always looking out for his best interests and served him as a father confessor, jack of all advice.

Jimmy Durante

Jimmy Durante and his entourage, including Gary Moore and singer Gerry Sullivan, were coming by train from Los Angeles. They were to give a performance as a benefit for the Community & War Fund. As publicity director, I was fretting about possible press coverage.

I decided to contact their press representative on the West Coast to get the exact time of arrival. "When are they getting in Friday?" I asked "You mean tomorrow morning," she said. I was amazed to learn there had been a switch in signals and no one informed me they were arriving a day ahead. Strange, after all these years, I should remember their PR person's name: Wahila Lahay.

I quickly called the Ambassador East hotel to be sure someone had informed them. "Tomorrow?" the registration clerk asked. "You mean Friday." And then he informed me there was no room for them at the hotel. I called Ernie Byfield, president of the hotel, prepared to beg for rooms. Then I came up with an idea.

I told Ernie the sad story and proposed my idea to him: Shift reservations at the hotel to provide accommodations for Jimmy Durante and his people. Set up temporary beds in the cocktail lounge across from the Pump Room, adjacent to the registration desk. I assured him I could produce reams of publicity.

Ernie, a resourceful and fun loving guy, knew an opportunity when he heard one and quickly installed beds in the lounge. He produced red flannel nightgowns for everyone and prepared a table laden with delicacies for their arrival. Ernie was Chicago's

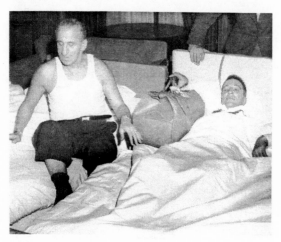

Jimmy Durante and cast abed off Amassador East lobby.

outstanding hotel operator, responsible for Pump Room gimmicks like the flaming sword. It was a favorite stop off destination for celebrities.

When someone once asked Ernie about the flaming swords. He replied: "They don't hurt the food much and they look good."

Members of the press were not averse to covering the stunt. Photographers and writers turned out in force to record the event.

Jimmy Durante and the entire cast came to the reception. Tired as he was, he entertained at the piano and willingly signed autographs. Everyone gathered around the piano and joined in as Jimmy played and sang. All the dailies printed photos of the entertainers in their nightgowns, allegedly forced to sleep in the lobby. The story emphasized the hotel shortage in Chicago during the war.

Serving the Disabled

I've become philosophical about my misfortunes. I occupied myself writing this book after my Stone Fish infection. An unexpected difficulty may have provided me with what may be the final career of my life.

My wife and I, along with another couple, Herb and Nancy Baker, decided to buy series tickets for the tennis matches in the giant tennis arena in Indian Wells. Herb took sick (and subsequently died) and Sylvia and I, after selling most of our tickets, decided to see at least one of the matches.

Parking was fine because of my handicap sticker. But when we got to the gate we were informed no one was available to push a wheel chair and I couldn't ask Sylvia to push me a couple hundred yards on the rough pavement. So we walked to where we were told there were elevators, but crowds were waiting in line to get aboard.

Despite Sylvia's protests that I not do so, I pulled myself up about 74 stairs and then walked about 50 feet or more to our section. Our seats were down about 40 precipitous stairs. A slip would have meant sure death.

We had good seats and an excellent view of the matches but about an hour later I realized I had to find a head. A friend sitting nearby helped me up the steps and escorted me down the same 74 stairs. But the toilets were single person units, both used, people waiting in line, and the attendant nearby wouldn't permit me to use the facilities in an unused suite. I asked our friend to get Sylvia and away we went. I came away with the conclusion that the tennis facility definitely was not handicapped friendly. Later I found others of my friends had the same experience.

I sent a letter about the experience in total detail to the *Desert Sun* newspaper and, after the article appeared, my phone began to ring with calls from friends and strangers who had similar experiences. One man told me how he had to call ahead when dining out to be sure if the restaurant was wheel chair accessible.

I was amazed that the owners of the tennis facility never called to inquire about my difficulty and offer a return inspection. I called the box office to inquire whether special arrangements were possible for wheel chair confined people. "Oh, yes," I was assured. "But you have to call a year in advance."

I could see that a new challenge was facing me. I was determined to find out what was being done in the Coachella Valley about service to the handicapped.

Alerted by my experience, I began to see similar abuses. My manicurist told me of the elderly ladies who, even aided with a cane, couldn't get up the curb at the shopping center on Bob Hope and highway 111.

After dining at CC's (formerly Cedar Creek) on El Paseo, I was waiting in the reception area to be picked up. I noticed how difficult it was for the gray haired people who frequented the place to make their way up and down three steps in front. The manager told me there was wheel chair accessibility at the rear of the restaurant.

I found that many institutions in Coachella Valley were able to avoid accessibility laws under so-called "grandfather" arrangements, meaning their establishments were built before the law took effect.

In pursuit of information I called the three leading hospitals in the Coachella Valley—Eisenhower, JFK, and Desert. I couldn't reach anyone talk to and on several occasions left my name and number, but no one called back. I didn't know what I was after at that point, but I did want to know whether there was a facility or service anywhere that offended the services I was so familiar with at the Rehabilitation Institute of Chicago.

On a trip to Chicago, I met with Dr. Henry Betts, former medical director of the hospital and now chairman of its Foundation. I also traveled to Roosevelt road to meet with Marca Brisco, who, while confined to a wheel chair, led the way to the erection of Operations Access, a building totally devoted to the needs of the handicapped. Over the years Marca had been an outspoken advocate of the needs for laws to protect the disabled. She urged me to start something similar in Coachella Valley and offered full cooperation.

When I returned to the desert, the vision of my destiny began to dance before my eyes. I could see there was a need for an information service in the Coachella Valley for the disabled. Many people volunteered assistance and money when I began to talk about my plans. Don Reuben, learning of my plans for a printed publication, which I planned to call Disabled Digest, suggested it might be well for me to consider a web site to reach literally millions.

When I was in Chicago, Marca Brisco urged me to acquire institutional sponsorship and I immediately thought of Eisenhower. I couldn't make contact with the Foundation office and, although several of my friends were on the board, decided to start with the physical therapy department. Its director, Derek Spinney, was very excited about my plans, and told me he would arrange a meeting with the Foundation office. This didn't happen and I called again.

A meeting was arranged with Spinney and a representative of the Foundation, Mary Kaye. She was not too encouraging and talked about how overburdened their staff already was and they had no budget for new projects. At that juncture, I had asked for no money and no staff assistance.

At lunch the next day at Tamarisk Country Club, I sat near Harry Goldstein, chairman of the hospital and an old friend. I told him of my experience and that I couldn't get a full hearing.

"You call them tomorrow," he said. "You'll get a hearing." I told him I would only meet if those present could make a decision.

The next day I received a call from the president's office asking when I could meet. Harry Goldstein was there along with the president and CEO of the hospital, G. Aubrey Serfling, and Mary Kaye.

I again addressed the issue, explaining I was not after funds, that I only wanted institutional sponsorship in order to give my efforts credibility. I told them that I had already met with Michael Smith, managing director of the Northern Trust bank of Rancho Mirage, which was building a new bank at Frank Sinatra Drive and Highway 111. I informed them that Smith had agreed the bank would become a sponsor and offered the facilities of his new branch for meetings and other services.

There was a considerable amount of discussion about whether my effort, particularly in the arena of accessibility, would bring problems to the hospital. I assured them the newsletter would only take positive approaches, recommending institutions and companies that offered maximum accessibility.

Understandably hospital officials were concerned my efforts might evoke negative public relations were my publication point a finger at a business in the community where the owner was a supporter of the hospital or on the board.

After that meeting, I had a private luncheon with Serfling and some progress was made on my plans. At that time, I spelled out my vision for a full facility possibly on Eisenhower grounds, a building entirely devoted to the needs of the disabled similar to Operations Access in Chicago.

We agreed to have another meeting and subsequently he called to suggest I call for another appointment in July. We made plans to have a meeting shortly with Michael Smith. In early November of 2002, Serfling agreed the Medical Center would be co-sponsor and would appropriate an initial grant to pay for a feasibility study.

Boxing as a Metaphor

I'm a peaceful bookish fellow but can be very aggressive with a pair of boxing gloves on my hands. I keep waiting for someone to mistake this benign looking gray—haired man for a person who can be pushed around.

I was giving boxing lessons to a 22 year old black, Jeremy Dible, an employee of the gym where I work out every morning and bang away at a heavy bag Sunday mornings. I sometimes work out on a speed bag and a heavy bag on a terrace behind our home.

The young man saw me hitting the heavy bag and stayed a while to watch. Generally on Sundays I asked him to move the portable bag to a comfortable spot in the empty exercise room where I can work out.

We got talking and he confided he wanted to be a professional boxer. This gave me an opportunity to work out with a young adversary. I saw that my limited skills could carry him to the next step where he could get appropriate professional training and avoid physical damage.

A likable young man, he called me boss even though I assured him Morry would be appropriate. Whenever we parted he hugged me and inquired about my wife.

We worked very hard on his left jab. I taught him a few combinations—a jabbing left, a right cross, another left jab and then a step in uppercut. How to bob and weave. I taught him to keep his gloves up at all times and to stop wasting energy with all that dancing around. I persuaded him to stop boxing with his back exposed to avoid kidney punches.

Some of the friendly old timers at the gym who know me come to watch. One hollered, "Don't hurt him!" I thought they were talking to my sparring partner. The man later told me he meant me.

I gave Jeremy all my old boxing paraphernalia—headgear and heavy gloves. I urged him to get a mouthpiece to save his teeth and to start running to build up his wind. Sylvia came up with a good suggestion: rent Rocky, a great fight film showing how Sylvester Stallone trained to get ready for movie battle.

Other than the exercise plus the feeling I am helping a good kid, I achieved something for myself. Since my Stone Fish accident, I found it difficult and painful to make lateral moves with my feet. Facing Jeremy and moving around to ward off his attempts to hit me, I found that I had been moving laterally as an act of self-preservation. Tennis, next? Even though my extra curricular pursuits generally have been along sedentary lines, boxing somehow has always been a part of my life.

It all started when my older brother, Harry, who ran a shipping room for our uncle's wholesale beauty culture company, would come home at night and show me, his 10-year-old brother, what he had learned about boxing from his assistant. My brother and I would box most evenings.

He would tell me about his young assistant: How he only earned very little but wore good clothes and smoked expensive cigars. He told Harry he was starting to do some professional boxing, winning small purses from his matches. His name was Barney Ross.

(He later held both the lightweight and welterweight titles. A WW11 hero, he was awarded the Distinguished Service Cross and a Presidential Citation.) Stretching just a little, I could say Barney Ross, one of boxing's greats, taught me to box.

One reason boxing was important to me was that I felt I had to know how to handle myself in an environment where occasionally I ran into bullies given to picking on kids who looked like they could be intimidated.

When I attended Wright Jr. College on Chicago's far west side I joined a boxing class and discovered my skills were ahead of most of the kids in class.

My greatest moment came (I relish the memory to this day) when one of the basketball jocks from Tuley High School, who was in the class behind me, joined the class and was asked by our coach to pick out an adversary for a trial bout. He saw the ex—editor of the Tuley Review and the literary magazine and pointed to me, thinking he had an easy one on his hands.

The more he tried to hit me, the more he became angry and exasperated. I successfully defended myself and hit him a few times to teach him a lesson. The coach halted the bout.

In later years I taught our sons never to pick a fight but only to use their fists for defensive measures. One summer our son, Richard, came home from summer camp and complained he was being picked on by one of the campers.

So we worked on his boxing. We soon got a call from the camp supervisor that Richard was winning all his bouts and some of the mothers were complaining he was too skilled and was hurting their kids.

Many years later, I offered to give my grandson, Jason, some boxing lessons. Jason was a Princeton football player, more than 6'3" tall, 235 pounds, and a superb athlete in several sports.

He looked at me quizzically. "Why, grandpa?" he asked. "I just thought you might want to know how to box in case you get into a fight on the football field." I replied. He answered that they never fight although they are rough on each other during games. I had seen him knock down an opponent and reach down to help him up.

What if a guy started a fight with you? I persisted.

"He'd be crazy", was his answer.

Boxing gave me a feeling of self-confidence when I was drafted and occasionally found myself in confrontation with rednecks in basic training. I never backed down. Bullies generally are easily intimidated if they feel they could be hurt in a fight.

Many years passed before I found boxing in my life again. While working out at a gym in Palm Desert, I found that my trainer, Gypsy, knew a great deal about boxing. He knew a lot of other stuff, including how to kill an adversary. But he was a gentle mountain of muscle with me. He was an American Indian and had formerly been a Green Beret.

Gypsy and I would box in one of the vacant handball courts twice a week. He urged me to get gloves, a teeth protector and headgear. He came to our home one day and installed a heavy bag and a speed bag so I could work out between our bouts. Unfortunately he disappeared one day.

He was a lovely guy and sharpened my boxing skills. He could have killed me had he ever really tried to hit me seriously. Mostly he protected himself from my attempts to lay one in. Once I caught him in the mouth and he started to bleed briefly. But he took it well and laughed. There was great amusement in the gym that I had tagged Gypsy.

Why do I consider boxing metaphorically?

Because I was afraid to get hurt when I was a kid and my wonderful mother, like many mothers from the old country, taught me to turn the other cheek and never get involved in a fight, especially with the goyim (gentiles). This was a doctrine of many Jews. Never bring attention to yourself. Never fight. (Until the Six Day War.)

When I learned how to box, I stopped being afraid. This feeling of physical self-confidence has served me all my life.

(Transitional postscript: I showed up at the gym for my regular Sunday workout and was told my young protégé, Jeremy, no longer worked there. But a young black man, who seems to have replaced him, asked if he could learn boxing from me. His name was Doni Parries, 22, a handsome young man, proficient in several sports, a third year college student studying computer programming. Luckily, Jeremy had not taken the boxing gloves I gave him. Doni and I boxed several Sundays and I acquired the purple bruises on my right forearm to show for it.)

The latest episode in my boxing career: Joshie, 14, my handsome grandson from Toronto, visited over the Christmas holidays. Several times I challenged him to put his dukes up so I can teach him a few boxing tricks. He smiles and takes the appropriate stance. I'm running out of potential pupils. Sylvia? My granddaughter Tali?

I Sing for My Supper

We were having lunch at Tamarisk Country Club—Sylvia, Marshall Wais, Bob Dickerman and me—when my good wife asked my two friends where they were going to be on June 6. I realized it was my birth date she was talking about—I'm not that dumb—and I also quickly realized she had a birthday party in mind.

Without being asked, I blurted out," I don't want a birthday party! If you want to do something, just get a room with a piano, somebody who can accompany me, some sheet music, a few lights and a microphone!"

I then went on to say, "I just want to sing and I don't want guests. That would be a good birthday party for me. "

It's a well known fact to friends and family that I love to sing. Enthusiastically but not particularly well. I have a player piano, 400 rolls of music and a microphone at home.

The next day Bob Dickerman called from Los Angeles to tell me that he and Marshall didn't particularly care what I wished, that they were organizing a birthday party and had already booked the Garden Room at Chasen's restaurant in Los Angeles.

"All you have to do is sing and supply the guest list "said Bob. "Marsh and I are paying for everything." I was much relieved.

Sylvia and I assembled a guest list of friends and associates mostly from the west coast. I didn't feel too many people had to travel far to hear me sing. A few did come from Chicago and Boston. At that our guest list numbered about 125—friends, a few clients, a small gang from the Young Presidents Organization, a few LA staff members, a few relatives and contacts from the Motion Picture Academy.

Now the problem that faced me was that I was apparently expected to perform—perform!—as though I knew how to sing. Previously my vocal efforts were confined to showers, golf carts, home, small parties and other venues where not too many people were present. Some of my friends flinch when I launch into "Glocca Morra" or "Nola." I win bets at piano bars that I actually do know the lyrics to the latter song—yes, there are lyrics—and I win an easy five bucks with that performance.

Being a trustee at Roosevelt University, I called Dr. Rolfe Weile, president at the time, about my problem. Could he get someone at the Chicago Musical College, which was part of Roosevelt, to help prepare me for that ordeal? I told him I just wanted to be comfortable with five or six songs, all of which I slightly knew.

He said it no problem. He enrolled me as a part time student at the college and obtained the services of a department head to work with me on my songs. A rehearsal hall and accompanist were provided. I attended class for two hours Monday nights. I told my instructor I wasn't interested in scales and stuff like that. I just wanted him to help prepare me for my performance.

The party was held on Friday evening. When you entered the private dining room at Chasen's, guests were greeted with a large banner atop the entrance which announced "PAVAROTTI, CARUSO, SINATRA AND ROTMAN." A brainchild of Betty.

Marsh and Bob had arranged for an orchestra and Marsh brought several cases of Cristal champagne from his private cellar.

Our invitation, which Sylvia prepared, invited guests to bring along sheet music if they wished to sing as well. Several did. Dale Wasserman, who did the book on " Man from La Mancha " and "Cuckoo's Nest, " brought along his pianist composer to do songs from their new production. Dale had threatened me with bodily harm if I tried to do "The Impossible Dream." He had already heard it butchered too many times. But he apologized later.

Marsh and Bob made gracious introductions. Bob pointed out that " Morry had always wanted a big party in his honor. But he didn't want to pay for it."

Among others, Marsh's stepdaughter, Julie, a handsome young lady, stepped to the microphone and caressed me with song. My uncle, Harry Harris, a professional songwriter, wrote and sang a special song for the occasion which related how he and his wife had fled to California from Chicago once they heard me sing.

When my turn came, I donned a straw hat and did a buck and wing to start my performance. (My uncle said I started with the wrong foot). I did my "Nola"—just to relax my guests, my teacher told me—and followed with "Glocca Morra," "People Will Say We Are In Love," and a few others. I was ready for show business!

A memorable evening.

Bernie and the Hollywood

Madam

My mind was spinning with all the names that popped into my head, all somewhat having a connection to one another, while Sylvia and I watched the Heidi ("Hollywood Madam") Fleiss story on television. It was especially absorbing to me. We always felt nice girls from good families (her father was a doctor) didn't go in for that kind of thing. In the Fleiss story you find she became a madam to make big money. It almost put her father in jail when he tried to help her.

What was the connection between all of the above?

Bernie Cornfield, founder of Investors Overseas Service, became Heidi's lover, protector and sexual gadfly, and showed her the world of riches and razzle-dazzle she sought: Private planes; enormous suites in hotels; baronial estates in Europe. This was the world Heidi wanted and ultimately went to jail for conspiracy, tax evasion and money laundering.

I never met Heidi although I did spend time with Bernie at his sumptuous quarters in Geneva, Switzerland, through recommendation of two good friends on his board. On a European trip with Sylvia, I stopped in Geneva for a 48—hour visit to discuss business with Bernie while Sylvia went on to Rome to await me.

My friend Bob Nagler was the reason I was seeing Bernie Cornfield. He had recommended me. Bob had been a Dreyfuss vice president when Cornfield lured him to Geneva to start the

Fund of Funds, an IOS vehicle. Bob's package included a ton of IOS stock. The other friend on the board was Bill Damroth, former partner of Sir John Templeton (Templeton Damroth.) Bob thought I might be of some help to Cornfield because he was aware we were doing business in Switzerland with Nestle. Bob and his wife, Ellen, took up residence in Geneva after he left Dreyfuss. They were later divorced.

Bob met me at the airport in his vintage Rolls Royce convertible and drove me to the Richmonde hotel. "First I must tell you," he started to say, "I am planning to resign in the near future because I don't like some of the things I am seeing in the company." This was a shock to me. He advised me he still felt it might be worthwhile to talk to Bernie. At the time Bernie had hired Clay Felker, later founder of *New York* magazine, to do his glossy company publication. Bob explained there was something for my company to do there because Felker was leaving the assignment.

Seeing Bernie and his operations was worth the trip. Because Bernie had a passion for delicatessen food, he insisted on having a real New York deli on the first floor of his office building. When I was ushered into his office, I felt I was in a pasha's harem. Soft hanging fabrics abounded. Moroccan cushions all over the place. Bernie sat behind a little desk as we talked. Pretty secretaries came in and out.

Bernie had a major problem and felt he would have severe legal troubles unless resolved in short order. In brief, Switzerland limited American companies to a handful of employees. Each had to have a Swiss permit (permis). Bernie figured out he could house employees at various local social agencies to which he would contribute money but working for him on his payroll. The whole thing was very illegal. Switzerland was eventually going to prosecute him, which they did. Bernie later went to jail. I am not sure of the exact charge.

I told him figuring out how to manipulate the law in his favor required a good lawyer and not public relations counsel. We did, however, take on an evaluation of their various publications and was paid for our services.

Bob Nagler set up an offshore financial consulting service after leaving IOS. I introduced him to Bruce Rappaport, of Geneva, and they struck up a consulting relationship. Bruce, an Israeli, was formerly a ship's chandler. He started a company to stock warehouses at various ports to provide prepared frozen food to ship's crews, following ethnic tastes. Today Bruce owns banks, ship lines and other companies. His palatial home sits on the shores of Lake Geneva.

Bill Burgess comes into the story now. As I wrote this, Bill called to arrange a dinner date with us. He had built a company called Electronic Specialties. Robert Vesco, owner of a small company, came after Bill in a takeover fight. Bill tendered all his stock and made a lot of money out of the deal. What he didn't know at the time was that Bernie Cornfield was the banker backing Vesco. Bill later regained control of his company. He died in later years from cancer of the prostate.

Vesco took control of IOS. One of his first acts was to raid the treasury of its cash. He also flew into Switzerland in his own plane and cleaned out Cornfield's warehouse where the company kept millions in Piaget watches and other expensive prizes awarded salesmen for sales success. Vesco has been in exile for many years now, last heard from in Cuba. Cornfield is dead. And Bob Nagler remarried his wife before his death.

The Oswald Gun

During my career as a newspaperman I had my share of covering slayings and all sorts of crimes but it was during my years in the public relations field that I was marginally involved in two crimes of the century: The assassinations of President John F. Kennedy and Martin Luther King.

Our agency role in the King slaying essentially was to counsel the Memphis police department how to handle the horde of reporters expected for the trial of James Earl Ray. Our firm had opened an office there after the assassination to assist the Chamber of Commerce create a more favorable image for the city and I was the key agency representative.

I got involved in the Kennedy slaying one morning when I received a phone call from a man named Milton Klein, who owned a chain of sporting goods stores in Chicago. I knew Milt from community activities in Chicago and at one time our firm had helped publicize his magazine, *Gun Digest*.

He was frantic, reporting that reporters were climbing the fire escape to interview him at the hotel he was living in. He explained that the FBI had traced the Mannlicher Carcarno rifle used to shoot the President to the Klein direct mail division. He said the federal agency had admonished him not to talk until they went through his sales receipts. Could I help him?

It was over the Thanksgiving holiday and we were expecting family but I hurried downtown to meet with him to get a handle on the situation.

In short order, I was able to reach the No. 2 man at the FBI, with whom I had previous dealings, and he briefed me on what the FBI wanted. I reassured him we would cooperate. I then called the top-level media people I knew to explain the FBI's instructions and assured them we would break the story the moment the FBI gave clearance. They all agreed to cooperate.

The next day I met with Klein's staff and covered a number of matters I thought important. Stop advertising guns. Advise the staff to talk to the press only through me. I even had a conversation with the switchboard operator to brief her.

I was concerned people would break windows of the Klein stores because emotion was so high in the city about the killing of a beloved President and the papers were pointing to a local connection where the assassination gun was bought.

My contact at the FBI called and informed me when Oswald was killed and I was able to fulfill my obligation to media.

The Lid Flipper

Three brothers named White launched their little company making bottle tops and had lunch with each other every day sitting around a table in the office, in some instances dining on some of the bottled products for which they supplied tops.

As the organization grew, they established the same luncheon dining custom for other employees added to the organization. When the organization got very large they still observed the custom, offering soup and bottled products at each table at no charge.

When we would come for meetings, we, too, would lunch in their vast dining room covering almost a whole floor, with several hundred employees having lunch with the Whites.

George White was the founder, a cordial white-haired gentleman who may have corrupted me by opening a bottle of scotch after our meetings and inviting me in for a smoke and a drink. I was not an unwilling supplicant and learned to appreciate fine cigars with him. Two other brothers were William and Phil, all cut from the same gracious pattern.

When we were retained to do their public relations, we were asked to deal with a major problem facing the company. Competitors were developing twist—off caps more rapidly than White Cap could engineer up to compete. Also there were complaints that some of the bottles broke at the top when people pried them off carelessly.

The White Cap solution: develop a key for prying off the cap. They showed us the implement and we began to prepare a campaign to introduce it. In the process of preparing our press material, one of our people describe the tool as a lid flipper. The client saw the value of that phrase and registered the tool as a Lid Flipper. That became the phrase used in PR, advertising and sales promotion.

It has been our experience that occasionally an idea created in a public relations campaign can become the centerpiece of a marketing activity. An example was the feedback we got from shelter magazine editors that color coordinated kitchens were the new idea, leading our client in the appliance field to make available various colors in built-in appliances.

We had an experience at White Cap, which proved to be an object lesson for all of us in the firm. One of our executives was riding the Northwestern train on his way to work. Next to him was a man he didn't know reading a legal brief. On top of it was a heading dealing with the sale of White Cap Company. That's really all he saw but he recognized a possible breach of confidence.

Upon arrival at the office, he conferred with me. He asked if I knew the company was being sold and with whom should we talk to at the company. We didn't know at the time that the man on the train, reading the brief, was a family member, who served as house counsel. The decision on our part was to call the top executive we reported to and ask him if the company was being sold. If so, we had to start preparing press material.

The executive hit the ceiling. He didn't know the company was at play and he was in the midst of negotiating his contract. In retrospect, should we have first consulted with the chief executive officer, in which case earning the enmity of our principal contact?

Hindsight tells us that was the appropriate approach at the time, particularly since someone was very careless about reading confidential material on a commuter train.

We had moments of uneasiness at the company but apparently, in the eyes of the Whites, we had acted appropriately and were not blamed for the explosive experience they must have had with one of their executives.

The White Cap Company was later absorbed by one of the conglomerates in the canning business.

The National Swimming Pool

Institute

I became an expert on swimming pools quite by accident. I didn't own one nor did I intend to install one but my friend, Sid Baren, started me on a quest when he called to inquire where he might get information on installing a pool at his suburban Chicago home. I confessed my ignorance but said I would check it out and see if I could be helpful.

There were many pool manufacturers in the phone book. I checked but found no listing anywhere of a centralized body offering information on pools.

My curiosity challenged, I called a few manufacturers and installers in the pool field. Several told me there had been aborted attempts to launch an association, such attempts abandoned by political infighting. Several said they would assist me when I told them I would be interested in starting a pool association for the field. I was seeking information for friend Sid but I saw an opportunity for an excellent public relations account.

I sent letters to a several people in the pool business and received encouraging response. After several months I announced that the first meeting of the National Swimming Pool Institute would be held in Chicago. I enlisted my attorney, Morris Leibman, and he drew up a set of bylaws. We selected a logo and legal name, the National Swimming Pool Institute, and sent out a mailing announcing the first meeting at the Sherman Hotel in Chicago.

Admittedly it was an economic gamble at that point but I assumed we would recoup for our time and expenses through registration fees. About 50 companies did register and we held our first meeting during which the bylaws were ratified and the organization officially launched.

We were paid for our time and expenses by the association and continued to work briefly until the officers of the Institute decided to carry on with an internal staff. My friend Sid built his pool and I had the satisfaction of knowing I had launched a major association.

Tuley High School

Our family was migratory even in Chicago. I can recall a series of moves from one apartment to another in an effort to lower living costs. There were at least a dozen moves in my early lifetime, which meant personal dislocation for the entire family as we left friends behind and tried to integrate into a new environment. My move from Marshall High School was a particularly difficult one for me; a personal heartbreak because I was leaving behind my buddies.

I was saddened when we moved from Douglas Boulevard. The boulevard was in the heart of the 24th ward. Down the center was a strip of grass criss-crossed by walkways, where my best buddy, Maurie Fulton, and I would play football with a gang of neighborhood kids. He later became a partner in Fantus Factory Locating Service, and, as the wheels turned, became a client of mine when I was in the public relations business.

I can recall my last day at Marshall. I walked down the aisles as we assembled in our homeroom and I shook the hand of each classmate in farewell.

As it turned out, the move to Tuley High School was especially lucky for me because I found my future profession and making new friends wasn't as difficult, as I had anticipated. At Marshall High School my vision of success included a position on one of the teams and a letter on a sweater (mostly to attract girls). I saw my buddies on the teams achieve celebrity status. They got the prettiest girls and landed the best noontime jobs at the hot dog stores across from school.

When I transferred to Tuley, I found a different world. There seemed to be no one parading around with an athletic letter because athletics was under-emphasized. The school had a pretty good basketball team and there seemed to be a good tennis team.

The emphasis at Tuley, a rundown old red brick building on Rockwell street near Division street, seemed to be on more cerebral stuff—the orchestra, drama offerings, the high school newspaper, debating and other activities for which one earned acclaim but no letter. The school was later named Clemente High after a Puerto Rican baseball player killed in a plane crash.

I wandered into journalism quite by accident when a buddy of mine asked me to accompany him to the office of the high school newspaper, *The Tuley Review*. A wrestler, he went there to hand in an article he wrote on the school's wrestling team. While there I began to talk to the editor, a short nervous guy with a palpable tic. His name was Syd J. Harris.

Syd asked if I had any writing experience and whether I would like to write for the paper. As a trial he gave me an assignment to write a report on the forthcoming student operetta. When I handed in my copy, he was complimentary and asked me to continue to write for the paper. My story appeared on the front page under a banner headline with my first byline—by Morris B. Rotman. Thus began a career that spanned the rest of my life. In subsequent years, I became editor of the paper, co-editor of a literary magazine, and was asked to edit the school's "annual", although it never came out for lack of funds.

When I became editor I inherited a private office shared with the staff and the paper's sponsor, Oscar A. Olson, a sparkling blue-eyed teacher who brilliantly taught Shakespeare and chemistry. His Macbeth class generated a lifelong devotion to the bard, which ultimately led to my involvement in the erection of the Globe Theater in London under the direction of former classmate Sam Wanamaker.

Sam's brother, Bill, a good friend at school, became an excellent Beverly Hills internist and also became, as he describes it, my "west coast" doctor when I had health problems while on business there. Once he made daily visits while I remained at the Beverly Hills hotel with a case of viral pneumonia. I wouldn't permit him to take me to a hospital because I wanted to conceal my illness from Sylvia, who, coincidentally, was coping at home with Richard's lobar pneumonia.

Bill also made daily visits to the west coast home of Manny Pasthoff (later Post) who died of health complications. Manny was circulation manager of the *Review* when I was editor. Another good friend to this day is Ernie Rosner, who wrote clever profile pieces for our paper. Ernie became a successful businessman engineer, the holder of several patents.

Tuley was literally a cornucopia of talent. Fine musicians, poets, writers, artists, scientists and the drama class where Sam Wanamaker was an early star in its productions.

Syd Harris was a brilliant, precocious writer. My collection of memorabilia includes a copy of the *Review* where he wrote an erudite critique of James Joyce's "Ulysses."

Isaac Rosenfeld, now a literary cult figure for his subsequent essays and books, wrote satirical columns for the paper. I prize his book of essays, "An Age of Enormity." My bookshelves have a corner devoted to books written by Tuley graduates, including Oscar Tarcov but principally by Saul Bellow. My little textbook "Opportunities in Public Relations," stands meekly in a corner. This book hopefully will sit there, too.

Saul was a respected person at school even at an early age. He preceded me by several classes and I met him occasionally outside of school. History reports Saul's subsequent success as a Nobel Prize winner, a winner of the National Book award and one of the most acclaimed writers in the world. Our paths crossed later and I had some dealings with him

When I represented the *Sun-Times*, I also found myself in a position to be of some help to Sydney, at that time writing for the paper.

Not content with the education provided by Tuley, although there were many excellent teachers, some of the students organized an evening school at a local church at which students lectured on their expertise. My recollection is that Bellow taught anthropology.

One of our class presidents was Harold Persky, who won early graduation and went on to become an acclaimed physicist. As did Jerry Lettvin, later also a psychiatrist who wrote funny pieces for our paper.

When I became editor, I used illustrations by Mitch Siporin, whose art later was displayed by a prominent gallery in New York.

The music class was conducted by a much beloved teacher, Irving Letchinger, who produced an accomplished orchestra. He died in April 2002.

I was preceded in school by Anatole Rappaport, who achieved fame as a pianist, and Rosalyn Turek, a harpsichordist, later to become a foremost interpreter of Bach.

Our class valedictorian, Nick Turkevitch, became research director and a principal in the Chicago office of the Darcy McManus advertising agency.

Still hungering for a letter on a jacket, I prevailed upon Oscar Olsen to permit us to have a large "T" manufactured with a quill pen on it, which our staff wore on leather jackets and sweaters. I wore the jacket on a visit to a basketball game at Marshall High School, where a girl, upon seeing my letter, exclaimed to her girlfriend," Oh, it's just for journalism." Slightly deflating me.

At first Olson wasn't sure I could handle the chores of the editorship, principally the writing of the front page editorial column, considering the quality of the previous editors. When I wrote my first column he told me I would do. He was quite pleased when I pompously used Shakespearean references in my column to describe the antics of a fellow classmate at a school meeting, writing that he was a "titanic bottom braying in an ass's head. "At that point of my life I didn't know from simple language but Oscar was impressed. I also wondered whether the student understood the insult.

My closest buddies and I found time for an occasional bit of mischief. My friend, Norman Dolnick, and I, noted most students hung their umbrellas outside their lockers on rainy days secured inside the locker. We also knew they rushed to class when the bell rang so we opened all the umbrellas just before the bell. We were delighted to see our assistant principal scurrying to close them all before the students crashed into them.

I used to parade around school with the page proofs of *The Tuley Review* in my hands. I generally was more preoccupied with those proofs than my schoolwork. One day after chemistry class I got the bright idea of inserting a test tube of hydrogen sulfide in my roll of proofs. I punched a small hole in the cork stopper. As I sat in class innocently going about my business, our teacher began to sniff audibly. Then she opened the window. She looked about to see if a student had had an accident. Then she dismissed the class. She understandably didn't like the rotten egg smell.

Tuley may not have had its athletic heroes but it fielded a heavyweight team of future intellectual, literary, artistic, musical, scientific and other icons. I never quite understood how it happened in a middle class community with a high degree of illiteracy. Maybe it was due to the pressure at home to hit the books. With the Jewish students, it was the heritage of the tradition of Jews being people of the Talmud and Torah. Maybe it was the desire on the part of many of the kids to rise above their humble beginnings. In my case it certainly was a mother who read good books and urged me to do likewise.

Sylvia and Me Plus 3

It is one of the strange accidents of fate that I casually met Sylvia, admired the way she looked, dressed and talked, and then regretted she was someone I would probably never see again. Lots of omniscience I didn't have then and little did I know she would pop up later in my life.

I had wandered into the Lincoln Library in downtown Chicago and was inspecting the stacks of books when this lovely young lady asked if she could help me. (I remember to this day, some 58 years later, how she looked and the suit she wore). I told her I was looking for nothing special, all the while sizing her up as someone I would like to know. But I don't recall even asking her for her name. Nor was romantic aggressiveness a virtue of mine at the time.

A couple of months later my friend Herb Natkin called and pulled me out of my post military slump by suggesting we go out for dinner. He said he had a date for me. He informed me we were meeting another couple at the Belden—Stratford hotel for cocktails. Like the song goes, and then again she walked into my life, the girl from the library stacks at Lincoln Library. I flipped when I saw her!

She was with another guy and sat down next to me. From that moment on, ignored was my date and ignored was hers. We chatted all evening and found a great deal to talk about. We discovered we had friends in common and similar interests.

The next day I called Herb and asked him to get her telephone number. When I called her, she accepted a date and even volunteered to meet me downtown. She lived on the north side and my home was on the northwest side. No car, I had anticipated a long bus ride to pick her up and then see her to her door. At the time I was living with my parents.

When she suggested a rendezvous half-way, I was impressed with her graciousness and thoughtfulness. The rest is our history.

Sylvia and I met in the lobby of the Drake hotel. As I approached her, I called her "Shirley," having forgotten her name in my nervousness. We got over that gaffe luckily and had a drink in the Allerton Hotel rooftop pub, after which we walked to Tony's Cellar, a basement dive on Rush Street, now no longer there. There was a jukebox, and I asked her to dance. Unfortunately, the jukebox offered only one record, a song called "People Will Say We're In Love," the great love song from "Oklahoma" by Rogers and Hammerstein.

We danced again and again. And again and again. At one juncture, now totally smitten and in complete leave of my senses, I said to her," You know we are going to get married." She looked at me, probably now suspecting she had gone on a date with a madman. "But I just met you," she replied. "I hardly know you."

Something that should not have happened happened in short order. After that initial date, I saw her much as I could. At one point she told me about the guy in the service she had been seeing. That she was between jobs as an executive secretary. We both realized that we were falling in love as the days went by.

About six weeks after that there was a nuptial on March 1 in her family's apartment, a small wedding before a modest group of friends and relatives, catered by Ashkenaz Delicatessen on Morse avenue. As I stood before Rabbi Silver, very nervous, my right buttock began to twitch furiously. I wondered whether the wedding guests could see what was happening to me.

Sylvia's father, Sam, had made an arrangement with the rabbi to give us an envelope containing a $1,000 check, before beginning the rituals. As the rabbi reached into his breast pocket to hand me an envelope, I sensed what was happening and told

Sylvia and Morry wedding picture.

the rabbi to continue on. Finally getting to know Sam, I realized later that he wanted his gift to be a public offering. Had I known how much he gave us, I might not have been so cavalier but none the less felt it was wrong to start my wedding that way.

Sam and I always had an amiable relationship. I discovered he was a troubling factor in Sylvia's life, as well to as his wife and offspring, Ruth, Ethel, Bert and Justin. He was a strong character, dominating, always trying to run his kids' lives. He was away when Sylvia and I started seeing each other.

Sylvia was relieved he was away because she was fearful he would like me, thus losing her interest in me. A family perversity! If he liked me, she felt I couldn't be totally worthwhile.

When I first met Sylvia she told me she was between jobs, having worked in the defense industry to do her part for the war, but had left that employment and had just returned from a trip to Richmond, Va., to visit relatives. I told her I might be helpful in finding her a job and called my high school friend, Dolnick, who was working for the Chicago Housing Authority. Norm reported his boss, Micky Shufro, needed a secretary and Sylvia subsequently got the job.

The whole thing turned fortunate. "Mick" Shufro needed a war veteran to rent his own apartment to so he could move to another place. During the war, the government mandated only a veteran could rent vacated apartments. A case where my veteran status paid off. So we had the promise of an apartment and Sylvia and I then could proceed to get married.

Incidentally, when we talked about marriage, we had a total income of $100 a week between her salary and mine. Little did we anticipate that Sylvia would quickly become pregnant and deliver Betty Ruth on Feb. 24, almost our first anniversary.

Sylvia and I were lucky to get the apartment on the south side of Chicago at 5221 S. Harper Avenue, the upper story of a real estate office. To us it was heaven—a nice bedroom; a fireplace in the living room; a rear porch looking out on an ample garden, and access through a window to the rooftop of the real estate office below. We quickly converted it to our patio by laying out linoleum and buying deck chairs. All for $37.50 a month!

We spent most evenings on that patio, watching the crowds go by, observing life on Harper. We also were treated to a free window show, watching people in an apartment hotel across the street. When we had our first child, Betty Ruth, one of the ladies across the way would call us if she felt Betty might be crying or trying to escape confinement from her little wooden playpen.

I had an extra bonus. Across the street, about a hundred yards south, was the Hyde Park movie theater. Once a week they would change the marquee and I would shout corrections from my rooftop perch. Invariably there were errors in spelling. I may be the only person in history to have edited a marquee.

At the time, I was an assistant city editor and rewrite man at the City News Bureau of Chicago, working occasionally on the night shift. This was a deterrent to my marriage, leaving my bride alone nights while I worked. I started thinking about moving on to public relations. Meanwhile, the apartment was a happy place for us. Friends and family would come to visit and we got involved with a pleasant group in the area.

Since the Lake Park avenue police station was only a block

away, I invited reporter friends to come to the apartment, occasionally for a meal. Some of them even began to dial their beats from our telephone. We never anticipated that extra expense. Gradually, as Betty grew, we stopped inviting the press to drop in.

We installed a crib in our bedroom and lived happily on Harper. Betty was a beautiful, aggressive tyke. I felt she was the most beautiful child in the world. I would parade around the neighborhood and take her to the park with her sitting on my shoulders, much as Richard did with his daughter, Talia. As she grew older, we would find Betty standing up in the crib, teething on the wooden rail, gazing at us as she awaited our awakening so she could be fed. The night before, Sylvia would leave crackers on the rail.

Now I felt I had to find extra income to offset the loss of Sylvia's salary. I began to think about getting into public relations. When I was at City News, I always had a little part-time job of one kind or another. One of my buddies, Phil Weisman, the sports editor, with whom I often double dated before Sylvia, would tell me about his extra-curricular activities. He did part-time publicity for some people. One, Danny Thomas, became a big hit while appearing at the 5100 Club on the North Side. He later rose to fame in Hollywood and on television.

When Sylvia was working at the Chicago Housing Authority, she heard about Shufro being offered a job as publicity director of the Community and War Fund of Chicago, the "Red Feather," agency (from its use of a feather to depict its fundraising goals) representing more than 150 charities in the Chicago area. She asked him if I could be interviewed for the job. I had an extra break: Prof. Wayne McMillan, of the University of Chicago, who knew Sylvia, was on the Housing Authority board, and was in a position to recommend me. I got the job.

It was difficult leaving City News. Also, for the first time in many years I was not chasing and writing the news. I found it hard to tell Gersh I was departing.

Working for the Fund offered a wonderful opportunity to meet leading business executives, entertainers, media and others in the Chicago firmament. I was proud of my private office, my secretary and all the trappings of the job.

I got to know Walter Paepcke, chairman of Container Corp. of America; Clarence Randall, of Inland Steel; Bill Street, head of Marshall Field's; Elmer Stevens, chairman of Stevens Department store, and many others. Later, when I took over William R. Harshe Associates and needed contacts for sales, some of these men were most helpful in their recommendations and door openings.

All of a sudden I felt like a factor in the community. I used to pal around with Nate Gross, a columnist on Chicago's *Herald American* newspaper. My friendship with columnist Irv Kupcinet came later. Because of my job, my prominence elevated me to become president of the Tub Thumpers, an organization of Chicago press agents.

I stayed at the Fund about two years but after a while felt I had to move on when I ran into an unexpected difficulty. I sensed that my boss, Chuck Dilday, a rotund Irishman, felt my accomplishments were getting too much attention from his superiors. He would often put his name on my reports. He would take credit for successes for which I was responsible.

I started to think about other employment and stepped up my pace for outside projects, including publicity assignments for several synagogues.

A project that whet my appetite for a public relations career was a brochure I wrote for American Marietta Corp., relating the life history of Grover Hermann, its founder and chairman. The assignment came to me through a veteran Chicago public relations counsel, Frank Lindsay Rand, who was in search of a writer. I quickly realized this was a field I had always wanted to get into anyway. I finished the assignment and Frank expressed his gratitude for a job well done.

Meanwhile, Sylvia and I, in anticipation of a second child, started to think about moving. At first, we considered building a home in the part of the South Side called The Highlands.

Our second offspring, Jesse Louis, was born Oct. 28, 1947. We had moved to 1631 East 70th St. The landlord, a fine old gentlemen, lived just below us. We had a friendly relationship until Jesse moved in overhead and spent most his time thumping back and forth in the apartment.

I received a call one day from Milton Kreines, a printing broker, asking me if I would be interested in taking over a publicity project in connection with the 100th anniversary of KAM temple, Chicago's oldest synagogue. Milt explained that he knew about me because he had played cards in our apartment with the former occupant, Archie Herzoff, publicist for Balaban & Katz theaters.

I met with the committee from the temple and came to terms but indicated I needed an automobile and couldn't handle the assignment unless they could help me buy a car. I didn't want to commute to the temple on long bus rides. In those days, at the end of the war, cars were still in limited supply. They produced a board member who owned one of the city's largest Chevrolet dealerships.

I called the dealer, who was aware of my need, and all he asked was which color car did I want. I ended up buying a beautiful green Chevy convertible, the envy of all our friends.

I apparently did such a good job the congregation's president asked me to join its board after finishing my professional assignment.

I discovered in reading the history of KAM that President Abraham Lincoln had written a letter to the congregation on an important occasion. I convinced Max Schrayer, KAM president, to offer a reward in a search for that lost letter. It was reported in newspapers throughout the country. We never found the letter, but it gave the temple miles of newsprint.

It was about this time that Sylvia came up with the job opportunity at the Fund. While I was there, I made the acquaintance of Bill Harshe, a Chicago public relations counsel. He was on the board of a Fund agency and managed to convince my boss to loan me for PR for a charity. Bill and I hit it off rapidly. We made the rounds of the newspapers together and Bill was amazed at how many of the reporters jumped up to greet me. They were all graduates of City News Bureau, who had moved on to the dailies.

During the course of our working together, Bill sounded me out whether I would be interested in working for his firm, Harshe Associates, at twice the salary I was getting at the Fund. I wasn't too sure because I loved my job, despite the low pay. But then Bill made a mistake. He told my boss that I was leaving. I was incensed at what I considered a breach of confidence. I called him and told him I was upset with him and turned him down.

Over the next year, my discomfort with Dilday grew. I reentered negotiations with Bill. My success seemed to make him insecure. I told Bill I would move only if I became a partner in his firm.

Bill agreed to my terms. Sylvia and I went on a short vacation to Jamaica. When we returned, I joined William R. Harshe Associates as a vice president. Bill agreed I would have 45 percent ownership in the firm but, since the company was making no money, this arrangement proved to be meaningless. In about a year, I began to hold and build the firm's clientele. Bill's history was that he was able to sell business but couldn't hold most of it. The clients became stabilized when I came on board. I learned later Bill had had a number of previous partners.

By this time, Sylvia was heavy with Richard Everett, who was born on Nov. 24, 1951. We had outgrown our present living quarters. Isaac Gershman played a crucial role in this event when I talked to him about our plans to acquire a house.

He discouraged us from building but said he would ask Mike Fields, the owner of the building where City News was situated, whether he knew of a house in the suburbs for us. Mike told him that his next-door neighbor had sold his house and was living alone in a big old house on Palos road in Glencoe while his wife had already moved to Florida.

We bought the old house, a three-story red brick Georgian, needing lots of repair but very livable. It cost $24,000, including more than a half-acre of Glencoe land and a houseful of old furniture. It was torn down in the 1990s and a million dollar French provincial mansion stands on it now.

The kids seemed to love living in the suburbs. Glencoe had a great school system. Sylvia proceeded to remodel the place room by room. I was able to make the down payment on the house by borrowing from Sylvia's brother, Justin, and my older brother, Harry, who gave me his savings book and told me, "take what you need."

Subsequently, with a little more affluence, we next moved in 1961 to a lovely ranch house at 1256 Fairfield road, near the Glencoe golf course. The house was built by a prominent contractor for himself and his family. He died before he had hardly spent any time there. It was a beautiful, modern home with lots of windows and wood. In 1969, Sylvia told me she wanted to move downtown because two of our kids, Betty and Jesse, were away at school and she anticipated Richard shortly going off to college. She didn't like the idea of living alone in Glencoe with our golden retriever, Sandy, while I traveled.

Sylvia let out the word to her chums we were looking. June Betty Manning, who had more connections than Bell Telephone, called one day to tell us Dick Himmel, a prominent Chicago decorator, was vacating his penthouse apartment at the Outer Drive East apartments on the lakefront.

We bought many of Dick's built-ins and ended up renting, later owning, the apartment, formed out of three apartments on the 37th floor, with gorgeous views of Chicago's locks, the park and a vast panorama of Chicago skyline.

There were three bedrooms, enough for Richard, who would commute to New Trier, and for Jesse or Betty, when they came home on holidays. Jesse at the time was at Ohio University in Athens, Ga. and Betty was at the University of Arizona in Tucson.

I was able for the first time to set up a completely private office with a magnificent view of the lake. Being virtually three apartments made into one, the apartment had three outside patios and a second kitchen in a room we had made into a den. The building had a large swimming pool with all kinds of other facilities.

After living there for about 12 years, we began to think of another change, this time moving to 1212 North Lake Shore drive. We bought an apartment from Eddie and Edith Anixter, who had the apartment built by one of Chicago's leading designers. We subsequently bought an apartment at 2650 North Lake Shore drive essentially for Betty to live in which we would utilize when we were in town.

Because of my travel to Los Angeles, I had joined Tamarisk Country Club in Rancho Mirage, Ca, near Palm Springs, but had never used the club much. When we began to experience a volatile atmosphere in Jamaica visits, we decided to buy a little condo in Rancho Mirage, near the club. Every couple of years we seem to have moved, each time to a slightly larger facility and ultimately settled down in the Springs Country Club in Rancho Mirage, where most of this material was written. In October 2002, we sold our house in the Springs Country Club and moved to an apartment on the third floor of a high rise in the Desert Island Country Club.

By now, Jesse and Richard were married, each bringing us two grandchildren. Betty was then working in a management position at Border's Bookstore.

The two grandchildren in Canada are Joshua and Talia. Richard went to Canada with his then bride, a Canadian, who didn't want to raise her family in the United States. Richard remarried, a lovely lady, Gloria Stein, and she brought along two-step grandchildren, Julia and Hart. So now in effect Sylvia and I enjoy six grandchildren. Jesse and his wife Diana have two wonderful offspring. Betsy, an aspiring actress, has enrolled at the University of Colorado at Boulder. After nearly a year at an advertising agency, Jason, is considering joining a management consulting firm. Meanwhile he is working as a trader on the Mercantile Exchange

Jesse, meanwhile, seems too be following some behavioral patterns established when he was in his teens. He always had a summer time or part time jobs—working with a construction crew, selling records, flipping pizzas at a neighborhood restaurant, or running children's parties while he serving as a disc jockey.

His aunt coined the name for him," the Mayor of Glencoe," because of his whirlwind of activities. We frequently had squad cars visiting our home because Jesse offered a free printing service in his darkroom for local cops.

Now, in addition to pursuing his thriving marketing business, he serves as chairman of Deerfield's cable and television authority and has negotiated the suburb's TV contracts for 11 years. Recently he also served as the political advisor for the man who successfully ran for the mayor of Deerfield.

Sylvia and Morry 58 years later.

Grandma teaches grandson how to play tennis.

Same kid on the Princeton football team.

The Lincoln-Belmont Booster

My late partner, Bill Harshe, asked me one dark night, when we lost our way driving back to Chicago from Plymouth, Ind., "In what other business, except rum—running, could you be lost in a fog at night outside Gary, Indiana?"

The same applies to being a newspaperman. In what other business, except journalism, could you find yourself dealing with victims, policemen, firemen, doctors, undertakers, politicians and a host of other sinners and saints and other just plain folks as you tried to wheedle a morsel of fact out of them in pursuit of the news?

Starting as a cub reporter at the *Lincoln-Belmont Booster* was hardly glamorous. Essentially most of it was drudgework and frequently your effort never saw itself transformed into print. But it was a heady experience carrying a card that said "Press", emboldening you to feel you could pry into the affairs of other people on the assumption you had a right to know what was going on because you belonged to the press.

The *Booster* functioned out of a double store at Lincoln and Belmont avenues next door to a bowling alley owned by a ward politico. There was a busy, small staff that got out the paper weekly and later started a Sunday edition. The paper grew into a chain covering almost the entire north side of Chicago.

Rather than returning to Wright Jr. College, I stayed on after a two-week trial to help launch the chain's second newspaper, the *Lake View Booster*, which covered an area near Chicago's skyline occupied to a great extent by Scandinavians, Danes and Irish.

I began writing little items for the paper—weddings, deaths, celebrations of all sorts and other grist for the local news mill. Leo A. Lerner, the brilliant editor of the paper, encouraged me as I worked my few weeks there. Finally, he suggested I stay on and continue my education at night. He took a personal interest in me and guided me in my work. He ultimately fired me, but that's a story for later. Incidentally, we remained good friends the rest of his life.

Later, when I was in the public relations business, Leo came to my office and sought my advice on trouble brewing at Roosevelt University about the acquisition of the Auditorium Theater. Leo resigned as chairman of the board, being adamantly opposed to the university diverting its efforts and funds that way. Leo and his wife, Dena, also came to visit when Sylvia and I bought our first Glencoe home. I remember him telling our two boys, Jesse and Richard, they could go to work for his papers when they grew up.

Leo was an outstanding editor, who wrote a well-read column on the front page of the *Booster*. He was a community leader and at one time served as chairman of Roosevelt University and chairman of the board of the Chicago Public library. He could make a magnificent speech with little preparation. In many ways he was an inspiration for me.

His suggestion was a blessing. The folks were bleeding economically. Our little store frequently was a chamber of horrors. Besides, we were working just to survive. I leaped at the chance to go to work full time, giving up my various part time jobs. I continued to work at Bert Shoes near the paper and the customers I waited on couldn't believe me when I told them I was a reporter on the *Booster*. I don't think they were as impressed as I was.

When Leo made his offer of continued employment, I leaped at the chance to switch from school books and part—time endeavor to newspaper work.

I was slightly in awe of the staff. There was an editor named Raymond Henagow, a wizened man, short of stature, slightly effeminate, a perfectionist with copy. The other important figure seemed to be Frank Boege, a corpulent man whose hair was lodged on the back of his scalp. Frank was the circulation manager, who seemed to have his hand in everything.

There were also ladies who attended the switchboard and a few who seemed to sell advertising over the telephone. One woman used to sell fur coats over the phone in her previous life.

There was also Mort Hart, a short plump photographer, with whom I later became friendly, who used his dark room to print pornographic pictures for the local policemen and a few members of the staff. His trophies were nude photographs. Mort seemed to be able to get all kinds of females to pose for him in the buff. He amazed me when he talked a new editorial associate into taking her clothes off for his camera. She was a shy journalism major, but not that shy.

One day Leo, probably perturbed by the cost of his morning orange juice, asked me to find out why oranges had become so expensive. I went after the story with a vengeance, contacting a relative who sold produce on the South Water Market, and he led me to an excellent source for the orange story. It wasn't an especially important story but I came in with a full account of what had happened: a freeze in Florida, lifting orange prices. Leo was pleased with my story.

Meanwhile, I did the rounds of police stations getting stories on accidents, shootings, suicides and other news about which I wrote when I got back to my desk. I fraternized with policemen and firemen and began to feel I had found my life's work.

Leo asked me to write a gossip column to replace Betty Bialk, who had resigned to move on to a magazine job. She wrote under the name of "On Betty's Beat" and I was dismayed to learn I was to write the column under that name because she had developed a following. It wasn't until later that I was given a byline on the column, but this time it was "Murray B. Roth", anglicized because they felt my family name was unacceptable in a community heavily populated by people of Teutonic origin.

I was filled with bravado. My shield and sword were my press card. One day I decided to attend a meeting of the very active German Bund that met in the Lincoln Turner Hall on Diversey Avenue. I wrote a full account about their program.

The beginning of the end of my career at the *Booster* (revived later) came when Leo called me in and told me he wanted me to write a long feature story for the front page of the new *Sunday Booster*.

It occurred to me that a neighborhood Catholic facility, the House of Good Shepherd, had never been written about and, in the tradition of fools daring to tread, I rang the front bell of the establishment at Addison and Clark.

A nun answered the bell and, when I informed her of my mission, informed me they didn't give interviews to the press. I told her I was preparing a feature article and was obliged to go ahead and needed verification but I would submit the article anyway.

She kept me waiting and a few minutes later a man appeared, the legal counsel, who happened to be visiting. We went over the same story. He left and reappeared with the Mother Superior, a kindly, sweet lady, who came out to size me up and then invited me into her office.

She relaxed after a while and took me on a comprehensive tour of the facility—a structure built on a cruciform architectural pattern with one section of the cross for nuns of the order, another for novitiates and a third for young women who had been placed in the House of Good Shepherd by the courts. Another section was for staff. In the center, at the base of the cross, was the altar, which meant they worshipped separately.

During the time we spent together, the Mother Superior asked my reassurance she would have an opportunity to see what I wrote before it was printed and, being a novice journalist, I gave her my assurance, not knowing this was not generally accepted journalistic practice.

I dug in and produced a fairly long article. I realized the meat in the stories was about the wayward girls, not the nuns and the edifice itself. I did some interviews of neighborhood people, called friends of the family in social work and hit the Chicago Public Library where I discovered a raft of stuff on kids who got into trouble, and were sent to the House of Good Shepherd.

One Sunday, in the office, I was pounding away on my story when by coincidence Leo proudly was showing friends around his new publishing home, a one-story building entirely devoted to his growing empire. Leo approached my desk and inquired what I was working on. I told him I had just about finished my Sunday paper project and he extracted copy from my typewriter and began to read.

He had with him several friends, among them the prominent writer, Ben Aronin. Leo took them into his office and I could see he was going over my story. Leo congratulated me and, after making a few corrections, marked the copy for publication.

My Good Shepherd story covered the entire front page of the next edition of the *Sunday Booster* with my byline. As I read it today, it stands the test of time as a fairly well written piece, considering my status as a fledgling in the business.

I didn't realize that Henagow did a slow burn that my piece was slated for the front page with the blessings of his boss. He later told me I had done something completely improper bypassing him, and that he had spotted a number of errors in my copy.

From that moment on, Henagow became my nemesis, my most adversarial critic and, aided and abetted by cohort Boege, he decided to teach me the craft of journalism, which meant that I had to write and report by his rules. I was a pretty good writer of feature stories but I had never learned my who, what, when, why and wheres which were, according to him, de rigueur in every news story. Journalistically speaking, I began to stumble and fall. I could not write a simple news story to satisfy him. I quickly degenerated to replaceable status.

One day as I chatted with a girl I was dating, standing in the paper's printing plant, in front of her Leo told me I was fired and that my work was unsatisfactory. I was crushed and pleaded for a second chance.

My mother caught me weeping in my bedroom and tried to comfort me. The next day, I pulled my self together and went job seeking. I went to see Paddock Publishing, another newspaper chain, and, seeing my background, the editor instantly offered me a job. I was not to work there. The next day Leo called and told me he and another man, Morris Kaplan, were starting a shopping newspaper in Cicero and Berwyn, Ill., and needed a circulation manager. I realized this was a terrible demotion but I was determined to prove myself to them and took the job.

As it later turned out, Leo tried to lure me back to the *Booster*, a story to be told later in this account of my career.

The Suburbs

I was farmed out to Cicero, Ill., west of Chicago, famed as a stronghold for the Capone mob.

We weren't exactly a newspaper in the strictest sense of the word. Ours was a shopper paper, distributed free of charge, chock-full of advertising. The paper was launched by Morry Kaplan, a short, feisty intellectual, who was fired from his job as editor of the town's leading newspaper. The *Cicero Life*, for allegedly encouraging the formation of a Newspaper Guild unit at the paper, in essence a union.

I still have a card attesting to my membership in the Guild signed by its then president, Heywood Broun, famed New York newspaperman, who wrote a much admired syndicated column.

Kaplan felt the *Life* had a monopoly in town and was determined to offer advertisers a shopper newspaper at lesser advertising prices.

I felt it was quite a comedown for me, acting as a circulation manager after I had been a reporter and columnist, but I was determined to show Leo and the crowd at the *Booster* that I had the stuff and they would regret canning me.

Gradually, I began to add news stories to our weekly while still seeing to the distribution of the paper. Kaplan converted the *Shopper* into the *Cicero Times*, a weekly, and later added Berwyn, Stickney and Oak Park editions, all the same paper with front page makeover to give the semblance of a localized paper in each community.

In addition to being reporter, editor and circulation manager, I added to my duties the running of a Greyhound ticket office. I also conducted tours of Chinatown for local club women. All for $28.00 per week. I recall I also swept the floor.

Our office was a half store on 26th street in Cicero, the other half occupied by a barber shop. I was soon joined by Mike Lerner, brother of Leo, who came on board to sell advertising. Mike was a happy-go-lucky guy who added merriment to our little office. Our most serious discussion every day was what to eat for lunch. One day Mike was asked by someone why we had no women employees. His answer: "Then we'd have to put a door on the toilet."

We subsequently moved to 2138 S. Lombard avenue, Berwyn, again a store half a block from Cermak avenue.

I gave my editorial job a lot of vigor (when I wasn't wearing my circulation hat, selling bus tickets or running tours of Chinatown.) The ham in me came out when I invented tales about Chinatown for the club ladies on our bus rides with me at the microphone.

I had a crew of young kids who delivered the papers. It was my job once a week to give them their routes, distribute stacks of papers, and then drive around the neighborhood to check their diligence. Occasionally I caught a kid dumping his load.

One of my boys told me one morning that he was on the Morton High School basketball team and occasionally worked out with Ralph "Bottles" Capone, Al's younger brother. I was very curious about this. How does a gangster get to play with high school kids? He told me that Capone frequented the gym almost every day, worked out with the team and then coach Billy Cepak, a former professional boxer, gave him a massage on a table in the locker room.

The next copy of the *Cicero-Berwyn Times* carried a story on the front page, which said "Ralph Capone Uses Morton as Country Club." It turned out I was more diligent than smart.

I did a whole column on the front page, feeling the story deserved major attention, but unfortunately it also came to the attention of the Capone family.

I was working at my typewriter when two huge guys came into the office. They were broad shouldered, wearing fedoras. One guy asked who the editor was. I told him I was. "Who wrote that story about Capone?" they asked. I told them I did, all of a sudden realizing I was in a tough spot. They looked at each other. One leaned over the counter, grabbed a fistful of my shirt, and advised me never to print that name in my paper again. I never did.

Incidentally, a previous editor of a similar paper in Cicero had been killed by the mob for some infraction. The fact that I was a 20-year-old kid probably saved me from a beating.

My story had an interesting by-product. The coach was fired. There was a also a shakeup in the management of the school.

Another story that created some excitement and fame of sorts for my little paper came about when I picked up rumors that the proprietor of a popular Bohemian restaurant, "Klas," had not come back from a trip to Czechoslovakia where he had gone to see his family in the wake of the German march into Sudentland.

The city abounded with all kinds of rumors about Adolph Klas and I stitched them together into a somewhat inventive piece on my front page, "What Has Happened to Adolph Klas?" I then went on to speculate that he may have converted his family's fortune into cash, may have tried to smuggle the money out of the country in a "false bottomed suitcase" and may have been apprehended by the Nazis.

My story was filled with legally safe suppositions. I went on to relate that rumors had it that Klas was in custody. That the Nazis were "unpleasant" to him. The next day the headline in the Czech paper screamed "Adolph Klas Tortured by Nazis." I didn't write anything about torture. The paper actually went on to elaborate on my tale, describing methods of German torture and the nature of the alleged infraction.

The next day June Provines, who wrote a popular column in the *Chicago Tribune*, did a long piece in her column entitled," Cicero Restaurateur Tortured by Nazis." She took her story from the Czech paper and printed it as fact.

I wrote to her and told her that she had printed a story that was based on supposition. She later replied and expressed her regrets, and indicating she was generally more careful. She also printed a retraction. But that wasn't the end of the story.

The State Department became alarmed and began an investigation. Cunard Lines, on which Klas had traveled to Europe, also got into the act. I had unwittingly started a whole hullabaloo.

There was a story in the daily papers interviewing Klas as he returned to the U.S. during which he proclaimed that he had not been under arrest and the whole episode was the imagination of "a reporter on his home-town newspaper."

Klas called me and asked me to visit with him at his apartment above his restaurant. I was somewhat apprehensive about the visit. "You caused me a lot of trouble!" he declared. But then he went on to concede that he had some difficulties getting out of Czechoslovakia. He added the publicity may have helped him. He also added that business in his restaurant had improved as a result of the news stories.

Morry Kaplan informed me one day that he was thinking of launching a new weekly in Chicago, in an area called Pilsen, which was to be my next job in journalism for a couple of years.

Laughs off that Nazi jail tale

Amused over rumors he had been thrown into a German concentration camp, Adolph Klas, well known Cicero restaurateur, was back home today after a trip to Czecho-Slovakia.

He said the journey, made with his wife, was enjoyable and that he was at no time troubled by the authorities.

"Some of my Chicago friends must have gotten worried because I didn't write home often enough."

FRIENDS ALARMED

Credence was given to the report after a community newspaper printed it, bringing alarm to Klas' relatives and friends.

The newspaper story stated Klas had sold property he owned in Sudetenland, taken by Hitler last fall, and that he had been arrested while trying to smuggle money from the sale out of the country.

German authorities allowed Klas

Mr. and Mrs. Adolph Klas

to sell the property, according to the story, and then betrayed the Chicagoan by arresting him after promising not to do so.

RIDICULES STORY

"Ridiculous!" Klas said today. "No such thing ever happened. Somebody must have a vivid imagination to think of such things."

The story previously had been proven false by Henry K. Weber of the Cunard White Star line offices here. He cabled the line's offices in Prague and was assured that Klas was free.

Klas arrived in New York last week on the Queen Mary.

Klaus Returns Home.

OSUD ADO RA JE ZJIŠTĚN

ZNÁMÝ MAJITEL RESTAURANTU ODSL V NĚMECKU DO KONCENTRAČNÍHO T\

KLASE Z (

Byl prý odsouzen na šest let, poněvadž chtěl p do Čech svoje vlastní peníze, které utržil za majetek, prodaný v sudetském distriktu.

MAJITEL POPULÁRNÍHO RE STAURANTU V CICERU ADOLF KLAS — NAHOŘE VLEVO — JEHO VYHLEDÁVANÁ NOST.

Czech newspaper goes all out on story telling how Klas was being "tortured".

The West Side Times

The *West Side Times* was situated in what was the original home base of Czechoslovakian immigrants, who later moved to the western suburbs of Chicago. There was still an ancient Bohemian synagogue on Ashland Avenue. On the corner, virtually across from our office, was a well-known restaurant, "Little Bohemia."

Our principal advertiser was the Leader department store on 18th street and we carried advertising from various and sundry local establishments. We were a full—sized newspaper as contrasted with the tabloid we published in the suburbs.

I felt like I was master of my little geographical domain, which existed in a circulation area from 26th street to 12th on the north and south side of Chicago, from Ashland Avenue on the west to approximately Halsted on the east.

I became busily involved in integrating myself into the community, visiting the various social agencies, meeting the community leaders and establishing rapport with political and religious leaders. I founded a group made up of religious leaders but was disappointed I couldn't get participation from the Catholic churches. I also patrolled the police and fire stations for news. I was determined to turn the *West Side Times* into a professional enterprise.

Morry Kaplan served as publisher and looked over my editorial shoulder. He was responsible for keeping the paper afloat, which frequently wasn't easy. He borrowed money from various sources and we kept publishing.

One evening at press time he handed a folded check to our 26th street printer, who insisted on being paid in advance before turning on the press. He knew the printer habitually placed the folded check into his pocket without looking at it. This time Morry gave him an unsigned check and the press run was begun. The next day the printer wasn't too happy about that subterfuge.

Another neighborhood weekly, *The Bridgeport News*, was printed at the same plant. I became friendly with an elderly couple who owned the paper. One day they approached me with a proposition. Become editor of their paper at an interesting increase in salary, also an assurance of ultimate ownership of their paper. Apparently they had no heirs.

I thought long and hard about their offer but declined. Long before I had made up my mind that I was not forever going to be limited to a small geographical area of the world. Taking their offer would be a guarantee I might be confined to Bridgeport for life. My desire to escape limited boundaries has always been a pervading influence in my life. I thanked them and turned down their kind offer.

I had the responsibility of not only reporting on and writing most of our paper, but getting the paper distributed by a small army of neighborhood kids. One day I noticed one of my boys was wearing a shirt that seem to be pitted with holes. I was curious if this was his only garment but he explained that a neighborhood industrial plant, Kramer & Sons, was spewing out fumes and everything in his home bore similar holes.

I went to his home and verified that indeed there was a serious problem. My front page told the story in detail. After my article appeared, the health department started an investigation and I did a follow-up article.

Later, I learned something about what happened as a result of my news story. A year or so later, when I was in my military uniform, fresh out of basic training, my uncle Harry took me for a visit to the home of a good friend. The host, a man named Romanoff, asked me what I did in civilian life and I replied that I had been a newspaperman.

He looked at me in amazed recognition and said, "You're the sunavabitch". "You're the guy that caused us all that trouble."

He went on to explain that, as a result of my story, his firm, Kramer and Sons, of which he was executive vice-president, was shut down and was forced by the Chicago Board of Health to install a filter on top of its plant at considerable cost. He added that it was a plus in the long run because the company was able to salvage valuable minerals with the filter, previously escaping in the open chimney.

Later I became a good friend of Howie Chapman, whose family founded the company, and Howie frequently told people I was the guy who had almost put them out of business.

There was a strong competitor in the neighborhood, which published a weekly with a following among the Czechs.

One day the *Chicago Times* began a series asking "Who Does Hitler's Dirty Work in Chicago?" I looked carefully at the series and discovered that the address of a printer, who printed lots of Nazi propaganda material, was the very same address as our competitor's newspaper.

I went to press with a double column on the front page: "Who Does Hitler's Dirty Work in Pilsen?" They shut down their paper that week.

I was able to supplement my income at the paper by selling advertising, calling on local merchants when I had extra time.

One of my good friends was a man named Max Stein, who sold advertising for us. He mentioned that Kaplan was closing down his suburban operations and was planning to take over my job. I was amazed I hadn't been told and confronted Kaplan. He said he had planned to tell me and asked me to stay on in a lesser capacity. At that time, he forced a decision I had been contemplating. I told him I was ready to move on to metropolitan journalism. I must admit I was a little piqued at how he had treated me. I resigned and started making the rounds of the dailies, again calling on the City News Bureau of Chicago, where I could never get an interview with the boss, Isaac Gershman, because I lacked academic credentials. But I decided to try again.

The Community War Fund

I had some misgivings about leaving City News, but the job at the Community and War Fund of Metropolitan Chicago was a marvelous opportunity for me.

Sylvia heard about the opening through her boss, Mickey Shufro and I went through a screening and was hired by the Fund.

I had my own private office plus an attractive secretary. The hours were respectable and I got an increase in my compensation over my City News pay. No more night duty away from my bride! And the opportunity to save a little. Also, our second child was on the way. It was a dream job for a person breaking into public relations.

My task was to publicize the Fund, the largest fund—raising entity in the country, encompassing most of the health and welfare agencies in the city and war related agencies like the USO and Russian War Relief.

In effect, I was the press agent for the Fund. There was enough material to maintain a steady flow of information to media. There were meeting announcements; stories about volunteers, and a multitude of releases about agencies within the Fund. On top of that, there were celebrity entertainers like the late Danny Kaye, who came to give a benefit. I recall spending time with Olivia de Havilland, the movie star, a sweet, obliging lady.

Danny Kaye wasn't cooperative one early morning when greeted by me and a band of photographers and models attired in Indian outfits to publicize the "Red Feather" name of our campaign. He stepped off the train, saw the group assembled to greet him, and fled into a waiting limousine.

Kaye must have awakened in a surly mood that morning and was quite profane and insulting as he fled. The press photographers instituted a ban on his pictures, which put a crimp into our ability to publicize his benefit appearance.

I began to get involved in special events as a means of generating publicity and went to see a theatrical agent, who booked celebrities in Chicago, in an effort to seek further cooperation from him. He in turn directed me to Frankie Harmon, who owned the Shangri-La Restaurant on Chicago's State Street, featuring exotic oriental food and fancy mixed drinks.

Like in a gangster movie, he said, " Just go over to Frankie and tell him I sent you. " I didn't know what I was going to get, but Harmon told me I could have his entire restaurant one late afternoon, food and drinks, all free of charge. We filled the place later for a benefit for our women's division and a horde of press people, and got excellent publicity.

One of the virtues of the job was that I began to deal at a very high level with the media. After all, this was the charity activity for the whole community. I was in a position to demand certain kinds of editorial support most PR people would beg for. I got the papers to agree to print a regular front-page column on Fund activities, illustrated with the Fund's Red Feather, and assign someone daily to cover the Fund.

One campaign, when Clarence Randall was chairman, he was invited to speak at the Chicago Commodities Exchange. As he began to talk, the closing signal went off and all the traders began to swarm out of the trading room.

Randall stood on one of the trading pits and shouted "Hey, fat man." A large individual stood in the doorway , frozen. Meanwhile he blocked the doorway so no on else could get out. Randall shouted," You're not walking out on Clarence Randall. You're walking out on thousands of widows and orphans!" Randall gave his whole pitch to that one man who was blocking passageway. As a result of his speech, he was able to get pledges from the traders in excess of $50,000.

William R. Harshe Associates

All the skills I had developed in previous years, going all the way back to high school when I edited the school paper, were utilized in starting my professional career in public relations.

Writing news releases was the basic tool. Writing and designing pamphlets; writing speeches; designing promotions; setting up photographs for the media and other similar activities were some of the skills I needed when I joined Bill Harshe.

Bill had noticed me when we did a project together while I was at the Community and War Fund. He was a director of the Illinois Society for Mental Hygiene, one of the Fund agencies. The head of the Fund, Bob Coburn, gave me permission to assist in that project because we were between campaigns, a light period of work. While visiting the newspapers together, Bill had seen the warm welcome I was accorded at most of the papers, particularly the *Tribune*, where many City News alumni were now employed.

I felt a special identification with Bill's project, a seminar dealing with the problems of returning servicemen finding it difficult to adjust to civilian life. By coincidence, I had been involved with setting up a similar activity because I found it extremely difficult to overcome my feelings of depression at being rejected by the Air Force when so many of my friends were still in service. Besides, the girlfriends I left behind were now occupied with other people or married.

Bill was a cheerful man with a wonderful disposition, always smiling. He walked with a rolling gait like a sailor. He projected bonhomme whenever he walked into a room. He was instantly liked at first glance. He was well connected in Chicago and he and his wife, Millie, were part of a near north side society crowd. His father had been executive director of the Art Institute of Chicago and was famous for urging acquisition of its present Impressionistic collection.

The firm, William R. Harshe Associates, had just moved from 8 South Dearborn Street, where the First Chicago Bank now stands, to an office in what was then Diana Court on Michigan Avenue. The Marriott hotel now stands there.

There was a small staff—a few writers, Bill's secretary, and a lady at the switchboard.

Bill slid me into authority, obviously uncertain how to break the news to his small staff that I was in charge. There were a few confrontations. I discovered his secretary kept her record of accounts payable in her stenographic book and it took some persuasion on my part to have her get a ledger. There were no files of media, which meant each writer had to develop his or her own mailing list each time a story was written. His secretary, a belligerent young woman, was replaced by Dorothy Helders, a gracious middle-aged woman, who took over the bookkeeping chores. I discovered she owned shares in the firm. Bill made a deal with her, offering her stock instead of a raise. Later, I purchased her shares.

I soon organized a mailing program and bought automated equipment and instituted a program where gradually I was introduced to clients. Each writer functioned in a singular way with no firm representation after Bill sold the account. I changed that, too, and got staffers to talk to clients in the collective third person "we" rather than the singular pronoun "I", reflecting organizational strength.

That was a hard sell because I knew many PR people dreamed of the day when they could start their own business. I worked hard to convince them that there was client longevity if the client didn't feel he was paying for one person. Besides, I said, clients don't like the dilemma of deciding between firm and individual staff member. We started holding our clients with my arrival in the firm. And we started adding new clients.

I soon discovered my own naiveté in not having demanded a contract with Bill when I joined the firm. In his mind, with his intentions presumably honorable, I was a partner but, consistent with his cavalier way of doing business, he had no formula for deciding on a split in equity. I discovered there were really no profits and we were living off loans and cash flow.

When I later acquired the business I paid off one loan from a relative of his where Bill had borrowed $10,000 at ten percent interest annually and had paid the interest for a period of ten years. I later made a deal with the relative to pay off the loan.

There was also the problem that Bill was charging many expenses to the company. He entertained at home a lot, which was good for business, but placed a burden on our ability to pay bills.

I talked about our loose relationship with Bill a number of times. He put the matter off because he said he had had a number of previous partnerships that were unsuccessful. He thought ours would work but he was reluctant to put the arrangement to paper.

Luckily, Bill's old classmate at the University of Chicago, Morris (Mossy) Leibman, took care of the firm's legal work. I spoke to him about my dilemma and he prevailed upon Bill to incorporate the company with Bill owning 55 percent of the shares and me, 45. He also included a survivor's arrangement where the surviving stockholder could purchase the other's stock at book value at death. The arrangement saved me financially when Bill died. Leibman remained my friend and lawyer for most of my business career. He was quite famous for having advised four Presidents of the United States.

Bill was not reluctant about introducing Sylvia and me to his well connected friends, but the fact that I was Jewish made him unwilling to introduce me into certain client situations where he felt there could be prejudice. The first instance was when Bob Carey, one of our account executives, who handled the Bismarck hotel account, told Bill the president of the hotel, Otto Eitel, was prejudiced against Jewish people.

When I heard this, I told Bill we should have no clients who would not accept me as a professional and the test would be that I would take over the Bismarck account, which I promptly did. I worked closely with Eitel, an urbane, cultured man who came from a distinguished family with old Chicago roots.

I became Eitel's friend and confidant to the extent he would ask me to help him decide on many issues including food additions to his menu. I took over the direction of Carey's accounts. We lost only one because of the problem Carey alluded to, a suburban bus line.

Whirlpool Corp.

We ran into the issue again when we learned Whirlpool Corp., St. Joseph, Mich., then called 1900 Corporation, makers of kitchen appliances, was in the market for public relations counsel. Bill didn't tell me about it and sent Carey to make the first call. I was very disturbed and again the matter of alleged prejudice came up. We agreed I would direct the account if we landed it, which we did.

I enjoyed a 30-year relationship with the people at Whirlpool. Elisha (Bud) Grey, chairman, was a charming executive. At one time he asked me to propose reasons why the company should or should not change its name from 1900 Corp. to Whirlpool, its principal consumer line. The company name was its address when it first started. I wrote a memorandum with a dozen reasons why the name change should take place.

There was a great concern how Sears would feel about the name change. The company made the Kenmore line for the chain. It was felt Sears might be concerned about its products being in competition with an aggressive Whirlpool brand.

The company's executive vice-president fired us in the emotional climate of a bitter strike but we reclaimed the account some years later when Jack Sparks became chairman. Jack was a young advertising manager during our first relationship. Both of us were two young guys starting out and we had a friendly relationship. He was pleased we were chosen again to represent the company but he let his staff decide.

Once, when I arrived late for a meeting, having lost my way from Chicago, Jack came to the front of their headquarters to razz me when I arrived. I recall with fondness Len Schweitzer, advertising manager, and Fred Upton, executive vice-president, whose family founded the company.

John Meck.

One of the first manufacturers of television sets was John T. Meck Co. of Plymouth, Ind. Meck was a sometimes nasty, infrequently pleasant client. During one visit, Meck invited Bill and me to dine at his home before driving back to Chicago.

The next morning, when I arrived at the office somewhat bleary—eyed from lack of sleep, Meck called. He demanded to know whether we had started on projects discussed the previous day. I told him I had just arrived at my desk. "You have negated my hospitality!" he exploded and hung up the telephone.

The Sniperscope.

We enjoyed a most pleasant relationship with executives at a firm in Indianapolis, Electronic Laboratories, which was born of World War II need. Among other things, the company manufactured the "Sniperscope", which was used in a variety of military ways for night vision. I had the task of going to the Pentagon to get clearance for us to release the information on the once secret weapon. That was almost a cloak and dagger trip requiring the utmost of secrecy.

OFFICE OF THE DIRECTOR

Federal Bureau of Investigation
United States Department of Justice
Washington 25, D. C.

May 9, 1946

Mr. Morris B. Rotman, Vice President
William R. Harshe and Associates
8 South Dearborn Street
Chicago 3, Illinois

Dear Mr. Rotman:

I wish to acknowledge your communication
of April 30th and I do want you to know that I
appreciate your calling this matter to my attention.

It so happens that we have been familiar
with the equipment for some time and have had demon-
strations of it. As a matter of fact, it has been
utilized in certain variations of our work. In view
of the nature of the use of the material, it would
be most inappropriate to publicize its use by the
FBI, for reasons which I am sure you can appreciate,
and accordingly, it would not be possible to take
advantage of your kind offer.

With best wishes and kind regards,

Sincerely yours,

J. Edgar Hoover

My correspondence with J. Edgar Hoover

Baby Sparkle Plenty.

At one time we represented a large number of toy manufacturers, among them Ideal Toy and Novelty, of NY. Their biggest
seller was a doll called "Baby Sparkle Plenty." Another doll ,
Baby Coos, represented a child dressed in velvet pants and a
striped T-shirt. It reminded me of my baby son, Jesse. I had an
outfit made to Jesse's size identical to the doll. The photo of the
doll and Jesse together went around the world.

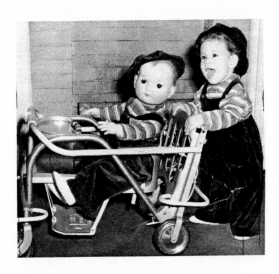

Son Jesse and Baby Coos doll.

In later years, Jesse had occasion to make a speech before the Toy Manufacturers Association, and showed that photo as an illustration of how long he had been involved in the toy business. He brought down the house.

Martin-Senour Paints.

A few of our firm's early clients were acquired by acquisition of the business of Paul Ridings, a Texan who decided to leave Chicago and take up his late father's former teaching post at Texas Christian university. One of the accounts was Martin Senour Paints, which became my cornerstone account when I took over the agency after Bill died.

After we seemed to go along smoothly as a business enterprise, Bill informed me he was thinking of moving to Nantucket, where his father was buried. He said we should open up a New York office, which he would man. From Nantucket? I asked myself. I was filled with dismay at this announcement because I felt the need for his salesmanship in the Midwest. Also I doubted we could afford the move.

Bill went ahead and rented a house on Nantucket, made

some furniture purchases, and started vacating his Chicago apartment. In the midst of all this activity, he was rushed to the hospital with a stroke. A portly man, he had been asthmatic as a youngster and ignored doctor's warnings about diet and exercise.

I went to the hospital to see Bill. He was cheerful and ebullient, full of grand schemes. He had summoned Dorothy Helders to his bedside with instructions to process the purchase of a new Cadillac, which I knew we couldn't afford.

On my second visit, I could see that Bill"s wife was in a state of alarm. The doctors were hovering over him. One emerged to announce that Bill had expired. He was only 42 years old. But his early respiratory problems militated against his recovery from a sympathectomy operation designed to alleviate the symptoms of his stroke.

I was a pallbearer at Bill's funeral in the Episcopalian church and could hardly contain my tears. Despite his careless ways as a businessman, he was a joyous, generous person and actually gave me my big break.

Harshe-Rotman, Inc.

Now I was faced with a lot of considerations. Should I close the business? Could I carry on? How do I get new business? If I carried on, would our clients and staff accept me as the principal? If I kept the business, should I change its name?

A complicating factor in my life at that time was that Sylvia and I had bought our first house in Glencoe, the down payment money mostly borrowed, and I wondered whether I should cancel the purchase in fear I would need every cent I had if I decided to go ahead with the business.

Necessity not caution prevailed. I decided my growing family needed a home. I vowed I could not afford to fail and told staff and clients I was carrying on with the same firm, no change of name, and assured clients they would continue to get the same level of good service they had when Bill was alive. I was confident we could keep most of the business with a couple of exceptions where Bill's presence and personality were a factor.

I traveled in a taxicab with Bill Stuart, president of Martin Senour, to make a condolence visit to Millie Harshe, Bill's widow. He was one of the clients about whom I was worried. In the cab he and I discussed the future of our firm and Stuart told me he would give me a chance to prove myself but he was uncertain I had the panache to make speeches before his marketing organization or do the entertaining of shelter magazine editors in New York, a requirement of service on this account. I quickly realized I had to master certain social skills in order to survive as head of our small PR company. Bill Stuart and I enjoyed a wonderful relationship for years and occasionally enjoyed playing golf together.

My friendship continues to this day with his son, Spencer, then marketing vice president. We talked about his joining our company but he moved on to fame and fortune by founding a very successful executive search firm, Spencer Stuart Associates.

Todd Co.

We had a client in Rochester, N.Y., the Todd Co., makers of check writers, which Bill personally serviced. I had never visited the firm although I was their principal contact on the phone. I telephoned Irving Greene, executive vice-president, to arrange an appointment.

Greene was most cordial when I arrived. An extremely tall, dark man with a balding pate, he heard me out. I could sense some skepticism as I offered my assurances. He finally said, "OK, go tell your story to Walter Todd down the hall." I spent some time with Todd and he said the decision to continue had apparently been made by Greene and he just wanted to meet me.

When I returned to Greene's office, after my visit with the chairman, he showed me a letter he was prepared to hand me, canceling our services. We held the Todd account for many years and Irving Greene became one of my best friends.

It was almost a year before I added my name to the name of the company out of sheer insecurity and also a firm belief that nothing substantial should change for a while to give the firm continuity.

I asked advisers what I should do about the company name. One man close to me suggested I change the name to Harshe-Morris on the assumption this would anglicize our firm.

I concluded that future sales prospects would be amused when I identified myself as the Morris Rotman of "Harshe-Morris. " I stayed with the old name until I began to build the business in my own image.

At first I was somewhat tremulous about the idea of becoming a salesman. I tried Bill's style in the first few calls—cheerful, airy etc. It didn't work with me because it wasn't me. I decided to read books on salesmanship, not being too sure what was involved in the process.

I went to see my uncle, Sam Friedman, a seasoned salesman, who built his fortune running a school for beauticians after a life selling cosmetics. He was not formally educated but talked with a friendly self-assurance. His advice: sell what you know, be yourself and inspire confidence. Simple advice, but helpful to me.

I had several disastrous experiences before I began to feel a sense of self-confidence. The executive who made me feel most diminished was the man who called in his butler to serve tea in his office and leaned back to listen to my tongue-tied pitch.

Kal Druck.

We were having problems in our New York operations, which had now become a major outpost, because Leroy Bieringer, whom we had sent from Chicago to New York to run our operations there, suffered a serious heart attack and was hospitalized.

This represented a major problem with a number of our large clients, principally Hertz and Mosler, but we handled client contact out of Chicago while I sought a permanent solution, feeling Lee might not be up to the strain of running the office once he returned.

I thought about Kal Druck, whom I had met at meetings of the Public Relations Society of America. I was impressed with Kal's presence, his booming voice, and the contacts he had as result of major client relationships with his previous agency, Carl Byoir.

Kal had left Byoir and set up his own small organization. By coincidence, we shared an account, Fantus Factory Locating Service, and I could see he was getting major results with his half of the account. I approached Kal and he scoffed at the idea he would leave Byoir and join an organization smaller. I proposed we would change the name of our New York operations to Harshe—Rotman & Druck and he would own 50 percent of that company. I also assured him I would be pleased to exchange his stock ownership in the eastern operations for ownership in the parent organization.

I pointed out that combining our large client list with his, making available services in our various offices, and bringing together our personnel would give him an added advantage in sales situations.

Kal did a great job in bringing in large clients from contacts during his Byoir days. We added as clients International Telephone & Telegraph, the U.S. Independent Telephone Association, the National Coffee Association, and others.

One day Kal came to me and told me point blank that, since he had done such an exemplary job in New York, he was entitled to own half the company. He demanded I give him half our shares without cost. I of course resisted and offered to sell him more shares but he brought in his attorney for a major confrontation.

After endless negotiations, during which Kal wouldn't budge from his demands, I came to a point of final determination. I advised Kal that unless he desisted from his demands, I would ask him to leave the company.

He backed off and I made available more shares to him, still retaining control of the company. I assured him we would later be willing to trade his shares in the New York Corporation for parent company stock and change our name to include his. That's how we became Harshe-Rotman & Druck.

Another major crisis came later when Kal sold his home in Scarsdale and bought a place in Florida. He began to work three or four days a week and terrorized the staff with his demands to meet his limited schedule. He resigned when we tried to renegotiate his compensation to reflect time he was now spending in the business.

By now, our firm had ancillary services for our clients: a design studio, a photographer on full-time availability, and a company owned lettershop not so much for profit but to control mailing schedules for list security. Outside letter shops, I learned, were providing our mailing lists to competitive firms. Some of these confidential lists were provided by our clients.

We often could not get letter shops to respond to our need for instant mailings in client crisis situations when we had to move fast to service the press. My older brother, Harry, was brought in to organize and run our letter shop. He also became part owner of the shop. We acquired an international public relations service, PR International, mostly to acquire its various relationships around the globe, and a two-man firm, Manley Markell, specializing in financial public relations.

Harshe-Rotman & Druck

With Kal Druck coming into the firm, we were able to solidify our eastern base and start a period of rapid expansion. We retained Hertz and were able to take advantage of our excellent relationship with Bob Shropshire at Nestle and soon added that account.

We were now in a position where large firms seeking public relations services would include us more often than not when inviting major firms to solicit their account. Among our new clients were the U.S. Exhibit at the World's Fair, the Wachtler campaign and others.

With Kal heading eastern operations, I found more time to expand our services, particularly abroad, and called upon various firms in our network of international representatives. I felt it was important being able to offer services wherever our clients would need representation.

We established a solid relationship with Jacques Blumenthal's firm in Paris, Information Et Enterprise, and purchased a substantial interest in a London based firm, Cutbill, which changed its name to include ours. I was proud of our name on a marble plaque on Albemarle Street next to the Brown Hotel.

Our Chicago and Los Angeles operations continued to grow. On my visits I would spend time with the Academy, the Avocado Growers, and Mattel and generally I would swing through San Francisco to meet with Castle & Cook and Clorox in Oakland. I also began to participate in the affairs of Marwais Steel, then situated in Richmond. I would make an occasional visit to Rochester, NY, to call upon Bausch & Lomb, Graflex and Taylor Instruments.

We added American Motors in Detroit. Kal headed up the account and recruited my son, Jesse, to be the account supervisor.

We were amused at the repeated misspellings of our corporate name, receiving letters addressed with garbled spellings of our name as a result of which we developed a large graphic for our various offices illustrating the most humorous aberrations.

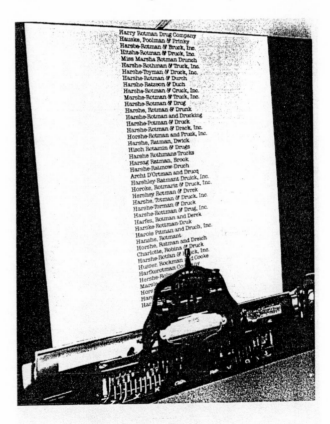

Display of company name misspellings

Office wall display with misspellings of our name.

Ruder Finn & Rotman

I had been approached many times by other firms seeking to merge or acquire us.

One day I got a call from a public relations headhunter in New York asking whether I would consider a merger with Ruder & Finn of New York. I had never thought too highly of their operations. Their Chicago office was very weak, but I felt we might be able to put our organizations together and become the country's largest independent.

At about that time Peter Gummer, of Shandwick, called me from London and asked if I would meet him in New York, that he would fly over just to discuss merger with me.

I made plans to meet Gummer and Ruder & Finn in New York the same week.

I was intrigued with Gummer's concept of bringing together a number of firms which would retain their identities in their respective markets but identify themselves as being part of Shandwick. It seemed to be the resolution to the concern most firms had about losing personal identification.

Gummer was interested in us because of our U.S. strength plus our cash reserves. Unfortunately, Gummer's cash position was low but he had verve and style and I felt his idea was right.

My meeting with Ruder & Finn went well. One thing I learned, however, was that Bill Ruder was withdrawing from active participation in the firm. That's when I should have backed away. Bill and I were old friends, and he was the reason I was so interested in the firm. But R&F had facilities and services, as well as an excellent client list, that I felt would mesh with ours.

When I went back to confer with our attorney, Lee Freeman, and my key people, I was urged to pass up the Gummer deal because of his paucity of capital.

We started the merger with R &F with great fanfare—stories in the *New York Times* and other publications. I began to feel I could work comfortably with the organization. Finn and I had an understanding wherein we would equally share management of the merged company. We would change our corporate name to Ruder Finn & Rotman. David would be chairman and CEO while I would become president and chief operating officer. I chose that title rather than co-CEO, which was offered by Finn, because I felt that title innocuous.

In our negotiations, David Finn asked me if I would support his involvement in the publishing of art books, a personal project. David did the photography, the company's art department did the design, and David distributed these books widely allegedly for corporate public relations. I thought it was a good idea at first, but initially I had no way of knowing how much it was costing the company. It turned out to be a lot. There was no disclosure whether Finn had personal financial gain from this activity.

In the first year of our relationship, the company lost about a million dollars. It plunged into developing a long neglected computer operation. I could see the funds we brought in disappearing. My son, Jesse, who was executive vice-president of our New York operations, was forced out.

Despite David's assurances we would jointly run the business, he ran the company unilaterally. I was not consulted on many decisions.

The culture of the company was completely different from the one I ran in Chicago. So many things were annoying. For example, David once insisted, in order to save money, we bring our own sandwiches to a board meeting. The team I had put in place to run the joint operations, consisting of Al Gertler, our president, and David Witkov, our treasurer, were both ignored.

David once admitted that a major cause of our growing estrangement was the fact I wouldn't place my travel business with his wife, who ran a travel agency and, incidentally, charged personal items to the company. I felt I didn't want her to tell me when and how to travel. I really didn't want to deal with her.

Finn had three of his offspring in the company, including two daughters, who constantly battled with one another, which was reported in the public relations press. His son, Peter, who wore wire rim glasses and sported a wispy red goatee, was in charge of the computer operations. After the breakup, he was promoted to executive vice president. There was another relative, a physician, who was on corporate retainer but essentially was paid for the Finn family's medical needs. Finn had a car and a chauffeur, who also served as the family butler in his home.

There were a lot of things my advisers missed in putting together the merger. My attorney was Lee A. Freeman, an antitrust specialist, who had been our firm's attorney for many years. The merger was initially negotiated by my old friend, Charlie Davison, vice chairman of Peat Marwick.

I soon realized our due diligence was inadequate and that the great promise of the merger was a foul mirage and I had to get out.

I told Finn I wanted him to buy back my stock , that I no longer wanted to stay with the company, nor did I want my name associated with it.

A long struggle ensued because of Finn's unwillingness to part with capital but I prevailed. Richard resigned and sold his stock. Finn held onto my name for another year and finally sent his hatchet man, Charlie Lipton, to tell me the company was dropping my name. Much to my relief.

Jesse, meanwhile, who had left the company earlier, moved his family to Chicago to seek his future in private industry. He ultimately developed a successful career in marketing and public relations, specializing in electronic products.

Richard 's wife, a Canadian, studying at Northwestern University, prevailed on him to move to Canada to launch a new career there. He, too, developed a successful public relations practice, mostly in corporate communications. After divorce, he married Gloria Stein, an architect by profession.

One of my considerations was that I open up my own firm again. I had threatened Finn with this eventuality when I was forcing him to buy my stock. Richard was strongly in favor of this but my attorney advised me a long costly battle would ensue with Finn, taking a great deal of my personal capital. I had done a disservice to my family with that merger and, of course, a distinct disservice to my career, by believing I could work with David Finn.

Rogers & Cowan

I was approached by an old friend, Art Winston, a management consultant, who inquired whether I would be interested in a possible merger with a west coast firm. Art was formerly Norton Simon's chief of staff at Hunt Foods.

He identified his client as Rogers & Cowan, the leading Hollywood PR firm, representing a long list of movie stars and studios. I told him the Academy would not look kindly at our merger with them but I would listen.

When I met with Art and Henry Rogers, I began to see the wisdom of the merger but I was not yet ready to bring the matter to the Academy. There were several things I liked initially. Henry was an urbane, well-dressed, soft-spoken man. I could see he could adapt himself to the kind of clientele we had on the west coast.

I also saw a kind of cross-pollinization between accounts we had and his. Movie star endorsements for our clients' products and appearances of those products in movie productions. I reasoned we could sell and expand west coast services to our clients.

We then got down to planning the new firm. We prepared a brochure with a combined client list and arranged to meet in Palm Springs for a three-day conference to negotiate details. We met at the Wonder Palms hotel, which was adjacent to the Tamarisk Country Club in Rancho Mirage.

We thought we could meet in secrecy but I discovered a host of Chicago friends in the club's dining room. Henry had arranged for us to have guest privileges at the club. One of my Chicago friends encouraged me to join, which I subsequently did.

I began to have some uneasiness about the deal, mostly because Henry and Warren Cowan operated on the principle they left nothing at the bottom line the end of the year whereas my own compensation was relatively modest because I believed in accumulation of equity in our stock. We had substantial cash and they were into the banks for loans.

Also Henry told me about a large unfunded insurance policy they carried for the two principals and Temme Brenner, a stockholder, who was an important factor in serving their movie star clients. Henry confided that Temme had cancer problems. I realized they would have to borrow more money to pay the insurance claim were Temme or one of the other principals to die.

Henry asked me whether I could spend time with Warren Cowan to get to know one another. Warren had not been in on most of our discussions.

We were then living in Glencoe, Ill., and Warren came for an overnight stay at our home. He was a dynamic, charming guy. At one time he was married to the movie star, Barbara Rush.

I recall the scene. Warren went to sleep in the vacant bedroom of our daughter, Betty, who was away at the University of Arizona. . He emerged from the bedroom and exclaimed, "You're putting me on! I found the last fan in America."

Warren discovered Betty's room was a virtual museum of Eddie Fischer memorabilia. Pictures of Eddie on the walls. Albums of his songs. Newspaper clipping of Eddie in various stages of his career. Eddie was Warren's client, a long relationship. He said he wanted to have Eddie do "something special" for Betty. I urged him to get an autographed photo.

After he returned to his office, Warren called and told us Eddie had invited Betty to come to Las Vegas, where he was performing, to be his guest for a weekend .We told Warren only if she could bring a companion. Betty thought we were joking when we called to tell her about the invitation.

Betty took along a classmate, Cindy. Eddie's Rolls Royce

was at the airport to greet them. There was a corsage of orchids for each of them. And they were escorted to a large suite at the Desert Inn hotel. That night Eddie dedicated his show to Betty and her friend while they sat ringside. The next day he took the girls to the Hoover Dam on a sightseeing trip. He spent an entire afternoon sitting with them pool side.

When they departed, Eddie drove them to the airport. He couldn't have been a nicer, more gentlemanly guy. I wrote him a letter of appreciation.

Unfortunately, when I put the numbers together with my advisers, I felt we were facing economic jeopardy in the merger. I asked Henry to revise the executive insurance policies but he was unwilling to do so. And I withdrew from further discussions, much as I was intrigued by the possibilities of the merger.

Morris B. Rotman Associates

Two dear friends volunteered to become clients in my new career as a one-man public relations company. One was George Mitchell, chairman of Mitchell Energy & Development, of Houston. The other was Marshall Wais, chairman of Marwais Steel of San Francisco.

Mitchell's company, after years of relationship with me, was on inactive status when I departed from Ruder & Finn. The firm tried to contest my serving this client by its claim that I was violating my non-compete arrangement. My attorney advised this claim was without merit because Mitchell wasn't then a client.

R & F was very vindictive because I had forced the company to buy me out and they did everything they could to obstruct my progress for several years. This stopped dead when I retained Don L Reuben, one of the Midwest's leading lawyers, former counsel to the *Chicago Tribune*, the Chicago Bears and a host of other leading entities.

I was introduced to Don by Lee A. Jennings. When I told Lee of my troubles, he said, " I know just the man for you." But I was fearful he had the wrong lawyer for me. Don Reuben had a reputation as being a tough guy, handling only big stuff.

When I finally met Reuben and he agreed to take me on, I asked him why he was interested in my small account. I'll never forget his reply, " Because I hate to see anyone screwed." Incidentally, he turned out to be a pleasant person and later we became pals.

Our relationship with our previous counsel, Lee A. Freeman,

ended when we consummated our deal with R&F.

George Mitchell had asked me to undertake a counseling arrangement with his company, visiting Houston headquarters occasionally, clearing copy and offering counsel on the phone. I retained this relationship and friendship with George and his company for more than 20 years.

Marwais Steel.

Marshall Wais was an extremely successful self-made man. He built Marwais Steel into one of the country's largest specialty steel producers; turning out thousands of tons of color coated extruded steel. His company had a number of public relations needs where he felt I could be useful. He asked that I provide the company with a couple days of my time each month, requiring only monthly visits to his headquarters in Richmond, Ca.

In military circles, Marshall was regarded as a hero because his company built steel shelters that protected our fighter planes and bombers from enemy attack.

He married Lonna Hannah and we spent lots of time together. They had a beautiful chalet above the old town of Eze on the French Riviera and we visited them there as their guests.

I introduced Marshall to Sam Wanamaker, who was raising funds to realize his dream of building a replica of the original Shakespeare Giobe Theater on its original site on The Thames in London. Marshall overwhelmed Sam (and me) when he pledged a quarter of a million dollars for the project and later contributed steel to build the proscenium in the theater.

Marshall was honored at a special ceremony at the Globe when a portrait of him was installed in the lobby of the theater.

Mayfair Regent Hotel

I took on a couple of interesting assignments during the period of my professional single-blessedness. One was to revamp the marketing activities of the posh Mayfair Regent hotel in New York. Another was a marketing program for the downtown revitalization of nearby Cathedral City, Ca.

The Mayfair account was a prize package for me. I had been recommended for the assignment by Don Reuben, who was counsel to Heitman Financial of Chicago, owners of the hotel. Heitman was a giant manager of properties and trusts for unions, school boards and others, headed by Norman Perlmutter.

The account was a joy for me personally. It gave me an opportunity to go to New York at will. Perlmutter told me I could bring Sylvia any time. I stayed at the hotel and could dine in the hotel's dining room, mostly catered by the famous La Cirque restaurant.

I interviewed various levels of staff to get an understanding of internal attitudes, including Dario Mariotti, managing director, and Michael Blackman, general manager.

I hired a New York public relations firm to do local publicity and cleared all hotel communications with the press. I came up with two promotional ideas, both agreed to by owners and management and heralded by the press.

Since the hotel had no exercise facilities for guests, other than some equipment in a suite, I proposed development of a putting green for guest use. Competitive hotels all had elaborate health facilities for guests.

An avid golfer, Blackman went at this idea enthusiastically and installed a putting green in a vacant suite with rolling contours and typical golf course flags. He ordered balls and putters imprinted with the hotel's name and launched a guest promotion. I was never sure how many guests used it, but we had loads of publicity for our claim of having the "only golf course on Park avenue. "

At our press preview, we took over an entire floor and laid out a competitive putting contest for the press and there was lots of merriment. And press coverage.

The other idea came out of the custom my wife and I had of requesting extra pillows for night reading every time we checked into a hotel anywhere. I noticed I had come to the Mayfair several times and made the same request each time. I asked myself, why didn't they make a note of my preference?

I proposed a "Pillow Bank" wherein the guest would be told the hotel stocked any special pillow a guest wished, and that it would be on his or her bed the next time a registration occurred.

Blackman and Mariotti were fully supportive of the idea. Blackman insisted the hotel "do it right" and purchase the best pillows available. Ownership agreed to his budget of $150, 000 for superior pillows, selected after an international search.

The hotel installed a giant armoire in the lobby displaying its pillows. A brochure was distributed at registration showing more than a dozen varieties of pillows available. Many guests wrote how pleased they were with the program. And the *New York Times*, among other publications, ran a full page in its Sunday magazine showing "the best new idea" in hotel customer service. They also illustrated the putting green.

NY Times proclaims Pillow Bank "year's best new hotel idea".

The Times also illustrated " The only golf course on Park avenue."

College of the Desert

After a speech before the Coachella Valley Women's Press Club, I was approached by a man who identified himself as a dean at the College of the Desert in nearby Palm Desert. His name was Roy Wilson, who later rose to political prominence in the community as a county supervisor. Roy asked me whether I would be interested in teaching communications at the college.

The thought appealed to me and I agreed to be interviewed by department heads there. I reasoned the task would be a snap with my more than 40 years of experience in the field. But I didn't count on the obsession with academic credentials.

One of the interviewers asked me if I had any awards or letters of recommendation. I said I could bring a suitcase full of framed awards and letters from many people of note.

Then there was the matter of my not having a bachelor's degree. I quickly learned I could counsel giant corporations but I couldn't really teach at the College of the Desert without academic credentials. The final straw that broke the proverbial back was when I noticed, before one interview, that I was competing for the job with a female undergraduate about 19 years of age. I withdrew my name from consideration with a polite letter.

The head of the department, Frank Attoun, asked me to reconsider. I told him I would if I didn't have to go through all that interview nonsense. I now understood why the college could not attract too many of my friends to teach, many giants in the business world, some without college degrees.

I became friendly with David George, then head of the col-

214

lege, who paid me a rare honor by sitting in one of my classes. David later lost his post because he foolishly got involved in a Pyramid scheme and was indicted along with a bunch of local luminaries, including the head of McCallum Theater. No jail, but a lot of careers affected.

Teaching was an exciting avocation. Maureen Daly, my old pal from newspaper days, paid me a compliment by signing up for my Monday evening class. She did her homework conscientiously and turned out to be my best student.

I had a number of interesting experiences with the class. This wasn't your typical undergraduate group. There were about 25 at the start although a few dropped out later. Most were in the field already; others were attending class for credit. A couple of students, who had jobs in advertising or public relations, were very serious about the class and wrote excellent report papers. One young woman asked pointed questions each session and my mental meter detected hostility. Actually, at the end of the term, she asked me if I would consider coming to her home for dinner to meet her husband.

I told the class we would take on a community project as a voluntary experience in public relations in training. The class selected the local "Foods on Wheels" and wrote a recommendation for a public relations program for the charity. Two of my class members volunteered to continue to devote time.

For the final exam, I asked the class to pose questions of themselves relating to what they had learned or read during our course. I told them I didn't object to their finding questions in their textbooks. But I pointed out I could tell by the final papers how much they learned and how much effort they put into the test.

I told the class I would host dinner at a local restaurant for those who stuck it out to the bitter end. We had about 20 of us at dinner and the class prepared a trophy attesting I was the "No.1 PR Coach." It's sitting in my office as I write his, an orange golf ball in its mid section.

Postscript: Frank Attoun, department head, told me he was

required to grade my teaching ability. He attended one class where I did my usual thing and another when I was absent.

We then had a solemn session. A very nice man, sincere and very soft-spoken, Attoun approached the subject diplomatically.

"You did very well considering your lack of academic training, and are graded excellent," he started. "But there were a few problems.

"You told one of your students she had on a lovely dress," he said. "This is inappropriate."

He also said that one of the students complained that each session I asked for a volunteer "scribe" to write at the blackboard during class. (My handwriting is terrible). There was an objection to the terminology. What was worse, a couple of young ladies who volunteered, it was said, were polishing the apple for better grades. This was unfair, some felt.

After my return from Vietnam, I neither had the endurance nor the ability to stand before the class and I did not continue my teaching.

Cathedral City

I was invited to compete for a local account. Cathedral City, Ca., a community adjacent to Rancho Mirage. The city was planning a revitalization of its central shopping core and I met with Susan Moeller, coordinator of the project, for an initial conference.

I told her at the outset I was planning a two-week vacation trip before I could start. She invited me to meet with a promotional committee made up of local businessmen and a few city trustees. After a brief time, I was notified I was the finalist. I quoted what I considered was a fair fee and submitted a memorandum outlining what I was prepared to do. We made plans to get started immediately after my return from my proposed trip to Indonesia.

When I appeared before the committee, I made my report outlining various alternative suggestions for marketing programs.

In the process of collecting my thoughts, I wondered why the committee felt the need for a new name for the revitalized area. My first suggestion was that the city just proclaim that it was "New Downtown Cathedral City." This wasn't a popular suggestion. The committee was gung ho for a big league promotion.

Before I left on my vacation, I did research in libraries and conducted interviews of city council members, leaders of the Indian community, and local luminaries. I studied books on names California gave various cities.

A number of thoughts began forming in my mind:

Half the people interviewed wished the city would come up

217

with a new name to escape its past reputation as a city formerly known for its brothels and gambling joints. When I talked to Irv Kupcinet, the *Chicago Sun-Times* columnist, about Cathedral City, he said, "Oh, Cat City. We used to go there to gamble."

My inclination was that it was easier to improve a bad image than to create a brand new one. I took into consideration the enormous costs the city itself, businesses and professions would have to assume were they to change building names, stationery, names on stores and the many places the name of the city appears on various monuments.

The objectives of my study:

1. Find a name for the new downtown.
2. Select a name that would reflect the ambience of the development.
3. Select one that would lend itself to trademark or insignia.
4. Select one that could be used if an ultimate decision was made to change the unpopular name of Cathedral City.

Dick Shaloub sat as head of the committee primarily concerned, I felt, with protecting his interests. He got very prickly and apparently became obstructionist to me, frustrating me at every turn, when I ventured the opinion the new downtown should provide a variety of unusual food experiences to attract crowds in addition to fast food. Not McDonald's alone.

Shaloub must have visualized his McDonald's sitting right in the middle of the new downtown, dominating the scene. At the start I didn't know he was the McDonald's man, who, incidentally, came to committee meetings in his shiny Rolls Royce.

Shaloub rented a private office in the former Cathedral City municipal center, which he shared with a rumpled advertising old timer, Chuck Davis, who warned me when I took on the assignment that he was planning to handle the promotional part of the Cathedral City study. "Don't expect to do any work beyond your original inquiry, he said. "I am going after that assignment.

" Meanwhile he sat at Shaloub's side during all our discussions. I felt this was a definite conflict of interest.

I had a contract with the city calling for half payment at the start of my engagement, the remainder when I submitted my report, plus $1,000 in out of pocket expenses. I had to press for the final payment, which took months after completion of my assignment, and even then some expenses were briefly held out. The explanation for this delay was that the committee (Shaloub) wanted a guarantee I would show up if I were called in for questions about my report. Try to keep me away!

I was scheduled to go to Chicago on my vacation and had forewarned Susan Moeller. Since I had an agreement permitting $1,000 for expenses, I felt there would be no problem being compensated for my travel expenses, consistent with our agreement, if I came back from my vacation for a week to work on the project.

I made appointments with Shaloub, who told me where to meet him (at his McDonald's) in Palm Desert, but was unavailable when I came back and said he never had an appointment with me. I also made a date with Chuck Davis, who never showed up at his office. My third appointment was with Mike Velasquez, then mayor pro tem, who also didn't show up and said we didn't have an appointment. The committee (Shaloub) refused to pay for my transportation expenses for the return visit to the desert. At that point, I realized there would be no peace with Shaloub, but I was determined to finish the job. My sense of professionalism prevailed

I presented a number of alternatives to the committee:

1. Improve on the present name and launch a program to announce a new downtown.
2. Out of consideration of its Mexican population, call the area The Zocalo. I recalled many visits to Mexico City's Zocalo, a central meeting place where people assembled and was popular with visitors. The great Cathedral was situated there and excellent restaurants abounded. I

could visualize colorful decorations, mariachi dancers and fiestas in the new downtown Cathedral City. I even suggested a symbol which would be very easy to design—a simple "Z" for Zocalo. I thought of the thousands of T-shirts etc that would be emblazoned with "Z.

3. Another suggestion was to call the area Santa Rosa Village, after the surrounding mountains. I showed the committee an unusual design for a rose. I felt this design would also lend itself to everything graphically. My research told me the head of the state's rose growers hobbyists lived in Palm Springs and I contacted him about whether a new rose could be developed named after Cathedral City.

4. During our travels, Sylvia and I were taken with the popularity of various fountains we had seen. We loved the circular fountain next to the Pompidou museum in Paris with its giant circulating Nikki St. Phaule figures. When we got to Saigon, we were delighted with a fountain with a submergible Punch and Judy show. The figures rose out of the water and then disappeared at regular clockwork. I showed the committee photographs of the two fountains and included them with my bound proposal.

5. Another idea was that the development be named after the man who had literally discovered Cathedral Canyon, an area in the nearby mountains which reminded him of a cathedral. His name was Washington. Why not honor him by naming the area after him?

6. In my research I also discovered that the Indians had a legendary hero. With so many American Indians in the area, why not honor them with a tribute to their hero? I could visualize Indian decorations, guest tribal dances, etc.

Shaloub finally said, after hearing my report, that the committee found my ideas unacceptable and asked me to try once again to come up with a new name. I should have quit when I was behind, but there was a matter of professionalism at stake if not to mention half my fee.

I scanned various books of California town names and could find little better than what I had suggested. It occurred to me that Cathedral City was midway between Rancho Mirage and Palm Springs. I also learned the area had once been referred to as Midway. I recalled the lovely esplanade that runs through the University of Chicago.

Shaloub apparently was in a hurry to end the meeting. He quickly told the committee my Indian idea was acceptable and would adorn a central area in the complex. He said the city would also plant lots of roses and maybe would consider some kind of fountain. I felt modest vindication.

It took me several weeks to get Shaloub to release the remaining half of my fee. I learned later they had decided to go ahead with a fountain. Sylvia and I were at a reception one night and she began to talk to a local architect who told her his wife was working on a fountain for Cathedral City. Her name was Jennifer Johnson and we had a delightful conversation later. When I told her the name Nikki St. Phaule, she exclaimed to her husband, " Nikki St. Phaule! He told the committee about Nikki St. Phaule."

I went by her fountain several times. She was laboring under a tent in front of the new Cathedral City town center and had completed several large terra cotta figures for adornment as part of the fountain. We had dinner one evening with Susan Moeller and the Johnsons. She invited me attend the municipal center open house.

Today, the clock tower makes its presence known at intervals. The civic center has been painted a color, which reminds many of infant effluvia. And the lamp poles are painted a purple many people find offensive and humorous. Susan Moeller recently revealed she has resigned her Cathedral City post and was taking a similar assignment elsewhere.

Vietnam and the Spice

Islands

Sylvia and I luxuriated during our fortnight in Hong Kong, one of our favorite cities and one of the most exciting spots on the planet. On a number of previous trips, we had been with convention groups or on business calls, but this time we decided to see things in Hong Kong never seen before by us.

After our Hong Kong sojourn, we traveled by air to catch our ship, The Voyager. We flew from Hong Kong, then on to Bali and finally to East Timor, where the ship awaited us.

Now that I reflect on the trip, I am reminded two doctors urged us not to go. Had we had the foresight to listen to them, Sylvia and I went to see our internist in Chicago, Dr. Charles Nadler, for preventative medical advice. "I won't tell you not to go," he said. "But the odds are 50 to 50 that you'll get sick on this trip." He gave us gamma and tetanus shots and a variety of prescriptions.

We also consulted Dr. Steven Becker, our otolaryngologist, about potential respiratory diseases. He also sounded an ominous note. His first words were " The first piece of advice I will give you is to tear up your tickets." He was well aware of the problems with pneumonia I had suffered several times on various business trips. But we were determined to go.

The Voyager was a comfortable ship with reasonably good meals. The passengers were an amiable bunch, mostly from England or Australia. One, Sir Bruce MacPhail, was managing director of the Peninsula and Oriental Steam Navigation Company, owners of The Voyager. He was on holiday with his wife and daughter and a son, who brought along a beauteous French young lady. Sir Bruce and I became friendly and there was an invitation to dine with him when we got to England.

We sailed blissfully, each day stopping at one of the numerous small islands, going ashore by rubber dinghy for visits to native villages where we shopped for trinkets or saw the usual native rituals.

One day we stopped at a little island called Waingapu. I was prepared for snorkeling with the mask and other gear I brought along. One dive and, to my disappointment, I discovered the sea was murky, offering no underwater visibility. Sylvia and decided instead to walk the beach, kicking the sand and occasionally wading in the shallow water.

When we got back aboard, Sylvia noticed three tiny black holes above my right ankle. She washed my ankle and applied an antibiotic salve but we soon discovered this was no negligible bite. My foot began to swell. I began to get feverish and seemed to go into toxic shock, almost drifting into unconsciousness.

She called the ship's steward and he came down with his medical bag, applying an antibiotic ointment to the affected area. Unfortunately, the small ship carried no full-time medical doctor. He was it. He had no idea what he was dealing with but did his best under the circumstance.

Sylvia and I went to the ship's dining room to get some food. I barely made it up the stairs. The passengers were alarmed by my appearance and offered help. But there was nothing to be done until the ship docked in Bali the next day. A couple from Australia accompanied Sylvia to a hotel after which she took me by cab to a hospital, a very large facility with seemingly hundreds of rooms.

The resident physician was a dermatologist, who had no idea what had befallen me but quickly started injecting me with Augmentin, a broad span antibiotic. Had she known what had infected me, Sylvia would have pressed for airplane evacuation. She tried to communicate with our emergency evacuation service to no avail. She did contact the U.S. counsel in Bali, who was helpful in getting us on our way to Hong Kong, where we were scheduled to catch our flight to Los Angeles.

We spent a night in a hotel in Hong Kong and boarded a flight to Los Angeles. By then, Sylvia was managing to move me about by wheelchair. A young passenger, sitting directly in front of us, spent his time getting slightly inebriated when he wasn't helping me make my way to the lavatory. Unfortunately, we didn't get his name but shall never forget him.

Still not knowing what had befallen me, we got into a limo and, after dropping off baggage, went to Eisenhower hospital for treatment. The physicians began treating me with heavy doses of Augmentin, and immediately orthopedic physicians began debriding treatment, cutting away infected skin. There was still no diagnosis of my infection and at each visit I was reminded that I was involved in "something serious". Later I learned there was serious discussion about amputating my right leg to save my life.

My friend, Bert Given, who worries about his friends and loved ones, kept calling every day from Los Angeles to get a report on my progress. He told Sylvia he was unhappy with my being treated without a specific diagnosis and insisted she bring me to Los Angeles for an examination by a tropical disease specialist, Dr. Clare Panosian, at UCLA.

One of the valets at Tamarisk drove my car with Sylvia alongside him in the front seat. I was surrounded with pillows in the back seat and we made our way to Los Angeles to keep my appointment with Dr. Panosian. Earlier I had learned she was widely acclaimed for her professional expertise in tropical diseases.

She was a pleasant soft spoken woman and went to work immediately submitting me to a series of blood tests. She finally told me she was certain I was infected by a strep A infection called necrotizing fasciitus, a flesh eating disease. She wrote a memorandum for doctors at Eisenhower and urged me to return home immediately for treatment.

Before going back home, we assembled a few friends, including Bert, for lunch at Junior's in LA. If I was going to die, I thought, I was going to heaven with a deli sandwich in my belly.

I reported back to Dr. Lawrence Cone, a disease specialist and oncologist, who had given me a physical prior to our trip. He read Dr. Panosian's memorandum with interest and went into action immediately. He was able to slow down the skin destruction on my leg. The skin had been ravaged up to mid shin and there was a hole over my right ankle almost to the bone.

I saw a plastic surgeon about skin grafts on my ankle. My leg was discolored up to the shin, a condition that persists to this day.

As the plastic surgeon was about to close up the wound, Larry Cone called and abruptly stopped him, telling him he had seen with the naked eye another infection in the ankle, which he later identified as a dipthoid. Apparently, I had picked up another infection in the open ankle hole on shipboard or traveling home by plane.

The recommended treatment was nearly a month in bed of intravenous injections of vancomyecin, a powerful antibiotic. I wore a permanent shunt in my arm as nurses from Eisenhower outpatient service came daily. Many of them being pretty and bosomy with a habit of leaning close to me, some getting onto my bed with one knee, my morale improved slightly despite the procedure.

A number of the nurses took personal interest in my case beyond the call of duty and offered advice and sincere nurturing. One escorted me outside when I started walking again, halting steps with a walker and then cane. She confided she was part of a chorus at a local church and I told her about my interest in singing.

She urged me to take voice lessons and lined me up with a lovely young lady who had a studio in Palm Desert. She had excellent voice training and we worked together for about a year until she married and moved to San Francisco. Before she left, she recorded my favorite songs on tape, one version herself singing all the songs we worked on, and another just the music so I could accompany myself.

The singing was great therapy for me. Occasionally I would go to my player piano equipped with a motorized drive and sing songs from my collection of more than 400 rolls. Despite my medical problem, I was determined to finish the Cathedral City assignment. I had done most of the research before leaving on my vacation and only had to collect my thoughts and submit them to my Macintosh computer.

I attacked the project with my right limb propped up on a stool and managed to complete a fairly respectable professional report outlining various alternative programs for the Cathedral City marketing committee to consider. I submitted the report first to Susan Moeller, city coordinator, who had retained me for the study.

A very intelligent lady, she understood her committee. She said I had fulfilled my professional commitment but also feared the recommendations I made were "too subtle." First time in my life anyone had ever made that charge against me.

As I began to feel better, I was determined to satisfy my curiosity about what kind of sea animal had infected me. I wondered why the ship operators hadn't alerted passengers to dangers of the sea. Why physicians at the Bali hospital had no idea what infected me even though I believed they must have encountered cases like mine before. Even Dr. Panosian had no idea as to the name of the sea culprit and promised to do some research. But I never heard from her. I finally decided I had to pursue the matter myself by consulting a variety of resources on the web.

The most conclusive answer came from Dr. Gregg Mitchell, son of George Mitchell, who was on the staff of the Scripps Oceanarium at LaJolla. In response to my inquiry, he communicated with fellow staff researchers in various parts of the world and the unanimous opinion was that I had been infected by a Stone Fish, one of the most poisonous creatures of the sea found in profusion in the part of the world we were visiting.

The Stone Fish lies burrowed in the sand and it was my misfortune accidentally to molest it as Sylvia and I strolled along the shore. It has three dorsal fins under which are poison sacs and attacks its enemies with a hypnotic injection. That's probably why I felt nothing when I was infected.

The Stone Fish. My worst enemy.

Since my misadventure. I have kept in touch with cases of necrotizing fasciitus. Twice I have lectured on my experience at grand rounds of physicians at the Rehabilitation Institute of Chicago. The newspapers reported the premiere of Quebec lost his leg shortly after being infected and there were reports of 12 women in England dying of the disease after caesarian birth. Now when I meet a physician and he gets curious about my experience. he always congratulates me about "still being alive."

The Rehabilitation Institute

of Chicago

A plaque on my office wall attests I'm a Life Director of the Rehabilitation Institute of Chicago. There is a photographic portrait of me on the 15th floor with the Institute's graphic symbol, "The Tree of Life," whose design and adoption I helped create. A letter in my files from Dr. Henry Betts says something to the effect that my name should be carved in marble for my efforts in bringing in major money contributions.

All of these testaments to my service hardly match the joy and satisfaction I have had over more than 30 years in helping the Institute reach its place in society and serve the physically disadvantaged. Nor does the recognition match the feeling I get when I see the Institute become the No. 1 hospital of its kind, according to the annual *U.S. News* magazine survey.

For about 20 years I served on the board of directors and was chairman of the Institute's public relations committee. During that time, I supervised the Institute's image in the media, in the community and among various publics important to the hospital.

I first became aware of civilian rehabilitation, as contrasted with veteran rehabilitation, in a lunch one day with an insurance man and banker, Howard Hurwith, who told me about the efforts of a handful of men to start a facility in Chicago. He asked if I

Photo portrait hanging at Rehab Institute.

would serve on its board and help the new hospital get acceptance in Chicago.

Physicians I knew weren't sure Chicago needed a facility like that in the mistaken belief most hospitals offered similar care to the handicapped. My physician brother—in—law told me how he personally handled the physical therapy for his patients. Like most physicians in the community, he wasn't sure of the need for a new hospital for the treatment of the disabled.

The first board meeting I attended was in Hurwith's insurance company office on Wells street. A handful of men crowded around a little table but they were a powerful group capable of accomplishing major objectives. Attendees included the heads of Standard Oil of Indiana, International Harvester, Searle Co., A.B. Dick and a few others. This kind of support reassured me of the possibility of the success of the enterprise. The more I heard about the mission, the more enthusiastic I became about the need for such an institution.

The hospital was able to acquire a building at 401 East Ohio Street, a warehouse owned by the Regensteiner family. The first official board meeting was held in the basement of the facility. When I suggested an open house be held for press and physicians groups, one of the directors said this was not appropriate because medical people ethically had to maintain a low profile and stay out of the press.

Luckily I prevailed. I could see that if I were to help the Institute I would have to convert some mindsets, the first being the board of directors. I had to convince the board I knew what I was doing professionally and they needed to support me in my efforts to win exposure and friendships for the Institute. At times, it was tough going.

My assessment was that the Institute had a number of major obstacles at the start which it had to overcome if it were to be successful. Probably the first was that neither the Institute nor its mandate were well known or understood in Chicago. Secondly, the hospital couldn't thrive unless physicians would refer patients and many of them were actually concerned they would lose their patients if they went to the Institute. Thirdly, the insurance industry would not pay for rehabilitation claims. Finally, the Institute had a token women's group, which was not involved in fund-raising or giving the hospital high visibility on the women's pages of newspapers.

At the time I joined the board, the Institute was not socially acceptable. My experience told me that executives and women activists were not interested in joining the board of an organization that had a low recognition factor and where other well-known people were not involved.

On a number of occasions, I mentioned the need for a more active women's board to stage events, to raise funds and to develop high visibility in the community. This was a delicate move on my part because the present small women's board was recruited with the promise it would not be called upon to do more than lend their names. The idea of an active women's board took wing when Mrs. Dorothy Browne, a director, took the lead in organizing such a group. Mrs. Browne also became an important benefactor. At one point she quietly bought the parking lot next to the Institute and later gave it to the hospital.

The women's board subsequently staged major events, and was responsible for contributing substantial funds to the Institute. It also got major recognition in the Chicago press.

I started to give a good amount of my time to the Institute. I was so imbued with the correctness of the idea that I began to get friends and family involved. Sylvia brought several of her friends over. Even my kids got enthusiastic. Betty volunteered some of her time and later went to work in the public relations department. Sons Jesse and Richard installed a fish tank with colorful tropical fish on the cafeteria floor and visited the hospital regularly to clean the tank and replenish food. It became a popular place for the patients to visit.

One day I took a group of my friends through the premises, including golfing buddies from Briarwood Country Club. When we visited the prosthetics laboratory, one of the men, Bobbie Berkenfield, who lost part of his hand as a combat flyer in the war, asked, "Gee, I wonder if they can give me a new hand?" Another friend, Marshall Goldberg, former all American football player from Pittsburgh, replied," No, but they can give you a hook." Funny, but true. Also, if he needed one, a new artificial hand.

The Institute recruited Bob Leys, an executive at Allstate, to head up its communication program with the insurance industry. He was able to convert Blue Cross and other insurers to begin paying claims for rehabilitation. This was a signal victory for the Institute.

Physicians like Drs. Clint Compere and Bob Addison at various times gave medical leadership to the Institute, acting as medical directors. Addison was responsible through the years for bringing in large sums from major contributors.

Subsequently the Institute hired two medical directors and neither had the personality to take a leadership role in the community. Dr. Henry Betts was recruited from the New York Institute of Rehabilitation, where he had developed a distinguished reputation in handling well known patients, particularly Joseph Kennedy, patriarch of the family of President John Kennedy.

Betts proved to be a winner in many aspects. He was sincerely interested in the welfare of the patients. Very important, he lent himself to the task of circulating in the broader public. His name began to appear in the newspapers through no effort of mine. He was lionized by some members of the board. He became a close friend of the Gaylord Donnelly family.

I was asked to speak at a party in his honor at the Racquet Club and my remarks included the jest that we had asked Dr. Howard Rusk to send us a medical leader with charm. I pointed out that what we got was a case of "overkill."

We were fortunate that the *Chicago Tribune* publisher, Harold Grumhaus, was on our board. He provided the Institute with access to the paper. At one time, the paper published a lengthy story about the hospital. The Institute was considered the special province of the *Trib* and some directors resisted when I suggested that the *Chicago Sun-Times* be urged also to take an interest in the Institute. Eppie Lederer (Dear Abby), whose column then appeared in the paper, came on the board. She was helpful and the *Sun—Times* began to cover the Institute. When I became public relations counsel to the paper, the relationship was further strengthened.

I suggested to Henry Betts we get someone to handle contacts with the media. The burden of serving the Institute's public relations needs began to eat into my business time. I approached Lois Weisberg, an old friend and former neighbor, about handling the assignment. The public relations of the Institute under her direction began to pick up steam when she came on board.

She suggested a film about the Institute and I went to the board for money. Our first film, "The Way Back," was completed on a budget of $12,000, mostly because Lois was able to get the services of a student director from Northwestern University, who wrote the script and directed the movie. We used professional actors to portray a young woman incapacitated by an automobile accident.

At first, we distributed the film ourselves to various community organizations and television program directors. The picture had many years of service and was shown nearly 500 times on TV programs around the country. We held previews for staff and board members and engaged the services of a professional film distribution organization.

We did a second film when Ella Streubel, my former colleague at our firm, became a board member and a member of the public relations committee. She was an invaluable member of the committee. Together we traveled to the studios of various Chicago film makers to select one to do our next film, "Touchdown," which featured a young athlete paralyzed as a result of an accident in a football game.

I feel the secret of our success in public relations was attributable to a number of factors: The hospital was gaining credibility in the community through its excellent service. Henry Betts' leadership and image was a very significant factor. Our ability to attract prominent Chicagoans to serve on the board was another. My own work for the Institute was successful because, being a member of the board, I could talk directly to the leaders about my plans and get their support without going through layers of management. The respective roles of Compere, Addison and Leys were very significant in breaking down barriers and earning support, particularly at Northwestern U. Hospital, the source of a large number of referrals.

Henry Betts began to get wonderful exposure in the press and the matter came up at a board meeting. One director suggested publicity for a physician was unseemly and I was able to ward off an attempt to limit Henry's social activities. There was a case where my peer relationship on the board was helpful. I said that we would be lucky if we could find a man of Henry's social skills through Central Casting.

My personal feeling is that the Institute reached a major crossroad when John Evers, chairman of Commonwealth Edison and chairman of the Institute's board, proposed the concept that all patients, regardless of their ability to pay, be admitted to the hospital and that the hospital develop a substantial free care fund

One of our major problems was that Rehab had empty beds, with an insufficient patient load. Visitors to the hospital felt the Institute didn't need funds because it was short of patients.

The need for an internal communications department was developing very rapidly as the institute grew. The department began turning out news releases and various publications including a house organ, which was distributed internally and to contributors and members of various boards associated with the hospital.

John Evers and I traveled together to New York to see Dr. Rusk to see it we could find out why the New York hospital was so successful. Rusk told us he publicized his hospital by "shouting from the housetops." Rusk did many of the things Henry Betts was starting to accomplish in Chicago to give the Institute high visibility and access to major donors.

At one point I recommended that switchboard operators and others begin answering phones by saying "Rehab Chicago" instead of the full mouthful," Rehabilitation Institute of Chicago."

At one of the board meetings, one of our directors proposed we change our name entirely because it was long and confused some people as to our true mission. He said some felt we were an alcohol or drug treatment center. I opposed the move, saying that we had already invested substantial time and money in developing our name.

When the new hospital was built at 345 E. Superior Street, I was given the honor of being chairman of the dedication.

Henry Betts informed me that a discussion had been held with Marc Chagall about his doing a design for a tapestry to be hung in the lobby of the Institute. There were substantial costs entailed for insurance, shipping, and weaving. All not so great, and we felt that it came nowhere near equaling the ultimate value of the tapestry itself. Chagall had promised he would come to Chicago to participate in the dedication but he died before completion and his widow came instead. I proposed the idea to the board and got approval and funds to go ahead.

I also asked the board for funds to develop an appropriate insignia and signage for our new hospital and got approval to retain Morton Goldschol's firm. He designed "The Tree of Life," which has been a popular symbol. One of our problems was the various plaques that adorned the old hospital honoring major contributors and others chosen for the honor. Goldschol came up with a design which enabled Rehab to still honor those previously so honored but in a more attractive format.

I suggested to Henry Betts we launch an archive program to assemble historical materials. I was able to get one of my friends, Marvin Berz, to handle the task. In short order, he assembled an archive library but his service was cut short by his untimely death.

I was elected a Life Member of the board in 1983. Although residing in California, I still attend board meetings when I can and meet with officers and others to give the benefit of my experience and recollections. On several occasions, after I recovered from my Stone Fish infection, I was invited to address the staff on the treatment of necrotizing fasciitus.

Young Presidents

Organization

As soon as I joined YPO, I became active in the organization. I was invited to join the board and the executive committee, and served for several years as chairman of YPO's public relations committee. I helped set the standard for YPO public relations and the organization sent a staff member to spend several months with me in my office writing a public relations guidebook under my direction for all chapters.

Being on the executive committee was an intimate and rewarding experience, working closely with Bo Callaway, who later became Secretary of the Army; Red Blount, later Postmaster General; Roger Sonnabend, head of the Sonesta hotel chain, and Seth Atwood, from Rockford, Illinois, an industrialist, one of the world's foremost timepiece collectors and authorities.

Today, YPO and its successor organizations, World Presidents and Chief Executives Organizations, which absorb the graduates of YPO who retire from the younger group at the age of 49, have given us friends in virtually every part of the free world.

Sylvia and I took advantage of most of the opportunities to travel with YPO and attend its Universities for Presidents both in the United States and abroad and, as a result, traveled with young presidents and their wives through most of South America, the Far East, Europe, the Middle East, Scandinavia, the British Isles, North Africa, the South Seas, Australia, New Zealand and Canada.

In every case, YPO's presence provided an open door to industrialists in these countries who were also members of the organization, to U.S. ambassadors who were anxious to entertain us, and even to royal families in a number of countries.

I cannot deny our business had enormous benefits from YPO. While the organization does not function like a service organization where you are required to do business with one another, many members feel that, all things being equal, the business should go to a friend. Over the years, I can recall dozens of accounts coming to our agency, either directly with friends' companies or on the basis of YPO referrals.

There are a number of friends who have called me when they heard public relations being discussed. It was helpful if they were either chief executives or on the board of important companies. I also looked out for their interests whenever I could and was constantly doing favors for YPOers.

I didn't realize at the time I joined that YPO would fill a vacuum in my life. One of the problems I had when I took over our business was that, not having gone to college, I didn't have a coterie of business contacts or fraternity brothers who could some day help me when they rose to positions of corporate eminence. I really didn't know much about running a business. I had no idea how one goes about structuring or managing a business. I had few people I could call upon if I needed help, advice or door opening.

My social orbit at the time was limited to people I knew in the community, met in the army, met in high school, met in journalism or at the Community Fund, or was fortunate to develop a relationship with in the course of events in business.

I soon served on various committees running several "Universities for Presidents." One of the members, Jim Lavenson, an advertising man, who later managed the Plaza Hotel in New York, became my partner in running conventions together.

When Lavenson left the Plaza Hotel after it was sold, he decided to go into business for himself. He looked around for a facility to buy which could not be sold from under him, as was the Plaza. He ultimately found the San Ysidro Ranch in Montecito, California. Bob Halliday of YPO and I lent our financial and moral support. Halliday was the former treasurer of Boise Cascade, a former partner in Arthur Andersen, and later went on to found a major company on the New York Stock Exchange, Wheelabrater Frye.

Jim and his wife converted a rundown ranch, formerly owned by movie star Ronald Coleman, into what it is presently — one of the world's most successful country inns, a mountainside retreat running at a high occupancy rate. It was sold after several years of profitable operations.

When we ran these various conventions together, Jim and I came to the conclusion that we couldn't do anything that was mundane or not unusual. We also felt that both of us had to have some fun in repayment for the hard work we were putting in on behalf of the membership.

We ran one convention in 1962 at the Arizona Biltmore Hotel in Phoenix. It really didn't have the facilities for the huge organization YPO had grown to. We expected about 800 people including wives to attend our conference and knew the Biltmore couldn't accommodate everyone.

The first thing we did was to find someone who could provide us with a tent, which we installed in the center courtyard of the Biltmore large enough to accommodate us at the various banquet functions. The people who had tents like that were mostly religious organizations, which ran evangelical assemblages in various parts of the United States. We soon found one we could rent. We also rented a wooden dance floor, and hired one of the top professional party givers in Los Angeles to provide the nightly change of decor at our various parties.

Additionally, YPO, which is both an educational and social organization, provided a superb intellectual broadening to Sylvia and me, to our sons Jesse and Richard, and our daughter Betty. From the very start, we tried to expose our children to YPO and happily there were second-generation friendships that evolved with sons and daughters of YPO members in various parts of the world.

Many people think of YPO as some kind of a tax dodge scheme to provide free trips for chief executives and their wives. But YPO, and now the two senior organizations, provide a unique educational apparatus at which both husband and wife can sign up for various courses at the "University for Presidents" or take part in seminars in the United States and various parts of the world on matters of significance to the individual members, to their wives, and to their families.

One of the highlights of my YPO experience was attending the annual week long seminar at the Harvard graduate business school, studying with some of the best minds in business education on the Harvard faculty. It was an emotional experience to "go to Harvard." Many of my closest friends from YPO days are those that I roomed with during the seven years I participated in the Harvard classes.

(Front Center) Steve Ross and wife dancing at my farewell party

the Young Presidents' Organization

cERtIfIcatE of DEpRECIation

presented with reluctance and awe for outliving his youth to:

Morris B. Rotman

in recognition of his constant criticism of the principles and purpose

of this organization, to which his contribution must

henceforth be vicarious.

Bo Callaway

President

Chief Executives

Organization

The last time I served as a convention organizer was for the Chief Executives Organization, a graduate group of YPOers to which one is invited to become a member.

George Mitchell, a board member of CEO, asked me to organize the conference in Scottsdale in 1983 and I chose Bob Dickerman as my co-chairman in charge of educational activities.

Bob and I came to the conclusion we wanted to do a one—theme program and we came up with the idea of a session called, " Strange Encounters with the Fourth Estate."

We felt there was a unique opportunity for a dialogue between prominent media people and members of our organization and decided to take the educational budget and pay fees to prominent journalists because we wanted certain specific people on our program. This was an unorthodox idea because neither YPO nor CEO pays fees to resources. It got George into trouble with the board for permitting us to indulge in what they thought was an extravagance, even though we didn't exceed the educational budget. We just broke a time honored philosophical position.

We recruited the participation of Chuck Schneider, a member and also an officer at the Times Mirror Corporation in Los Angeles, which published the *Los Angeles Times*. He was exceedingly helpful in reaching some of the people we wanted.

We initially invited Walter Cronkite, but he was called away for the peace signing in the Middle East between Egypt and Israel. Walter prevailed upon Dan Rather to be the key speaker on our program.

Dan and his wife, Jean, and Sylvia and I slipped away for a day of tennis during the convention's only free day. We got a guest membership to the Gardiner Ranch and spent the afternoon playing tennis. After tennis, even though the kitchen was closed, it was no problem to prevail upon the staff to produce hot fudge sundaes when they spotted Rather.

We also had Howard Cosell to talk on sports; Ted Koppel, before he became as famous, to talk about international coverage; Paul Conrad, Pulitzer Prize winning cartoonist on the *Los Angeles Times*, who gave us a cartoon talk and explained how he works; Louis Ruckeyser, who talked on coverage of financial matters; and Robert Toth of the *LA Times* Washington bureau, who was kicked out of Russia after he was briefly imprisoned.

One of the reasons we wanted Howard Cosell was that we thought it would be a hilarious sequence to have him give out the sports awards at our annual banquet, bestowing the golf and tennis trophies in the mellifluous language he reserves for big league sports events.

He gave an absolutely brilliant talk but threatened to bolt the last evening before fulfilling his role as an award giver. I told him I would have the guards refuse to let him out of the ballroom if he decided to depart before doing his job. Howard was a tempestuous guy to deal with, but he gave a performance well worth his fee. In effect, CEO was a continuum of the YPO experience. There were excellent programs and the annual conclaves were held mostly in resort areas or big cities.

Many of us have relationships with one another going back nearly 40 years. An annual event is held each year, called a Nostalgia Weekend, and members come from all parts of the United States to bask in the glow of long time friendships.

Families in Business Together

Standing in a hotel pool on a hot day in Napa Valley, Ca., with a couple of fellow graduates of the Young Presidents Organization, I had a conversation that became a serious discussion on the complex ramifications of family run businesses. One asked how I had managed to woo my two sons into our public relations business.

I told them how I had originally discouraged my family members from coming into the business, not that they were not capable, but because I felt they might be happier pursuing different careers. I didn't want my sons to be discounted by our staff on the assumption they were in the business because of blood relationship rather than ability.

This attitude shifted one morning during a conversation with Joe Kubert, a senior partner at Booz Allen. We were on the commuter train from Glencoe to Chicago, talking about our sons' careers. Joe expressed amazement I was reluctant to bring Jesse and Richard into my business, and gave me valid reasons to open the door to them. He helped me to see that I had been wrong and should have encouraged my children to join the family enterprise when they expressed interest in it.

When I explained my change of heart to Jesse and Richard, I invited them to join the firm provided:

They really wanted to make public relations their life's work and would treat it like a profession;

They had journalism training;

They had job training for at least a year elsewhere preferably in the communications business;

They accept a basic requirement they begin under another supervisor, never reporting directly to me;

And finally, they would start at the lowest rung on the business ladder with their progress measured by a direct supervisor.

Ultimately, both Richard and Jesse came into the business and did very well, heading two of our offices, New York and Chicago. Jesse gained experience as managing editor of his college paper at the University of Ohio; Richard in summer time employment at the *City News Bureau* of Chicago and during one summer as a reporter at the *Washington Post*. Betty had journalism training as a shopper columnist at the *Chicago Sun-Times* but decided to seek employment elsewhere.

That conversation in Napa Valley led me to a new adventure through the Chief Executives Organization, which provides members an opportunity to develop and run mini-seminars under an individual action program. I decided to undertake a three-day seminar called "The Family in Business Together."

Both YPO and CEO had family business seminars but never one where the entire family unit was involved—fathers, wives, sons and daughters, and sons in law. We soon encountered other categories— widows inheriting the business, former wives and even a former son in law still in the business.

My YPO friends were encouraging and I was pleased by the reaction to my first letter promoting the seminar, which was held at the Center for Continuing Education at the University of Chicago (a rather spartan but comfortable conference center.)

Some of the leading families in YPO immediately signed up. Over the course of three seminars Bob and Mary Galvin had most of their entire family in attendance.

An educational advisor from the sociology department at the U. of C. helped to secure discussion leaders with training similar to that provided at the National Training Laboratories at Bethel, Maine.

The first seminar was essentially a Rotman family effort. Sylvia helped with registration, hospitality and meal planning. Jesse and Richard organized a panel discussion for younger family members. Betty helped with communications, and Richard conducted and narrated an architectural tour of Chicago.

I was determined we would split up the family unit into separate discussion groups, with no father at the same table as his son or daughter or wife. I wanted to be sure there would be a free flow of candid communication without the possible intimidation of a father.

Before the start of the seminar, Dr. Roy Menninger of the Menninger Clinic in Topeka, called me. "I hear you are in my field," he said. He explained one of his board members was coming to our seminar. He said he was writing a book on the subject. Could I send him an abstract?

I told him we had no more funds for resources but he was welcome to come and we would provide room and board but no funds for travel. Much to my delight, he called the next day and said he was coming. I had known Drs. Karl and Will Menninger in connection with other YPO activities, but had never met Roy.

He turned out to be tall, handsome man, with a halo of white hair. I told him he could roam about as he wished and need not make a speech if he didn't want to.

Roy came to me the first day and said he had observed something that should be rectified. Would I mind if he made a speech? To me that was like Sinatra asking his host whether he could sing a few songs at a private party.

We scheduled Roy for lunchtime the next day and he made a spirited talk. His main point was that he had observed YPOers acting like surrogate fathers to some of the young people, talking them down whenever they had anything to say that might be considered critical of their fathers. He felt this was counter-productive. Apparently some YPOers had asserted quasi-parental authority over their friend's offspring.

Roy suggested that each family find a nook or corner in the Center, their own sleeping quarters or an unused conference room, and start discussions about what they had learned so far, what their familial problems might be. Some families' talks went on far into the night. Assembled in our own rooms, my family talked at great length.

At lunch the next day, we listened to talks by some of the young people. One young lady talked about how she had been on family boards since she was 13 and just wanted to live her own life and not become a member of a family dynasty.

Looking directly at his father, a young man told us how his father said he would always be available and that he came first. "Just let me know whenever you want to talk," he said. However, when he asked his father for some private time after a ski run, his father suggested he call for an appointment tomorrow. "I just wanted to talk to him right away, not tomorrow. And I didn't want to make an appointment," the young man said.

Our second seminar gathered in Scottsdale, AZ, and a third in Palm Springs, Ca.

Dr. Menninger agreed to be our educational resource in Scottsdale and brought along his wife, Bev, who made an excellent talk on "Living on the Edge of the Spotlight." Roy also brought along Dr. Glenn Swoggers, head of industrial counseling at Menninger, who also participated.

Summarizing some of the difficulties confronting families in business together:

1. The father executive who won't get out of the way and allow his family member/successor an opportunity to run the business.
2. The selection of the wrong son to take over as CEO because of chronological placement in the family.
3. Daughters who feel deprived of an opportunity to become head of the family business because of bias against women.
4. The father/ executive who plays so close to the vest that the potential successor (widow, son, daughter) knows nothing about the business and is ill—equipped to run it.

Some interesting configurations of family business problems:

1. The son chosen to take over who wanted to do something else.
2. The second (or third) wife inheriting the business about which she is uninformed and is unprepared for the resistance she encounters when she began to take an active role.
3. The father who wanted to keep his talented son in-law in the business, after he and the daughter had divorced.
4. A common complaint was that members of the family unit, particularly daughters in law, were excluded from family business discussions as though they were interlopers.
5. One frustrated wife, a Canadian, complained she and her husband hardly saw each other because both traveled so much. They resolved that problem when, as a result of their experiences at our seminar, they went into the business of providing family business counseling. The Family in Business seminar provided the solution for their family problem and gave them an idea for a new business.

Its difficult for me to admit my own family became the classic Cobblers children In spite of many opportunities to benefit from lessons available at these and other YPO events, and despite having organized the conferences and participated in them, we failed to apply what we had learned to our own business and lives. We did not address the need for a succession plan, or a strategy for the business future, whether to stay independent or sell out.

I would urge anyone involved in a family business to read this chapter carefully and to plan their company's future wisely in order to avoid the pitfalls that have swallowed many family ventures. Conferences like the ones described here can increase the odds for survival and greater success if the lessons learned are not overlooked in the day-to-day busy-ness of the business world because most businesses do not survive into the second generation, as ours did not, and it's conferences like this one that increase the odds for survival success.

Desert Rats. King Rat

In the Coachella Valley I served for 11 years as the "King Rat" of the Desert Rats organization, made up of 75 graduates of YPO.

In the twilight of my professional years, I took on the role of leader of this lively group of men, who chose to continue relationships made in YPO. As burdensome as it was at times, I enjoyed my role and the continuing friendships with a bunch of swell guys. Our members come from all over the country, from Alaska to Florida, to vacation in California. Some have retired here permanently.

The organization has now grown in size and stature. We don't seek publicity, consistent with the YPO custom of being a low profile organization even though we have had occasional speakers of national and international repute. Our resources are unpaid and pay for their own travel and lodging, coming to speak to us because they themselves are graduated YPOers or friends of our members.

Among our speakers was David Hinson, when he was head of the FAA. Bob Galvin is a most popular speaker and will occasionally drop in from the skies to deliver a message to the Desert Rats. An extremely popular program was presented by one of America's greatest lyricists, Hal David, who brought along an accompanist and singer at his own expense. Dave wrote the lyrics to "Raindrops " and a score of other famous songs. He is an honorary Desert Rat. Maj. Gen. Kenneth Mills, now an honorary member, arranged a tour of the Marine Base at Thousand Palms.

What's significant about the Desert Rats is that it illustrates the binds that are engendered in YPO. Many members, once graduated from the organization, and, becoming 49ers, want to continue the experience of idea—exchange and socializing with peers. Many have friendships going back nearly two score years.

One of the unique characteristics of our group is that we meet in member's homes, most of them quite sumptuous. One member has a home that will accommodate 100 in its living room. A caterer is brought in and occasional entertainment is offered. A discussion group is generally held, led by the "King Rat," before the evening's events at which members and their wives have an opportunity to discuss various topics. The discussions are never hostile but frequently heated.

One of our members is Bob Pond, who led the drive to build an Air Museum near the Palm Springs airport. Bob and his wife, Josie, annually host an outdoor barbecue on their more than 20 acre ranch in Palm Springs. Bob has one of the country's finest collection of classic cars including about 18 Ferraris. Seeing the collection is an eye popping experience to the auto enthusiast.

The only requirement of membership is graduate status from YPO and a part-time or permanent residency in the Coachella Valley.

Two of the members assist me in Desert Rats duties. One is Ron Glosser, Akron, O., banker and former chairman of the Hershey Foundation. He has assumed the role as Chairman. The other is John Doces, of Seattle, who came to this country penniless from Greece, and built a furniture store chain. He sits on the board of most leading institutions in Seattle. At one of our meetings John, who originally trained as an artist, presented Sylvia and me with a painting he had made of a star, declaring it was in honor of our 56th wedding anniversary and that we were the stars of the desert.

The members of accomplishment are too numerous to cite here. I am pleased they like to see old friends in the Desert Rats and suffered my leadership. At a recent meeting, the group named me "King Rat Emeritus" and presented Sylvia and me a lovely glass trophy.

Convention On The QE11

Another highlight experience of my YPO career was when in 1973 I was asked to be a resource for YPO after I had graduated and was over 49. YPO frequently brings back what it calls 49ers or graduates to run courses and give lectures.

YPO had chartered the entire Queen Elizabeth 11 for a cruise from Southampton to Tangiers and back. The convention carried with it two orchestras, a platoon of educational, business and political celebrities, and provided an opportunity for one to indulge in a week long, sleepless seminar that sometimes started at 6 a.m. with aerobics and ended at 2:00 or 3:00 in the morning with movie previews at which stars and producers were present.

The convention committee did things in a big way. A tennis court was installed on the stern specifically for this cruise. I can recall one morning being awakened around 6:00 a.m. by Kemmons Wilson, founder of the Holiday Inn chain, asking me if I was up to an early game of tennis because the court was available then. I got there in time, but the wash from the sea made it a slippery enterprise, and Kemmons and I joined the women members doing their early morning calisthenics. Sylvia was amazed to find Kemmons and me lying on the floor with about 50 women in leotards, we in our tennis clothes, going through the various exercises.

The trip itself can only be described as a colossal experience, a merger of Disneyland and Harvard.

The ship carried a staggering array of educational resources ranging from top scientists to philosophers to political leaders and outstanding journalists. Class sessions were held most mornings and afternoons. Besides listening to prominent lecturers during the afternoon, one had a choice of discussion groups, various athletic activities, and all kinds of special classes in fields of business, humanities, the arts and family life.

I recall a lecture by philosopher Walter Kaufman of Princeton, whose ideas were challenged by politician/businessman George Romney, who grew so angry with some of Kaufman's ideas that his agitation grew to apoplectic proportions.

The YPO group that ran that particular convention, including Chris Bailey, Bob Nagler and Brian (now Sir) Wolfson, had plenty of clout and imagination.

At one interval, while sailing down the Mediterranean, an aircraft carrier, the USS Kennedy, moored virtually alongside of us, and gave us a special show of naval planes taking off and landing. They also gave us an exhibition of sea rescue techniques. The commander of the ship came over to the QE11 and sent instructions to the aircraft carrier while he was aboard our ship.

The QE11 trip occurred about the time the Watergate case was starting to occupy press and public. Heated discussions occurred during almost every educational session as many of the resources modified the original titles of their courses or talks and directed their remarks to a discussion of the consequences and morality of Watergate. The full story hadn't unfolded yet, and the newspapers were reporting only early details.

Art Buchwald' s talk, instead of dealing with Washington media, as he had originally intended, was an inside picture of how the press was covering the Watergate case.

My own topic was, "Corporate Consumerism, " and I converted it to "Corporate Responsibility in the Wake of Watergate."

I was challenged by some of my audience to make a prediction about the consequences of the break-in. Many took exception to my statement that the incident was a cover-up by the executive branch. I was bold enough to predict that, from the evidence

I had seen at that point, President Nixon would either be impeached or would have to resign.

A number of my friends in the audience were outraged by my prediction, and some friendly betting went on. I offered to back up my prediction with a money bet with anyone in class and a number took me on. Once Nixon resigned, I collected my winnings from, among others, Kemmons Wilson and George Mitchell. George offered me the job of professional seer for his company when he paid off.

My surmise about what would happen in the Watergate case may very well have been a wild guess. . On the other hand, it might also have resulted from the kind of training I had in journalism. The facts even at that preliminary moment, indicated to me the President was involved in a cover-up and possibly even the burglary and could not survive the ultimate investigation.

One of the special delights of the trip was the opportunity to spend time with Art Buchwald and his wife, Ann. Art and I were both invited as resources but, whenever the ship docked, Art and Ann and Sylvia and I slipped away from the crowd to find the best restaurant in town for a good, quiet meal.

As a former writer of the restaurant scene, Art had a special technique for finding the best restaurants. He would go into a store where wine was sold and have a friendly conversation with the proprietor to find out which he thought was the best place in town. As a result, in Majorca we had a meal at a marvelous French restaurant.

In directing us to the restaurant, the shopkeeper said it was on the "other side of the mountain." We took a cab and got there in about 20 minutes. The friendly shopkeeper didn't tell us the restaurant could be reached in about five minutes by foot, up a little hill.

Art was able to arrange a reunion at that restaurant with Faye Emerson, formerly married to Elliot Roosevelt, President Franklin D. Roosevelt's son, who hurried over to the restaurant to join us once word got out that Art was in town and wanted to see her. It was distressing to note that the once beautiful Faye, still with a lovely face, had transformed herself into a very, very buxom lady.

Incidentally, when the YPO planners invited me to be a resource on the Queen Elizabeth, I was given a major time period for a program called a plenary session. I was given no instructions as to what I should cover during this session except that I should do "something interesting" with some of the graduate YPOers, called 49ers.

I developed the idea of a panel discussion entitled, "Wise Old Men of the Sea," and reached out for some of the most charismatic and successful YPOers I had met in the time I had been a member. My panel ultimately included Tom Bata, of Bata Shoes, one of the largest shoe manufacturing and retailing concerns in the world; George Mitchell, son of a Greek immigrant, who in 25 years made one of America' s great fortunes in energy and real estate; J. B. Fuqua, principal shareholder of two New York Stock Exchange companies, a successful and self-taught industrialist and Bob Halliday, board chairman of Wheelabrator-Frye, a big board company.

My instructions to each of the panelists was to use no notes, no prepared text, merely to tell the audience how they did it, what they were currently working on, and what their plans were for the future.

All were remarkably good because they were uniquely successful and did it their own way.

J. B. Fuqua may have been the hit of the panel, although I suspect he did it unconsciously. He was describing to the group changes in his life. He pointed out that he and his wife Dorothy have a home in Atlanta, an apartment in New York, a boat, a private plane to take them about, but they really lived "very simply. " The roar of laughter that greeted his remarks caused him to realize he had made a joke. He was momentarily startled and taken aback, and then joined in the laughter. Simple living, indeed.

Speeches and Presentations

Public speaking is an important function for the public relations executive, whether before an audience or in making a new business pitch before a small group of executives.

At the start I had great uncertainty whether I could handle that part of my business responsibility but I knew I had to do it. I plunged in bravely and soon found myself liking the challenge of winning over audiences small and large.

Based on all my bad experiences, I pass on a few tips:

Prepare a speech carefully, but commit it to index cards with brief recollection paragraphs.

Abandon your file cards soon as you master the skill of speaking with prepared extemporaneousness.

Before your speech, spend a little time with your proposed audience to develop a mutual feeling of comfort.

Try to pick a subject of possible mutual interest in that early encounter so you can refer to that subject in the beginning of your remarks. It could be a name, a sport, or a historical reference. Anything, so long as you don't plunge in cold with your speech.

Do some advance research to establish familiarity with the company or audience involved.

Don't start out by saying you are reminded of a story and then, what's worse, tell it badly.

Try to pick out one person in the audience to whom you are going to address your remarks. Look at him or her and make yourself believe you have an audience of one while occasionally scanning your audience.

If you are going to use graphics, make absolutely certain the person in the last row can see it; otherwise forget it.

Don't feel you are above checking out the microphone or the characteristics of the hall or meeting place. Nothing can ruin your speech more than a lousy mike.

I now consider myself now fairly competent at the microphone but I went through hell in the early days because of my nervousness. Later, I actually had occasions when large associations, seeking a speaker at their annual conclaves, sought me out and paid my expenses and a decent honorarium for a speech.

Terrible experience: I was to be the featured speaker at a client convention in Miami Beach to an audience of more than 500. The client had an outside professional organization prepare a skit in which actors, singers and dancers portrayed executives on their staff and ours. One actor even portrayed me. The objective was to dramatize the inauguration of a brand new marketing program. As the last dancer went offstage, she accidentally stepped on the heels of the dancer before her and they began to argue loudly and profanely. The mike was open and the audience heard everything.

The chairman of the group was to introduce me next to provide the alleged high point remarks but, in his consternation over the backstage imbroglio, introduced the speaker after me as I approached the microphone. What to do? I sat down on the edge of the stage and laughed with the audience. When things quieted down, I made my speech.

I was invited to address a class at Duke University on public relations and marketing. No more than 50 in the room. As I began my remarks, I noticed a guy in the front row spread out his legs, lean back in his chair and slowly close his eyes to sleep or contemplate. I knew this would throw me off so I stepped directly in front of him and exclaimed: "Mister, I like to give my speech to one person in the audience and you're it!" He came awake quickly and said after the speech that he had found it an interesting experience.

Bad experience: I had been invited by the Houston chapter of the Public Relations Society of America to make a speech. Everything was going along swimmingly when my speech was interrupted by the delivery of a layer cake for the dessert. I was about 10 minutes from completion when the chairman of the event, impatient to serve the cake, stepped to the stage, just to the side of me, and applied an invisible hook to get me to stop. I retreated gracefully as I could.

I had an appointment with a prospective client who had a reputation as a most difficult fellow. I waited in his anteroom for about a half hour during which I read his magazines and looked at his scrolls of endorsement on the walls. After we started our conversation, I told him I knew a lot about him. For instance, he was into boating. He had gone to Yale. He liked to travel. How do you know all this? he asked. From his magazines, I explained. He was amused and my remarks served to break the ice. We got the account.

Some times an illustrative gimmick helps in a speech. I once affixed Band Aids to my upper arms with key points written on them to dramatize my speech. As I proceeded I took off my jacket and peeled off the Band Aids one at a time as I made my remarks. The audience applauded and I got their attention.

Another occasion, when we made our presentation before the National Bowling Council, we had special bowling shirts made for our staff with the name of the council inscribed on the back of each. At a given moment we all took off our jackets and turned around.

Roy Marks, of Bausch & Lomb, made a speech seemingly carefully dressed. In the course of his remarks, he took off his jacket and the audience could see he was just wearing a tie and a dickey. A simple sales message was written on his bare back.

Nothing is more boring to an audience than a slide presentation showing results of a publicity campaign.

"I want a bushel of clips!" one client commanded. During my report to his marketing organization, one of our staff people came into the room and poured out a profusion of clippings from a bushel.

Another time, we rolled out a carpet on which clippings were mounted. On another occasion, we used the feeding bag of a horse. Perhaps all this was silly but the audience took notice.

I was invited to be among the speakers at a special occasion honoring Sam Wanamaker for his work in founding the Globe Theater in London. I felt we might have a lot of flowery and ponderous speeches from the assembled academicians and friends.

Looking for a gimmick, I noted that about a half dozen gift bags were still at the registration desk for some who apparently weren't coming. I quickly copied down the names and read them off at the start of my remarks, stating if, they weren't present, I laid claim to the fancy soap contained in the gift bags. This launched a number of counterclaims from people in the audience who said they wanted the soap. Anyway, I had a relaxed speech.

Meshulim Riklis, the colorful New York financier, called me to invite me to make a speech before a rather sizable group of YPOers. They were assembling in Orlando, Fla., to attend a seminar being run by Riklis on financial relations. He asked me if I would cover financial public relations. My speech was scheduled for Monday morning but I arrived Sunday in time to hear Rik make his opening remarks. I noted he was speaking in his usual mixture of English sprinkled with Yiddish scatological colloquialisms.

I knew my YPO. Registrants at these things write furiously in notebooks for replay to staff or IRS. I noticed the audience seemed to be perplexed by some of Rik's words.

As I made my entrance Monday morning, Rik told me he would introduce me and then go to make phone calls. I advised him to stay because I was going to talk about him initially. He stayed.

I started out my saying I had noticed some of the words Rik used may have been unfamiliar. I stood before the blackboard and asked the audience to pronounce each word. There were about a dozen. I said the word Riklis used most frequently was a Yiddish substitution for the male appendage, "some times used interchangeably to describe your son in law." Rik later told me he enjoyed my remarks and wanted a copy.

I admire William Buckley's command of the English language. He has the ability to dredge forth words and phrases frequently incomprehensible to his audience. He made a speech in Chicago before the chapter of the Young Presidents Organization. I had the task of introducing him to the audience and I plucked some of his own words to use in the introduction. I'm not sure if they understood what I said but Buckley seemed to enjoy it immensely.

I worked up a glossary of the words he used and it was reprinted by the national YPO organization. I sent the following letter to Bob Galvin with a copy of my glossary:

HARSHE-ROTMAN & DRUCK, INC. PUBLIC RELATIONS

444 N. MICHIGAN AVE. CHICAGO, ILL. 60611 PHONE (312) 644-8600

MORRIS B. ROTMAN CHAIRMAN AND CHIEF EXECUTIVE OFFICER

Accredited by Public Relations Society of America

March 15, 1979

Dear Bob:

I am returning this booklet, as you requested. I've made copies of a couple of pages that interest me.

As I read through this tract, I recalled the time you and I appeared on television in what can hardly be termed a debate with Bill Buckley and Norman Thomas.

As I read through this thing, I realized why nobody can ever debate the man and expect to win, because he uses esoteric language as a kind of a put-down device, and his opponents are made to seem silly because they don't know what he is talking about and can't appropriately answer his questions.

On the first page, for example, he uses the word "condign" and my conclusion on reading the text is that neither Buckley nor Abrams were using the word appropriately. Then Buckley hauls up "utilitarian coefficient," followed closely by "empirical" and "ontological."

Try this on some of your executives the next time they are giving you an argument. Just remember that ontology recapitulates phylogeny or vice versa.

Cordially,

Morris B. Rotman

MBR/lag
enclosure

Mr. Robert W. Galvin
Chairman of the Board
Motorola Inc.
1303 East Algonquin Road
Schaumburg, Illinois 60196

CHICAGO NEW YORK LOS ANGELES WASHINGTON, D.C. HOUSTON LONDON

ROTMAN'S GLOSSARY OF BUCKLEYISMS.

At the request of the Forum Committee, Morry Rotman, the sage from Chicago, was asked to develop a glossary of the most difficult words used by William Buckley in his speech here. Following are the words and Morry's definitions:

COERCE - "Where people play golf."
FESTERING ANIMOSITY - "Two people in a stuck elevator"
ASSUAGE - "A massage limited to a certain section of the anatomy."
MOOT - "Water before a castle."
SOOTHSAYER - "Person talking with a loose bridge."
BUTTRESSED - "Kicked hard you know where."
REDUCTIONISM - "Making chicken fat."
GENITALIA - "Sexy Christians."
JUXTAPOSITION - "Sexual Excess."
PROLIFERATION - "Being against abortion."
EXTEMPORIZE - "What you say when your wife sees lipstick on your collar."
EFFUSIONS OF ECONOMIC ILLITERACY - "Not understanding Reaganomics."
MORALLY AXIOMATIC - "Settling an argument with your brother-in-law with a lethal weapon."
DIALECTICAL VOLTAGE - "Talk shows on television."
CATALYST FOR NATIONAL IMPOVERISHMENT - "McDonalds hamburgers."
SPIRIT ATROPHIES AND SOCIETY BECOMES MORIBUND - "Becoming a 49'er."
COGENT ARGUMENTATION - "An appeal for more allowance."
GOVERNMENT ORGANIZATION UNSUITED TO EFFECT ECONOMIC PROGRESS - "IRS."
CRASS MATERIALISM - "Paying what it's worth."
EGALITARIAN - "Fellow who hunts the American bird."
MONOLITH - "One lith."
ATTENUATION - "Listening when your wife talks."
SOLIPSISTIC - "Word buckley uses when he wants to evade a question."

Politics

Our firm did not consider itself particularly expert in political campaigns, nor did we seek that kind of business because of the financial risks often involved if the candidate wasn't completely successful in raising the money promised to him. Nonetheless we occasionally got involved in a political campaign that had intriguing characteristics.

I had my first political experience shortly after I joined forces with Bill Harshe. A group of his friends, principally attorney Morris Leibman, put their heads together and came to the conclusion that Adlai Stevenson would be an excellent candidate for Illinois senator.

Stevenson was assistant secretary of the Navy (1941-44) and special assistant to U.S. Secretary of State Stettinius in 1945. He attended the San Francisco conference that founded the United Nations.

John Bartlow Martin, Stevenson's former aide, who in later years became an ambassador to the Dominican Republic, wrote a definitive history of Stevenson's life, and made reference to the Harshe Committee, because my associate at that time was given the task of spearheading the effort to persuade Adlai to run and develop a campaign that would convince the Democrat slate makers he was a viable candidate.

Harshe went to San Francisco and met with Stevenson. He came back with an agreement that Adlai would run if the Democratic Central Committee asked him to do so. This was hardly an easy task confronting the group because the politicos had the impression that Adlai was a dilettante and an intellectual and not particularly a political animal. The name Stevenson was well known in Illinois because the candidate's father was a former Illinois Secretary of State, and the family still maintained control of a newspaper in Bloomington, Ill.

I was invited to join the committee and meet with them on Saturdays in Leibman's office. I was given the task of handling publicity and other communications that might be needed in the campaign.

Legend has it that Stevenson was "discovered" by Democrat powerhouse Jacob (Jake) Arvey, head of the Democratic Central Committee, but my recollection is that neither Arvey nor his Democratic cohorts were in the least interested in Stevenson until our committee came up with an artificially induced groundswell of demand for his candidacy.

We located potential supporters throughout the state, particularly in southern Illinois, and launched a massive postal card campaign addressed to the slate makers, calling for consideration of Stevenson as a candidate for the U.S. Senate. The number of cards that came in was quite impressive to the committee and, ultimately, after a lot of negotiations and assurances, the party bosses decided to consider Stevenson's candidacy.

We discovered Stevenson had a handicap we had not known about. Candidates need a wife to help in the social amenities of campaigning but Adlai's wife, Ellen Borden Stevenson, would not cooperate in any publicity activities involving the family.

Adlai Stevenson would have been an ideal candidate for the U.S. Senate because of his service in the League of Nations and his role as an Assistant Secretary of the Navy, but the Illinois slate makers had a problem and pulled a most unexpected switch on us.

The Republicans, with tremendous support from the *Chicago Tribune*, were slating Wayland (Curly) Brooks to run for the Senate, partially on his World War II military record. Stevenson's activities as an Assistant Secretary of the Navy were not sufficient to match Brooks' war record.

Meanwhile, the Democrats had another potential candidate in Alderman Paul Douglas, World War II war hero and professor at the University of Chicago. Douglas was planning to run for the gubernatorial post in Illinois, a job he was eminently qualified for, but the Democrats slated him instead for the U.S. Senate because of his war record, and chose Stevenson to run for the governor's office, a post he did not seek nor was particularly qualified for.

Paul Douglas went on to the U.S. Senate and Stevenson went to Springfield.

Harshe had a falling out with the committee after the successful nomination campaign because he felt our firm should stop contributing its time and should be permitted to turn on the meter for time and expenses. I would have liked to have continued, pay or no pay, but it was not a decision I could make alone. The late attorney, Lou Koehn, one of the original committee, once commented to me that, had Adlai made it to the White House in later years, I might have gone along with him as press secretary.

Coincidentally, Adlai's press secretary when he was governor and in subsequent campaigns, was William (Bill) Flanagan, who in later years joined our firm and, because of his excellent political connections, attracted an occasional piece of political business.

We were approached by a committee representing Nelson Rockefeller in his bid for the presidential nomination against Richard Nixon. The political convention was being held in Chicago and the Rockefeller group seemed to come in with a blank check to permit us to spend enough time and money to persuade the delegates to go for Rockefeller.

In a brief period of time, starting no more than several weeks before the convention, we turned loose our staff on a communications campaign which included a daily newspaper to distribute to the delegates, massive publicity heralding Rockefeller's candidacy, and a princely sum to buy whatever air time was still available.

Rockefeller had charisma, and our staff seemed to fall in

My press badge.

love with his warmth, his consideration and his appealing qualities as a human being. There was literally weeping in our staff
press room when we were told that, at the last minute, Rockefeller
had gone to New York for a meeting with Richard Nixon, and
some kind of a deal had been worked out whereby Rockefeller
would withdraw from the race.

Through the years, we were marginally involved in various
political activities in Chicago and New York. We launched a
massive campaign to see if we could persuade Illinois voters to

choose merit selection of judges rather than continue with political appointments. We came close but the issue lost. We also handled several referenda dealing with personal property taxes and other matters of public interest.

As our New York office grew, we added more personnel and brought in professionals who had special experience in political matters. Two staff members, Sheila Kelly and Don Kellerman, previously were aides to Senator Jacob Javitz and would take leave from our organization to assist the senator whenever he ran for re-election. Jack Javitz was always kind to us through the years and occasionally would recommend us for an assignment.

He asked us if we would handle a campaign on behalf of Sol Wachtler, a handsome former businessman, a Republican with the Ivy League looks of Jack Kennedy, then serving as Mayor of West Hempstead, Long Island. He was not sufficiently challenged being mayor of a small community, and the Republicans thought that they might have a chance with this attractive, Jewish Republican to unseat political powerhouse, Eugene Nickerson, as county supervisor of Nassau County, a powerful post with lots of patronage.

We said we would take on the campaign if we could handle not only public relations but research, graphic design, media purchases and also participate in the political strategy. By then our agency had grown to sufficient size that we had on staff, in addition to Kelly and Kellerman, a research scientist, Dr. Sid Kraus; our own graphic design department, and enough staff to carry out all communications activities needed. Our budget for that campaign was $750, 000.

Our staff created a centralized theme called, "Walking with Wachtler" and we had the candidate and his attractive wife walking through various communities in the county. One of our staff people briefed Mrs. Wachtler, who had an excellent wardrobe and good taste in clothes, how to dress for political appearances and how to handle press responsibilities.

We started rather late in the campaign, and Sol Wachtler lost by only 1200 votes, much to the surprise of everyone, including his own party, because he almost defeated Nickerson. Gov. Rockefeller was so impressed with Sol Wachtler's showing that he appointed him to the State Supreme Court and later, with our firm participating in the campaign, Wachtler won a seat on the Appellate bench.

We got an unexpected bonanza handling this campaign. We approached CBS about getting exposure for Wachtler. The TV producers thought it was rather interesting that a firm like ours, with a reputation in business matters, was handling a political campaign on a limited geographical basis with a fairly substantial campaign budget.

CBS asked if we would permit them to look over our shoulders with a camera recording everything we did, the network privy to all our deliberations and all our activities in connection with this campaign. We were filled with apprehension but recognized that the coverage could be massive for both our candidate and our agency. Knowing we had nothing nefarious up our sleeves, and with the concurrence of the candidate and his staff, we agreed to permit CBS to do its special documentary.

It did have its problems, and a few embarrassing things occurred, but the network did an excellent job. The show, an hour in color called, "The Making of A Candidate," with Eric Sevareid doing the commentary, appeared on the CBS network on the night of the Oregon primary. The film was also shown in political science classes.

There were two negatives that came out of filming, although in a final measurement of its value, both we and Wachtler benefited. It was discovered that, while CBS was doing it's filming our side had a spy in the enemy camp. We knew nothing about it, and we were not sure who made that arrangement, but there was a clerk working in Nickerson's office who was leaking information on a regular basis to someone on Wachtler' s staff. We were convinced the candidate himself knew nothing about it. There was an uproar when the discovery was made and a lot of nasty charges. That segment appearing in the film made it in my belief a more interesting documentary.

The other thing that happened was that the candidate himself, a man of strong intellectual beliefs, was made to seem like a puppet in one episode when the film showed our researcher gathering opinions at a commuter station and then the results of this research seemingly coming out of the candidate's mouth a few hours later. It was a juxtaposition of research and candidate philosophy caused by the CBS editing process.

Sol Wachtler was keenly embarrassed by the impression given in that one scene he was not master of his own thoughts and took positions based only on information gleaned from others research.

Our firm was mentioned a number of times in the documentary and, because it was photographed during actual working sessions, members of our staff were shown in action, making speeches, advising the candidate and working on various communications matters.

Unfortunately, in 1993 Judge Wachtler got himself into serious trouble when he was Chief Justice of the New York Supreme Court and had a long time affair with Republican fundraiser, Joy Silverman. When they became estranged, Mrs. Silverman claimed he had made extortion threats and obscene telephone calls. She claimed he was stalking her and had sent lewd anonymous mail to her daughter, threatening to kidnap her. He was found guilty and ended a brilliant career by going to jail for 11 months. There he was shackled and handcuffed and treated like an ordinary criminal. I had always predicted he would one day be governor of New York, but I was wrong. Very wrong.

Architects & Designers

Over the years I had the good fortune to work with outstanding architects and designers. Their skill and creativity—and that of musicians, painters and sculptors—has always been a source of awe to me.

Once I heard Ian McKellan recite Shakespeare sonnets and portions of plays for two whole hours, using only a chair as a prop. Dazzled by this display of memory and talent, I turned to Sam Wanamaker and asked how McKellan was able to memorize all that stuff. Matter-of-factly, Sam replied, "I can do the same thing."

Architects and designers start with an idea and end up with buildings of beauty and grandeur or a revolutionary new product. A better face on an old one. A way of communicating through design.

It was my practice to give little directions working with these professionals. I told them what I wanted and got out of the way. That's what I expected in my own work.

Frank Lloyd Wright was of great interest to me. I had read several books about him and Sylvia and I often visited one of the lakefront homes he designed just a block away from our home in Glencoe. While in Tokyo we went to see his magnificent earthquake—proof hotel.

I never expected to have a professional relationship with Wright and was delighted when our firm was chosen to publicize his appearance at a dinner in his honor in Chicago to inaugurate a Foundation bearing his name. I found him to be a soft voiced man with magnetic presence.

We staged a press conference and one reporter asked him how he would redesign Chicago. Not a man at loss for words, Wright answered he would burn down the city and start all over. He would build giant buildings reaching into the sky and provide parks around each building.

How high? he was asked. " Oh, about a half mile," he responded.

The next day the Chicago papers scoffed. There were editorials having fun with Frank Lloyd Wright.

About 10 days later, he called and said he wanted another press conference. He brought along his design for a mile high skyscraper. His design appeared on front pages all over the world.

I had a call from a partner at the Skidmore Owens architectural firm. Would we be interested in handling the PR for an Indian tribe? He said they were The Flatheads, who were building an immense spa on land they owned out west, with sources of hot mineral water.

How do I go about negotiating with an Indian tribe? I wondered.

My contact at Skidmore said it was very simple. "Do you have a pocket knife?" he asked. "You'll just sit by the road with the chief and talk. Take it easy, don't push. Just whittle away at your stick."

I had my Scout knife at the ready but the appointment was canceled, never to be renewed.

For a time we worked for the C.S. Murphy architectural firm in Chicago, a company with plenty of political clout, responsible for many large projects in the city. Charlie Murphy, son of the founder, brought us in. His principal function was contact and sales and he was very good at it.

We had some contact with Walter Landor, the eminent designer. I envied him because he conducted his business on a houseboat sitting in the bay near San Francisco. He did some work for our client, the National Restaurant Association and others.

One of my favorite designers was Henry Dreyfuss, who became a good friend. He closed his office in New York and moved with his wife to Pasadena, where he opened an office on a large estate. He tried to prevail upon me to do likewise but I didn't feel I could practice public relations in the serenity of Pasadena away from clients and press.

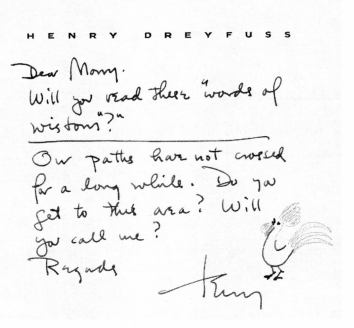

Henry Dreyfuss letter with rooster drawing.

Henry and I would correspond frequently. Each time he wrote he added to his letter a new design of a rooster, which was our corporate symbol. I saved most of his letters. Henry was a very successful designer, responsible for design programs for American Airlines and other large companies. Sadly, when his partner wife died, Henry took his own life. The world lost a great man, an extraordinary designer, and I lost a good friend.

One of our clients, General American Transportation Co., which was in the freight car business, hired Walter Dorwin Teague to design the company's first proprietary product, a molded plastic chair that could be stacked.

Teague's office was in the same building in New York that housed the Powers modeling agency. He decided to get a common denominator measurement of the human derriere by luring models to come to his office and sit on a block of clay. Not a bad job if you can get it. The multitude of impressions provided the basic seat contour of the chair he designed.

I had great rapport with Morton Goldschol, of Goldschol Associates. We teamed up on a number of projects over the years and even talked at one time about sharing in the building of an office on the north shore of Chicago to house both our firms. Again I had concern about being away from the action and Mort went ahead on his own.

He was a superb graphic and product designer and later teamed with his wife, Millie, to do documentary films.

Mort and I worked together on the Martin-Senour paint account, itself an unusual company that went from selling buckets of paint to merchandising through color. The parent company, Sherwin—Williams, impressed with our skills and those of colorist, Fred Rahr, hired us with the approval of Bill Stuart, Martin Senour's president.

I was responsible for bringing Mort into the picture at the North Shore Congregation Israel, where I was also chairman of the public relations committee. The new temple was a thing of beauty and elegance, designed by architect Minoru Yamasaki. Mort and his people did a complete graphics program including signage and memorials.

In institutions like the Rehab Institute and the North Shore temple, there is always a delicate problem of handling memorials. Most people who have made significant financial contributions to an institution expect their memorial plaques to be transferred to the new buildings.

In the case of the temple, Mort provided a solution consistent with the new ambiance. He designed an innovative way of memorializing the deceased, previously accomplished with lighted candles, by creating a handsome wall box where small lights marked the "yahrzeit "or day of death.

Traveling Man

I once overheard one of my children describing my work to a friend. "My daddy talks on the phone all day," was what she said. The description might have added that daddy travels all the time, too.

The person who seeks a career in public relations faces the fact that sedentary activity is not how one gets to see the clients, gets more business, calls on media people, cultivates contacts in various parts of the world, and helps to stimulate staff members working for the company in offices in other cities.

Paper work at my desk has always made me fidget and fret. My own personal system has always been that at the end of the day I always clean up all the correspondence, memoranda to the staff and all the postal detritus that accumulated on my desk, making a personal commitment not to hide too much stuff in my desk drawer for attention later.

I felt restive if I was not planning a trip and going to see someone, which means that much of my life was spent on airplanes traveling back and forth to various foreign outposts and cities around the United States where we had offices and clients.

I can't say I was infatuated with travel but I considered it part of my professional responsibility. If the next trip included a foreign port of call that happened to be one of my favorite cities, (like London, Brussels, Paris, Rome or Hong Kong), I looked forward to the trip, although travel can be extremely arduous and seemed to take its toll in later years.

When I was young and starting to build a business and traveling about 60 percent of my time, my wife ran the household, raised the kids and did her occasional sleeping in a pup tent with the Brownies or the Cub Scouts, things a traveling husband couldn't do.

At one time, one could look forward to fairly decent meals on airlines, but food became more and more plasticized and inedible as the years went on. If it was a short hop, like between New York and Chicago, I passed up the airline food and took my meals on the ground, particularly if I was going home or going to New York in time to go to one of the restaurants I loved to frequent.

On a number of occasions, flying from New York to Chicago at a late hour and knowing I would miss my meal at its appropriate time, I would stop off at Kaplan's Delicatessen in the Delmonico Hotel, which was virtually across the street of our New York office at 59th and Park, and have them put together a deli sandwich, slap on the strong mustard I prefer, a "new" pickle, and include maybe even a piece of their delicious pastry.

My other catering service on an occasional trip from California to Chicago was Nate and Al's Delicatessen in Beverly Hills, where I get a similar bill of fare.

I can recall many glances of enmity and even jealousy as I dined in delicatessen splendor while my seat companion had to deal with something inedible served by the airline. Raise your hand if you have ever tried to eat that hot glob in a foil wrapper served in coach class that American Airlines calls a burrito.

Incidentally, the habit isn't an exclusive idea of mine. I once traveled from the West Coast eastward with Frank Sinatra and his entourage, and he produced a giant picnic basket catered by Nate and Al's with dozens of pastrami, corned beef and tongue sandwiches. I must say that Sinatra knew how to eat, although I can't imagine how he managed to visit all the Italian restaurants in Palm Springs, Los Angeles, San Francisco and New York that display his picture in their front entrances with an autographed signature indicating that particular place was Sinatra's favorite eatery.

Traveling as much as did, I equipped myself with various devices and supplies that I carried in a small canvas shoulder bag for books, newspapers and miscellaneous supplies. You would also find therein a leather pouch containing a pair of soft leather slippers into which I slip my feet on long flights, a shoe horn to get my swollen feet back into my shoes when we land, a sleeping mask, and a pair of earplugs.

My travel supplies also included a small bottle, which contained a selection of various medications one should have on journeys to distant parts, including pills for stomach distress; antihistamines, and sleeping pills to knock me out on an overseas journey.

In my little bag you would also find a plastic tube of Dijon mustard, which I used liberally on airline steaks, chicken or sandwiches to make them palatable. In that little pouch is also a collection of mints and packages of nuts distributed to me on previous flights. I use the nuts primarily to pep up a salad and an unappetizing looking chicken dish.

You should see the looks of the stewardess when she served a piece of nondescript meat and passed a few moments later to notice it is now adorned by a liberal squirt of something. One stewardess asked me how it got on my meal, as though catering had made a mistake. On many an occasion, I shared my mustard with an envious seat mate.

The other thing I carry is a very thoughtful present my wife once gave me, a miniature fresh pepper grinder, which comes in handy on airline food that needs a pepper upper.

Most of the airline people do a job of heroic proportions. I don't come in contact with the pilots in the front cockpit except hearing their voices occasionally over the loudspeaker, and I wish some of them would spare me from their attempt to earn a mark in history along with Will Rogers and Bob Hope. I really don't want anybody too folksy flying my airplane. I also don't like to see those little wine glasses going into the cockpit while I am on foreign planes.

I had another habit while flying. I happen to be a frustrated singer, a would be tenor who actually enjoys singing and will even do so occasionally in front of friends with whom I feel comfortable. I have a player piano at home with 400 rolls, a microphone and an amplifier, and, for my own amusement, frequently sit at the piano during the evening hours singing away. I probably know the complete score of a half dozen musicals and frequently when I traveled would add a sheet of music to my briefcase, spending a few moments memorizing the words when my work was done or when not doing my reading.

A man studying music on an airplane must appear to people nearby to be a musician. The stewardess would inevitably approach me and inquire about the song I was studying. "Are you a musician?" I would be asked. I answered that I was a "vocalist," which wasn't really an exaggeration although I am not a professional, which I don't explain.

I fudged the situation a little bit when they sought to find out where I sing and with whom. My answer was that I sing with "various groups", not explaining that the groups are generally around my own player piano. Anyway, it was fun, and I got to meet a lot of stewardesses that way.

Anyone who has ever flown extensively has had all kinds of harrowing experiences to relate to the folks back home, and I am no different. I generally was most alarmed flying little puddle jumper trips through mountainous zones. I had my share of trips of that sort, mostly from Aspen to Denver after a skiing trip or in some foreign country like Kenya where the only available transportation was a little plane that looked like it was shot down in World War I. I had moments of apprehension in lightning storms over the Rockies when the shards of lightning seemed to bring an eerie, incandescent glow to the inside of the plane.

On a trip from Chicago to Palm Springs the pilot announced we were going to circle the field because his cockpit lights indicated he couldn't get the landing gears down. I asked the stewardess where we would land if we had to do a belly flop, mindful of the fact my wife was waiting at the Palm Springs airport. She explained to me that the plane would probably go into the Los Angeles airport because they had the best-equipped disaster service. That wasn't reassuring.

A former Air Force flight surgeon sitting next to me, on his way to attend a convention in Palm Springs, instructed me in techniques of crash survival by suggesting that both of us remove our spectacles, sharp objects from our pockets, place a pillow on our laps and lower our heads on to the pillow. I was all set for a crash landing as I could be, but the tower informed the pilot they could see his landing gear; it was down. The pilot landed safely in Palm Springs.

Friends in Honolulu came out en masse and threw a party in the airport restaurant for Sylvia and me as we were departing after a week's stay. Sylvia and I, bedecked with colorful leis, boarded our plane for Los Angeles and Chicago amid fond farewells from our friends, who were going to stay at the party and finish off in our absence.

We were three quarters of an hour out when one engine failed and then the other caught fire. The pilot decided to return to Honolulu, and our friends were amazed when we rejoined the party since they were positive they'd seen our plane take off with us aboard.

On another occasion, again out of Honolulu, we were traveling with another couple. Each couple decided to do some last minute shopping at the airport, promising to meet at the airplane ramp. Our friends got on the plane, and Sylvia and I waited patiently at the wrong ramp through some error in reading the departure information. Our plane and our friends took off without us, and they created quite a scene on the plane, insisting that the captain go back and find out whether we had been visited with a catastrophe while trying to board the plane. They, of course, continued on.

Trying to offset our stupidity, Sylvia and I discovered there was a plane leaving for San Francisco within five minutes and we could get seats. We flew to San Francisco and were able to get an immediate flight to Los Angeles. We met our friends in the Los

Angeles airport while they were waiting for a connecting flight, and our story seemed almost unbelievable to them.

I was waiting for Sylvia at the Savoy Hotel in London, having gone ahead for a few days business. She arrived at the hotel with our youngest son, Richard, a very shaken person. It seems her plane had flown the last two hours with only two engines, and for those hours she felt she was involved in a potential air disaster.

We had an extraordinary experience when Sylvia and I boarded a plane in Los Angeles, which was flying on from Honolulu to Chicago. We boarded the plane in the coach section, and noticed that an elderly gentleman was sitting in the middle seat and looked very gray, ashen and sickly. I commented to Sylvia that the man looked like he might not be able to finish the flight. My remark proved to be a prediction.

We were about a half-hour out and the stewardess was wheeling her cart down the aisle taking drink orders when there was a call for any doctor on board to identify himself. A young man dressed in an Aloha shirt, returning no doubt from a vacation in Hawaii, moved forward to offer his services. We could see the oxygen mask pop down at the seat of the man I noted in boarding the plane. Nothing had ever prepared the stewardess for this kind of contingency. She didn't know whether to continue to serve drinks, behaving normally, or abandon drink service while the emergency was being taken care of.

The young doctor pronounced the man dead within minutes and the attendants placed a blanket over him. Now they had an additional problem. Next to the man was a relative traveling home with him. We later learned that the man was traveling so he could die peacefully at home. But there was a stranger sitting in the next seat, and there were no extra seats anywhere. The attendants didn't know what to do with the body.

A number of passengers began to berate the doctor for bringing a sick man on board. He quickly denied it was his patient and said he was only performing a public service. They also verbally criticized the stewardess, who became very shrill defending the airline, while trying to calm people down and maintaining her composure at the same time. Meanwhile, she completely abandoned drink and food service.

The best flights I have had, of course, are on the private planes of friends who have the good fortune to own privately or where their companies own magnificent jets.

I have flown with Bob Galvin on his Grumman II, and his employees would not recognize the executive who dons a sweater and takes on the role of waiter while in flight, serving libations and dishing up an occasional tasty meal.

It is a lovely plane with accommodations for about 12 people, and Bob's wife Mary has furnished it with impeccable taste, including some beautiful miniature Impressionistic paintings of high quality. You feel like you are in someone's living room, and several of the couches can be utilized for sleeping purposes on long flights.

On one occasion, Bob was flying to Washington, D.C. for a committee meeting and Mary was on her way to New York. They invited Sylvia and me to come along. I had the pleasure of appearing to be the owner of the airplane when I stepped off the ramp first in New York City, with the limousine waiting for us, and it was a momentary heady experience.

I had arranged a business meeting in Delaware between John Rollins and E.F. McDonald, and Rollins sent his Gulf Stream to pick me up in Chicago, and then to Detroit to get MacDonald and bring us on to Delaware. Sylvia accompanied me because we were going to spend a couple of extra days with Rollins and his wife at their home. John, who at one time was lieutenant governor of Delaware, had extensive business interests which included Orkin Co and Rollins Leasing.

Sylvia and I were sitting alone in the plane as it took off from Butler Aviation near O'Hare airport, and I noticed that the plane had a working section with a lovely desk, an executive chair and a telephone on the desk. I asked the stewardess if I could make a telephone call, and she urged me to go ahead. I decided to call my office and tell some of our executives that I was flying overhead in a private plane.

The phone rang in our Chicago office, and I asked our switchboard operator to connect me with our executive vice president. He wasn't in. I then asked for the next two or three people in adjacent offices, and they weren't in. I then told to the switchboard operator: when she asked me if I wanted leave a message, that she should say that I called to check in on things.

"May I ask where you are?" she asked.

"Just tell them I called from an airplane while flying over Chicago," I said.

"Oh, you are always kidding," she replied, and I realized that nobody would know or accept the fact that I was trying to reach them from a private airplane while flying over the office.

PR Minefields

Being an objective counselor is fraught with minefields. The old saw—damned if you do, damned if you don't— applies particularly if you serve the role of the outside honest broker.

It takes courage to deliver an unpopular opinion, even if you know you may be risking your contract with the client.

The CEO of a company is at a loss to find someone completely objective. That is why YPO proved so valuable to many presidents by providing invaluable peer relationships. Occasionally, the executive finds he can talk with his attorney or accountant to get objectivity. The public relations counselor often falls into this role and in that position occasionally walks on eggs.

If you get too close to the boss, the staff may lay for you, jealous of the intimacy and bent on proving the relationship is unwarranted. You have to exercise both agility and charm to develop a relationship with the top man and still maintain good relations with the staff below.

When the outside counselor detects an unhealthy situation, a determination must be made whom to talk to. Your contact or the chief executive?

I was filled with personal anxiety when I broached a very difficult subject with one client. I reported it was becoming obvious to his staff and his board he was traveling with one of his female executives and sharing a room upon arrival. I reported it was not only improper but also contrary to his best interests. He was almost fired by the board for that.

I was summoned for a meeting with a client, who told me his

CEO had had an affair with a daughter in law, had fathered a child, and shortly may be sued. This was a most sensitive public relations problem. I was asked if I could keep it out of the papers. I urged them to settle because I felt certain the story would hit the papers and there was no way I could keep it out. Having been settled, the story never got into the papers.

One of our consultants made the mistake of taking out the secretary of our client. The date turned out disastrously when he made what she considered an improper pass. I was on the receiving end of my client's wrath. She felt I should be responsible for my associate's behavior. The moral here: Find your dates elsewhere.

Occasionally, a peculiarity on the part of the client can cause problems. One accidentally followed our then president, Kal Druck, out of the office and noticed him stopping at several windows as he strolled along. The client felt this indicated dilatory habits and refused to do business with Kal thereafter.

One of our clients was very critical of my handshake and complained about me to one of our executives. He said I had a weak handshake—like a fish, he said. I don't know if he ever shook hands with a fish but my handshake now is very firm.

One of the peculiarities and dangers of our trade was when the client's wife didn't see it in the papers; therefore our publicity program was no good.

Press Agent Stunts

Press agentry is indigenous to the public relations profession. Every day public relations people stretch their imaginations to find different ways to call attention to the opening of a new department store or theater, the introduction of a new product or service, or the initial listing of a stock issue on the NY Stock Exchange

I always stressed to our staff the importance of a basic creative idea to serve as a focal point of a marketing campaign. Capturing the imagination of the press and achieving press coverage is frequently our idea being better than someone else's.

We spent a lot of time thinking up new ways to deliver invitations to press receptions. We tried personalized delivery to the press by models attired in all kinds of outlandish costume; by invitations encased in eye-catching containers, or by teaser campaigns of successive mailings that finally included the actual invitation.

One of the best stunts I ever thought of was hatched while sitting having lunch one day with Ric Riccardo, who founded Riccardo's Restaurant on Rush Street in Chicago. One of our clients at that time was the Martin-Senour Paint Company. I had been searching for a way to show that the company's decorator paints, in thousands of colors, could be used for murals and other fine art. Across the street from Riccardo's, I saw an unadorned wall about eight stories high—remains of a giant building torn down to make way for a parking lot.

I asked Ric if he would cooperate with me in arranging for

the painting of a giant mural done, of course, with Martin-Senour paints. He saw the advantage of having such a mural across from his restaurant and offered to secure the artists and provide free meals to participants. William M. Stuart, president of Martin-Senour, was quite excited about the idea. *Life* magazine was interested. And then we ran into the insurmountable: the cost of the scaffolding needed for about six months of work. It was astronomical and defeated the project.

We couldn't get that one off the ground. Sometimes it's better if some of these ideas die at the source. Example: The public relations department of one of the major advertising agencies arranged for an elephant to be brought into a loop department store to roam around the third floor china shop. An elephant, not the proverbial bull!

A success, except the elephant couldn't be coaxed to leave, reluctant to get on the elevator. An entire third floor window section had to be removed so it could be hoisted down to street level. The ad agency later eliminated its public relations department.

A stunt of ours, which seems to have gone down in PR history (with some distortion), occurred when we were working for the Rival Dog Food Company of Chicago. Every now and then I used to get a call from a zealous writer who heard about the story and asked if I was involved in the stunt and whether I actually ate dog food.

One of our executives observed that the president of the company, to illustrate the palatability of a new all beef dog food meatball, would pop one into his mouth to prove that it was tasty and fit for human consumption. Our man proposed having a press luncheon at which the president and a dog would dine together for the edification of the press.

When he brought the idea to me, I questioned him very carefully whether there was any way to guarantee the dog would eat. He said he had a deal with the trainer to limit the dog's food that morning and indeed we would have a hungry dog on our hands.

With the press assembled and the cameras grinding away,

flashlight bulbs popping, the president picked up a fork and fed himself a beef pellet. The dog turned around and refused to eat, alarmed and excited by the commotion and the flash bulbs. (The trainer, a sympathetic soul, had given his pet a little extra treat that morning.)

The next day's front-page headline of *The Journal of Commerce* was "President Eats Dog Food But Dog Won't". It brought an immediate letter of cancellation of our services. This was not good news but I saw an opportunity to convert a disaster into a merchandising triumph and hastened out to talk to the president.

I told him that the story hit the wire services. He in turn said that the entire food industry was talking about it. I gave him a number of ideas on how we could carry on with a campaign using that misfired press stunt as a springboard. But he had already heard from the chairman of his company who advised him to take a lower profile in the future and fire the public relations firm.

He assured me that had he not had orders from his boss, Nathan Cummings*, he would seriously consider some of my ideas. "You know," he said, "When I walked into the room yesterday at the convention of the dog food manufacturers, everybody stood up and gave me an overwhelming round of applause. That stunt certainly made me well known." *(Founder of Consolidated Foods, changed later to Sara Lee Corp.)*

I would have preferred to have had a successful campaign and retained the client, and I still believe we could have turned the event into something constructive. Anyway, after that, when staffers talked to me about a stunt involving a dog, I passed up the opportunity. And I would like to assure historians of the public relations business that it was not I who thought of this stunt nor ate the dog food.

We had a lot of fun promoting a simple product, an inflatable, large plastic playball previously not on the market but now a staple in every store where playthings are sold. A man named Kip Livingston came to us one day to help him promote an inflatable ball which he had produced out of a plastic solar still for water developed by the military.

During the war, the ball floated in the water and transformed salt water into potable water. By removing the innards, Livingston felt he had a new product he could sell. We ourselves had a ball publicizing the product. We were successful in achieving major coverage because the product lent itself to frolic, fun, beaches and silly cavorting.

Life magazine covers plastic ball frolic.

Stunt at State and Madison.

Olsen and Johnson, the comedians, were appearing at the Shubert Theater in their variety show, "Hellzapoppin," and I convinced them to throw out plastic balls to their audiences during each show. Much to my discomfort, they would introduce me occasionally to the audience as the man with the plastic balls.

We staged a stunt at high noon at the windy corner of Madison and State, allegedly the world's busiest corner, with the cooperation of the police and the *Chicago Daily News*. The paper had a photographer stationed in an upper window at Carson Pierie department store while I drove by in a convertible with several models in bathing suits. I released the balls and the paper got pictures of the models scurrying around recovering them. Some photos showed passersby tossing the balls to the models. The stunt was given extensive coverage in the paper.

We managed to get *Life Magazine* interested in covering a story at the Gaslight Club in Chicago, which showed celebrants having fun with the balls. They ran several pages on the story.

On another occasion I approached *Life* about another product the company had developed, an interlocking plastic block that could be used in building structures, a plaything unknown then. The photo editor of the magazine was intrigued with the product and said he would be interested in the story if we had our client built a miniature city made entirely with plastic blocks. We hired Chloris Leachman, then a Chicago model and later a Hollywood movie star, to pose with the city of miniature blocks. Life ran a full-page spread.

Model Chloris Leachman, later a movie star, poses for Life with plastic block city.

New Business

If you want to have your own firm in the public relations business you need a zest for going after new business both from present clients and from new programs that come from the outside You have to deal with the inflationary factor in doing business, including additional rewards and compensation for the people who make your business successful; and you have to replace a certain amount of business lost for one reason or another, including budget cutbacks, political upheavals in client organizations, completion of projects initiated with a designated time span, and some loss of business because clients take their money and affection elsewhere.

One of the first things I did, a rather daring move considering the fact I had no money, was to hire two salesmen on a modest salary draw and commission basis to prospect for new business on the assumption that there were a lot of firms out there that didn't know much about public relations and had never been called on by a public relations professional. I felt that most PR people were too busy handling whatever work they had to find time to go out and knock on doors.

I hired two men, Fred Stein, an old friend from community newspaper days, and Fred Seaburg, a veteran public relations man along in his years.

In the first year, I invested about $12,000 in this project. We picked up a few accounts that way, including Dreml, a manufacturer of small craftsmen's tools in Racine, Wis. But I came to the conclusion, after about a year, that the man who ran the business had to do the selling. The integrity of an organization had to stand behind every sale. And a professional salesman, I discovered, was only concerned with bringing in new business, not whether we could make a profit nor whether we could actually achieve the objectives involved.

I also realized that only a professional actually working in the public relations field was capable of unearthing the client's needs and matching its fulfillment with services rendered in a responsible way.

Through the years there were many occasions when I went in to talk about one particular potential project and emerged with an entirely different assignment because my professional sense told me what was needed after a discussion with the prospect.

I found that candid and forthright discussions with my friends in a search for leads brought forth a number of prospects. Friends wanted to help and I was delighted and thrilled each time the phone rang and a friend told me he was thinking about me and had a lead on a potential new piece of business. I started a practice of keeping a yellow legal pad on my desk with a list of prospects, both active and long-range, and kept in touch with them virtually every month, either by an occasional telephone call or a reminder that I was still around.

It is an interesting coincidence that when Bill Ruder started his business with David Finn friends and clients would frequently send me copies of his direct mail letters, and I found that he had automated the process and yet kept it personalized, much to my envy. Years later we merged our firms and it didn't matter very much that Bill had done his direct mail better than I thought I had.

I also realized at the time that I had to get involved in the community so that I would be better known and ultimately meet people who might be interested in our services. I felt it was also an obligation on my part to exhibit a sense of responsibility about community activities.

I told Sylvia that, while she had an important role in helping me with the social aspects of our business, which she performed beautifully, I didn't want her to feel she had to pursue friend-ships for business reasons.

I cannot say enough about Sylvia's role in making our staff feel comfortable with her, never exerting power or influence in the office, keeping up warm relationships with present clients, and becoming a well liked and well respected person in the com-munity, working on things she was interested in. At the same time, she kept the family together while I spent much of my time traveling to other cities and countries as our business grew and my presence was needed.

Sylvia participated in many of the trips I had to make. In effect, she was a mother and a wife and a traveling member of the team most of the years of the development of our business.

There were a lot of adventures and misadventures, a lot of successes and failures, in the early years of soliciting new busi-ness.

I recall one day when one of my YPO friends, Elmer Rich, called to tell me that he had learned that his vice president of marketing told him that he was interviewing public relations people. Elmer was president of Simoniz Company, the car wax company. He indicated he may have called me too late and Paul Greenfield, his associate, may have already selected another firm. On the other hand, he felt he could ask Paul to give me an inter-view.

I arranged an appointment with Greenfield. He kept me wait-ing a short while in their reception room and then emerged to escort me to his office. A gray-haired, well-built man, he looked me over carefully as we began our discussion. Finally he said, "I was hoping you turned out to be a p—." He had already made his decision to hire a firm and now his boss wanted him to talk to me.

We got along very well and I could see he was intrigued I was talking marketing lingo and had some fresh ideas. I left his office with the account and he had to notify the other firm he had cho-sen someone else.

Simoniz was a lucky account for us. Through the years I

found that the best lead was one from a satisfied executive who moved on to another assignment. When Bob Shropshire left Simoniz and became marketing vice-president at Nestle, he retained us to do its marketing PR.

Greenfield also sought me out when he left Simoniz to become a partner in the Ed Weiss Advertising Co. The executives who purchased the agency found themselves in a nasty dilemma involving Weiss. Although he had sold the agency, Weiss maintained an office and secretary on the premises, frequently acting as though he was still the owner. His presence became a negative psychological factor and the partners tried to figure out how to ease him out without hurting his feelings and without outside publicity. That's when they approached Mossy Leibman, who in turn said they didn't have a legal problem and he recommended they talk to me.

I found a successful resolution to their problem. One of the ideas I developed was to establish a permanent collection of advertising and marketing books in Ed Weiss's name at the Chicago Public Library. This pleased Ed and paved the way for solutions to other problems.

Carl Singer was president of the national Sealy Mattress franchise, one of our clients. When he moved to become head of Scripto in Memphis, he brought us in, and did likewise when he became president of Renfield, the giant liquor distributors. While at Sealy, he asked me to accompany him on a trip to Tokyo while he negotiated a contract with a Japanese firm. I sat in on the discussions, but my major role was to help select a Tokyo advertising agency for the proposed venture and also to assess market potential.

I had another interesting experience with the Norge Company. I ran into a reporter from the Fairchild publications, who told me that David Kuttner, marketing vice president at Norge, was interviewing PR firms. My friend also admitted that he had heard about this about a week before and felt he might be giving me a late tip. This was about 5:00 p.m., and he happened to know that Kuttner was still at work in his office and supplied me with his direct telephone number.

I called Kuttner immediately. He told me he had already selected another firm, but I talked my way in and he agreed to let me come right over. We talked for a while and were very comfortable with each other, but he told me the other firm had already announced the new client to its staff. But I sensed an opening.

He had made a deal with a public relations firm to start three months hence, but neither he nor the firm had considered the fact that the appliance manufacturers trade show was opening in Chicago in about a month and a considerable amount of public relations activity had to be carried on immediately. I walked away with that assignment. The other public relations firm was not happy about that news.

He was sufficiently impressed with the kind of work we did in that short period of time that he retained us for a full program of public relations for Norge and excused himself out of the other commitment.

We worked through several presidencies at Norge, but with nobody more vivid nor more challenging than Judson Sayre, who came over from his presidency at Bendix to give new leadership to a floundering Norge. There was a bit of salesmanship required on my part in order for us to hang on to the account when Sayre arrived.

I received a telephone call from Sayre's secretary and she set up an appointment at his office. She then called back about an hour before our appointment and asked me to get a *Racing Form* newspaper. Mr. Sayre wanted me to bring it along, she said. I questioned her very carefully, but that's what he wanted. I managed to buy one, my first such purchase in my life, and walked into his office to find him with his feet on his desk, making a bet with one of the innumerable bookies, I found later, with whom he did business all over the country.

"Are you a betting man? he asked while still on the phone with his bookie. I realized that this was the moment for me to show the mettle of the man and admitted that I did occasionally place a bet, although I neglected to add that this occurred about once or twice a year during an outing at the racetrack.

"I have a pretty good parlay," he said. "How much of it do you want?" I gulped once or twice and said, "I'll take half." He laughed because he realized I didn't know he was placing a bet that involved a couple of thousand dollars. He finally let me off the hook with a very nominal amount of money on my part which, incidentally, I lost.

Then Jud Sayre told me that he had an appointment at his dentist and we would talk in a taxi. As we rode across the Loop, he quickly told me that Norge was spending a lot of money with us, that he didn't know what we did, that he didn't have time to find out, and he had made up his mind to fire us.

I made the right guess about Judson Sayre at that moment. He was one of the most capable men in the appliance industry, but his reputation was one of putting people to test however painful it was. Some said Jud Sayre delighted in shoving a hot poker into an unmentionable and painful place. That is what he was doing to me. He looked at me straight in the eye and waited for my answer as we stood at the curb in front of his dentist's office.

"Mr. Sayre," I said, " You didn't get to where you are by firing people without learning whether they deserved to be fired." I then went on to tell him that we absolutely refused to be dismissed without his hearing a presentation of what we had done for Norge, which I felt was considerable, and got him to agree to sit down for a report.

We made the cut and worked together for a number of years until the company was sold to Fedders. He was tough as nails, but our relationship was cordial, friendly and respectful. In fact, I genuinely enjoyed working with him. I must say he didn't put my feet to the fire once after that initial experience. He confided in me and I found him to be an open-minded man.

I had one experience that proved to be a disaster in more ways than one. I had been corresponding with an executive in Ripon, Wis., and one day he invited me to discuss a possible program for a new line of products. I set out in my automobile on a day when the snow began to fall in Chicago, and, by the time I got to Milwaukee, discovered it was just foolhardy to go on.

I slept overnight in Milwaukee and went on to Ripon the next morning, getting there several hours late after having called him to explain the circumstances.

The executive, a genial fellow, offered me a cup of coffee in his office. Then, before we began to talk about the project at hand, he excused himself for a moment. He told me he would be right back. His secretary came in to tell me a half hour later that he had expired in the lavatory and was dead. I took my leave and went back through the snow to Chicago. Nobody else knew why I was there.

On a number occasions, people have asked me what was the single most important activity that took our firm from total billings of $74,000 a year when I took over to more than six million in billings when we merged with Ruder & Finn. The answer is that I pursued every opportunity relentlessly and often carelessly in respect to my own health, endurance and safety.

I came down with pneumonia three times during my career when I neglected to rest and nurse a cold.

The incidence of the last pneumonic episode gets a footnote in my personal history for a special reason. I was on a European trip and kept walking in a cold rain in Geneva, Switzerland, and came home to Chicago with a slight cold. My wife and I returned to Chicago to discover that our youngest son, Richard, picked up a lobar pneumonia while playing freshman football at New Trier High School on a rainy day. He had neglected a cold in our absence.

I sped on to Los Angeles for an important meeting with Mattel. My associate in Los Angeles drove me to our meeting on a cool day in a convertible with a leaky rear window. I felt a sudden chill, and, when I got back to the Beverly Hills Hotel, I realized, having gone through it twice before, I had viral pneumonia.

I went down to the drugstore in the lower reaches of the Beverly Hills Hotel and purchased various supplies. I knew what I would need, including a thermometer, aspirin and other medication. I went to the haberdashery in the building and bought extra pajamas, then raided the bookstore of every book that looked interesting.

I called the hotel engineer and asked him if he would install a television set close to my bed because I told him I was going to be sick and would be too weak to move back and forth adjusting the set. He was curious enough to come up to the room himself. When he saw my appearance, he quickly complied by getting a long television connection and moved the set next to the bed. This was before remote controls.

I then called my high school chum, Dr. Bill Wanamaker, a Beverly Hills internist, and asked him if he would make a hotel call. Shortly after, he came over, and berated me for making a self-diagnosis, and then confirmed that indeed I had pneumonia. "You do the public relations and I'll do the diagnosis! " he shouted.

He told me that there were pretty nurses at Cedar Sinai Hospital, that there were television sets hanging on the wall operated by remote control and that he was going to move me to the hospital immediately.

I demurred because I knew Sylvia would be frantic trying to nurse one case of pneumonia in Chicago while I was ill with another form of the same ailment a couple of thousand miles away. We then conspired to call her and tell her that I had a touch of flu and would stay in bed for a couple of days to nurse myself back to health.

Bill came to the hotel twice a day to nurse me through my illness, and my daughter Betty, then at the University of Arizona in Tucson, came down to take care of her old man. I had a 24 hour nurse and a twice a day doctor.

Betty slept on a cot in my room and attended to me like a registered nurse. I was fortunate to have her at my beck and call especially when I awakened during the night in a cold sweat and my pajamas were soaked with perspiration. Many a night during her stay she produced fresh pajamas for me and wiped the moisture from my torso.

Food was no problem for me. I just couldn't eat during that ordeal. Occasionally Betty would order a refreshing milkshake from the hotel lunch bar. One day she went to visit Farmers Market and brought back a taco, explaining to me that she felt the hot sauce could cure my pneumonia. Taste of all tastes! Never before had I had anything so delicious, a taste experience never again duplicated. The first bite after a fast is a heavenly experience.

I would suspect that the most unusual pursuit of business involved solicitation of the Greek government tourist account. At the time our firm was closely connected with Senator Jacob Javits and through him we were recommended for the account.

I had the feeling that this was one I didn't want to pursue either personally or by our agency, and I insisted we check out the situation with some of our friends in the State Department and some important media people. I was uncertain whether we wanted to be involved in the country's political turmoil. In all instances, we were urged to go ahead, being informed that a relationship with the new Greek government would be consistent with American interests.

We were told that a presentation would have to be made in Athens. I was about to embark on a trip that started out in Paris, then to London, and then to Edinburgh, Scotland. I said I would be willing to make the presentation if I got the call when I was in either Paris or London but I was reluctant to try to get to Athens from Edinburgh, particularly since I was involved in a convention and looked forward to several days of golf on the Glen Eagles golf course.

I was standing in the lobby of an Edinburgh hotel, not the one I was staying in, when the concierge paged me by name about 11:00 p.m. one night, after I had attended a party there. He said he had a call for me from the States. How they ever tracked me down, I never found out, but I had an appointment two days hence in Athens, and the challenge was too much for me.

On the way there, I stopped off in Vienna to attend to a business matter and decided to visit the American Embassy to see if I could get a briefing on the situation in Greece. I was visiting with the commercial attaché, when I inquired about the name of the ambassador in residence. He told me Douglas Mac Arthur II was the new ambassador, having arrived that day. He looked at me in disbelief when I told him that the ambassador was an old friend of mine, and, while I didn't want to interrupt his first day's agenda, I suggested my card be sent up because I felt the ambassador would be disappointed were he to learn my wife and I were in the building and he had not been informed.

Much to the amazement of the attaché, Mac Arthur sent down word that we were to be ushered to his office immediately, and he explained that, while he had appointments pretty well stacked up hour by hour, he did want to greet us.

I told him about my problem, that I was on my way to Athens to solicit the government account, that I was doing so with some misgivings, and, while I was assured by the State Department that it was proper to do so, I wasn't quite sure that our agency should represent the political incumbents.

Douglas Mac Arthur summoned his secretary, told her not to interrupt us, pulled down a map of Europe, and gave us a political briefing on the importance of Greece to American defense interests. He told me it was important to the United States that a firm of our character and integrity handle the account. These were his words. He then proceeded to call the U.S. ambassador in Athens to arrange for a private interview with me.

I proceeded to Athens and checked in at the Royal Bretagne Hotel, where the tourism minister had arranged a reservation for me. I then called the American Embassy for my appointment. Then I went to my appointment with the Greek minister of information.

I confessed to him I was in doubt whether we were the firm for the assignment because I wasn't sure the present Greek administration would live up to its promises to democratize the country. He gave me a briefing on some of the things they had already done and cited examples where they had eliminated millions of dollars of graft and other abuses. I questioned him about their promises of a constitution and a free election and he gave me reassurances.

He then encouraged me to spend as much time as I felt I needed to talk to people, whoever I wished, in Athens. I told him I was going to visit the American ambassador and he replied that he knew all about it, but he didn't tell me how he knew. My assumption later was that phone calls from the Bretagne were carefully monitored.

I made a lot of contacts in Athens and sold myself on the idea that it was appropriate to take on the part of the account that I felt comfortable with. I made a deal that we would work only on the promotion of tourism and not work on political matters, although I realize now that there is a thin line of separation between tourism promotion and public attitudes toward a country's political activities.

One frightening incident occurred while I was having one of my interviews with the minister. We were having a serious conversation when three soldiers burst into the office without announcement. I was frightened out of my wits, but he was quick to reassure me that they were there to move his office. It was less expensive to use the army than to hire a mover, he explained.

We kept the Greek account for nearly five years. We were successful in arranging exposure promoting tourism. We brought over a number of journalists to see for themselves that the country was peaceful and that the Acropolis was still available for inspection. But then a new administration came in and the account went elsewhere.

Our arrangement with the Greek government was that an escrow account was set up at the Chase Manhattan bank in New York to cover our fees and each month we submitted an invoice and it was paid promptly after approval by our client. At the end of our relationship, a very large amount of money was unpaid, requiring my making a special trip to Athens to see if I could collect.

The Minister of Information expressed amazement that our

invoice hadn't been paid and promptly called the disbursement office. He found that the clerk in that department was uncertain how to convert pesos to American dollars and just sat on our bills. He issued an order to have our invoice paid promptly.

How does a service business like a public relations firm grow over the years? Ours grew from new business; expanded programs for clients; diversification into new services, and acquisitions or mergers, plus aggressive merchandising of our services.

As clients understood and appreciated what we could do for them, they were not reluctant to commit more funds to public relations activities, particularly when we were able to develop creative campaigns, which brought in sales.

When we started with Bausch & Lomb, for example, our budget only covered a portion of their needs in public relations. One day Roy Marks, executive vice president of marketing, approached me in the dining area of their Rochester plant.

"I want to tear up our PR contract," he declared, much to my chagrin. "Why?" I exclaimed. "I thought things were going well."

He quickly explained that other divisions of the company, aware of our presence, were demanding service. Not reluctantly, I tore up our original service agreement and cooperated in accepting a budget twice the size.

New business, of course, is the lifeblood of an agency. A turnover of a certain percentage of clients has to be anticipated, although we held many for twenty to twenty-five years.

In order to get new accounts, we had to be alert to opportunities by circulating in the business community; reading the trade and business papers; keeping in touch with a horde of contacts, and constantly giving our firm a high profile. A happy present client is frequently the best source of leads, particularly when friendly executives move on to other companies and recommend your services.

From the start, we carried on a public relations campaign for our firm as though we were a client and assigned a member of our staff to be the account executive on our company program.

We did monthly direct mail, tried advertising, urged our executives to make speeches, turned out publicity on ourselves, and even tried booths at sales promotion and marketing conventions.

I recall manning a booth at the marketing executives convention in Chicago, at which we showed case histories of our work, passed out literature, and displayed our client list. One executive came by and must have admired our initiative. He invited me to call on his company, Noreen, a hair care company in Denver. He was Harry Baum, president of the firm, and we served Noreen for many years.

The most unusual sale I ever made was on a plane ride between Chicago and New York. I deliberately seated myself next to a man who looked like ready money. He wore striped pants and a somber official type jacket, as though dressed for an important occasion.

During the flight I elicited the information that he was Ira Pink, president of Englander Mattress Company, and he said he didn't believe in PR when I told him about my business. He represented a real challenge and gently I tried to change his negative attitude toward PR. By the time I got to my hotel in New York, a message awaited me from Bill Harshe. A call had come in from New York to the Leo Burnett Advertising Agency, from Ira Pink, telling them to hire us for Englander's public relations. "What did you do to Ira Pink?" Bill asked.

The point of these brief accounts is that I spread the gospel wherever I could. I also made cold calls, visiting many business firms throughout Illinois, Wisconsin, Indiana and other states. In the early days, I made a number of sales by being the first public relations man to drop in and tell his story.

Our firm added volume by adding offices. At one time, we also had branches in Los Angeles, New York, Detroit, Memphis, and Rochester, N.Y., in addition to Chicago.

Our first acquisition was Ridings & Ferris, a small Chicago PR firm. It gave us billings, industrial accounts we badly needed, and additions to our staff. It also gave us the Ridings & Ferris affiliate office in New York. Al Gertler, an employee of Ridings &

Ferris, joined our staff at that time. He became president of our company in later years. Ultimately, we placed a full-time man in the Ridings & Ferris New York office and soon opened our own New York office.

Our California office came with the advent of a real estate promotion account. Dan Baer, an employee of ours in Chicago, had moved to California voluntarily to be near his folks who had moved from Chicago. We hired him on a half-time basis to service the real estate account. He went on full-time when we got the Academy account.

Our second acquisition was Manley Markell, a small firm specializing in financial public relations. Both principals, Manley and Mac Markell, came aboard in New York with a small handful of financial accounts. Mac's specialty was cultivating security analysts in secondary financial markets. The merger gave us an expertise and a presence in financial relations.

Leroy J. Bieringer, our executive vice president in Chicago, was transferred to New York to head up our growing operations there. We had a number of accounts in New York. At the time, Hertz was considering whether we were a capable "New York agency," and Mosler was becoming restive. I also had an excellent in at Nestle but needed a New York principal to pull everything together. This was when I sought out Kal Druck about joining our firm.

During the merger negotiations with Ruder & Finn, Lee Bieringer accepted a key position with a St. Louis based public relations firm, as head of their New York office, and liquidated his minority interest. He died in 1984.

We realized some of our clients would need service abroad, and we had no credentials or experience. We acquired a firm called Barnett & Reef, which in turn operated an international partnership called Public Relations International.

Sylvan Barnett and Arthur Reef had a great idea. They traveled the world and developed a network of leading public relations practitioners in most countries of the free world. In order to become part of the network, a practitioner had to buy a nominal amount of stock in PRI.

For a while, they were very successful and had a number of leading companies, including Deere & Co., Westinghouse, Goodyear and others. They earned commissions on all sales, but the business began to collapse when some of their partners decided to bypass PRI and serve some of the accounts directly. Some clients initiated the arrangement because they wanted to do foreign travel, or whatever. Barnett & Reef had no contracts which forbade their partners from directly serving the accounts, and this loophole killed their idea.

By the time they came to us, they were badly in need of capital and were down to a few accounts. We came to the conclusion the nominal price we paid was worth the international experience, the few international accounts and the list of qualified affiliates. Both Barnett & Reef joined our firm and ultimately left to take on key positions in industry.

During later years, as I traveled the world on business, I contacted PRI affiliates in Scandinavia, Europe, Britain, Latin America and Japan. We culled the list down to about a dozen and developed our own network of about a dozen "exclusive affiliates" at the time of the Ruder & Finn merger.

Marketing Slogans

I always felt simple slogans were the ultimate binding element in a public relations campaign in support of marketing. We strove to develop basic concepts in a slogan that was the cornerstone of a campaign. For example:

For the National Bowling Proprietors' Association we created the "Bowl Down Cancer" promotion, which was a public relations parlay providing benefits for a number of parties.

I felt we started a new concept in the campaign for the bowling association. Since our client did not plan to spend large amounts of money for advertising, we went to Wheaties and convinced them to advertise our campaign on their millions of boxes. In addition, they supported the campaign with several hundred thousand dollars of advertising. In return, the bowling association permitted them to offer a free game with every two games bought.

In effect this didn't cost the bowling proprietors anything. They got extra business and recouped cost of the promotion with the two games bought plus profits from shoe rental and other purchased items. "Bowl Down Cancer" virtually had a life of its own and went on for years.

Our slogan, "We're Glad Your Here," created for the members of the National Restaurant Association, was the anchor of a nation-wide campaign addressing a basic need of restaurateurs to create an aura of hospitality in food service places. I was quite pleased with our "Glad Your Here" program for the restaurant association. They were looking for a means of stimulating cordiality in food service places, at the same time encouraging employees to participate in such a program.

Our staff came up with the "Glad Your Here" concept. The scheme was simple provided employees cooperated. The slogan appeared on badges worn by staff; on table tents; in some cases on banners in the establishment, and on display at cash registers where payment is made.

We devised various prize contests for employees, both in the front and back rooms of establishments.

We made an arrangement with a printing firm to offer for sale the various promotional items needed by dining establishments. In the first year, most of the costs of the promotion were recouped by NRA on a shared—profit arrangement with the fulfillment house. I was pleased so many years after we developed the theme, to see airport signs in Chicago proclaiming "We're Glad You're Here."

One of our clients was A.B. Dick & Co., a family owned business specializing in duplicating equipment. When a new CEO came on board, we had our first meeting. I made a suggestion that seemed to startle him. I told him I was aware they had a meager advertising budget compared to most of the competition and suggested they pool all their funds into a sales promotion effort, possibly tying into a sports activity.

The result was that the company went into racing and, with our help, acquired several racing cars bearing their logo. Sales promotion contests were held; tickets to races were passed out by distributors; groups of customers were taken to the races, and the cars were exhibited in distributor parking lots. The company distributed T-shirts, jackets and hats advertising the racing promotion. Their advertising and point of sale pieces featured the racing cars. The company was now creating a lot of excitement with the same advertising dollar among their marketing organization and customers.

One of the reasons our agency grew at such a rapid pace in the early years was that I could see our competitors were concentrating on corporate public relations, neglecting the

importance of public relations in support of marketing. I began
to speak on importance of the bottom line, using the example of
a marketing program supported by a three legged stool, one leg
representing advertising, a second point of sale or direct mail
techniques and the third being public relations.

My feeling all along was that PR had a number of significant
traits:

a. It gave reach to an advertising program particularly by
reaching publications where the advertising dollar
wasn't spent.

b. PR was a device for urging supermarkets to get behind a
product and provide shelf space.

c. PR was a means of whipping up extra efforts in the
marketing organization by illustrating additional exposure support afforded by publicity.

d. A good local PR program involving a company spokesper-
son appearing on radio and TV and in the print publications served to provide enthusiasm in a market and
precondition the public for the advent of advertising and
sales promotion.

Silver Anvils

Among the various awards given to our firm through the years were the following Silver Anvils awarded by the Public Relations Society of America. The Anvils are the public relations industry equivalent of the Academy Awards. The awards and categories are as follows:

US Department of Housing and Urban Development. Community. Government

International Telephone & Telegraph—Institutional. Business

Monument Builders of North America—Institutional. Trade Association

N.Y. County Lawyers Association—Institutional. Non-profit

Aerosol Packaging Council—Promotional. Trade Association

Shinade Toys Div. of Operation—Bootstrap—Promotional. Non-Profit

Toy Manufacturers of America—Public Service-. Trade Association

U.S. Office of Education, Department of Health, Education & Welfare

Public Service. Government. With David Apter Associates

Memphis Area Chamber of Commerce—Public Service—Association

National Coffee Association-Consumer Relations

Mattel Inc.-Consumer Relations

U.S. Independent Telephone Association-Institutional. Business Association

Short Strokes

Edie McWilliams, the seminude "Vixen" of Russ Meyer film fame, noticing that Groucho Marx sat alone near the buffet at a party at The Bistro, momentarily abandoned by his companion, Erin, left our table and went over to say hello to Groucho. I had assured her Groucho wouldn't mind. "Oh, Mr. Marx," she gushed," Can I get you anything? I have always loved you." "Yes," he quickly replied. "Get me an erection." (This was before Viagra.) She came back to our table somewhat flustered. Apparently, she only gets flustered when she has clothes on. Groucho was always irrepressible. I once suggested to the Motion Picture Academy that Groucho be utilized as master of ceremonies at the Awards. They never asked him because they were afraid of what he might say unexpectedly into an open mike.

*   *   *

I was retained to develop a marketing plan for the new downtown revitalization of Cathedral City, Ca. Among the other suggestions I made, I said the name Midway might be one of the many acceptable names for a downtown location midway between Palm Springs and Palm Desert. One of the city councilmen rejected the suggestion by shouting "Midway? Everybody hates Bull Halsey!" He was still fighting the World War 11 Battle of Midway. Incidentally, I discovered later that part of Cathedral City was once called Midway. Fleet Admiral William (Bull) Frederick Halsey Jr. led the fleet in the decisive battle of World

War 11 that ended the advance of the Japanese in the Pacific. The US fleet demonstrated that bombers launched from aircraft could defeat a superior surface force.

*   *   *

The operating manager of the San Ysidro guest ranch of Monticeto, Cal., where for a time I was an investor along with Sidney Poitier, was telling me about the installation of jacuzzis on the patio of each cottage suite. I asked him how the jacuzzis were being accepted. "Hollywood directors and their script girls", he said, "spend a weekend here in isolation, ordering all their food via room service, and seem to use the jacuzzis an awful lot." The only problem, he added, was that he wondered where to find a semen extractor. Call the CSI!

*   *   *

I went to see one of Chicago's premiere personal injury lawyers, Paul Episcope, about my infection from a Stone Fish during a Spice Island cruise near Bali. He listened patiently to my account. I wondered about the cruise line's liability, which he dismissed. He inquired, "Then who you going to sue? The fish?"

*   *   *

We were asked to announce a new rectal thermometer produced by our client, Taylor Instruments of Rochester, NY. One of our executives, the late Bob Salins, privately suggested a theme for the campaign. "If you don't like our thermometer, you know what you can do with it."

*   *   *

Hollywood press agent, the late Henry Rogers, invited me to go to a fancy party honoring Audrey Hepburn, a client of his, in honor of the opening of "My Fair Lady," in which she starred. I protested I didn't have a tux with me although I did have a dark suit. We went to Kresge and found a cheap, black bow tie for a dollar. Hepburn was most cordial and invited us to sit at her table, cheap bow tie and all.

*   *   *

Norma Shearer, old-time famous movie actress, who stayed at the Beverly Hills hotel, sought me out at the pool. "You must come up to my suite," she urged. She wanted my opinion on the first sculpture version of the Irving Thalberg award in honor of her late husband, an award that would be given at the Academy Awards. As I marched with her to her suite I could almost feel my stock go up with the regulars at the pool.

*   *   *

I was standing at the ballroom entrance where former Illinois Sen. Chuck Percy was being honored. Former Pres. Gerald Ford arrived a few minutes late. We momentarily chatted. "Mr. Ford," I said. "You and I see each other frequently." He inquired where and I explained he and I share the same barber at Tamarisk country club in Rancho Mirage, Ca., near where both the Fords and the Rotmans reside. "Oh", he said, "You use Aldo (the barber), too. Isn't that wife of his a pistol?" We chatted for about two minutes about our common interest. Later, a *Chicago Tribune* reporter I knew asked me what Ford and I were talking about. I explained we were covering the Middle East situation. I didn't tell him we had talked about Aldo and his then wife, Barbara, who was a bountiful source of information about good restaurants in Palm Springs.

*   *   *

When Sylvia and I were in the early stages of our marriage and our first child (Betty, our first anniversary present) was on the way, I sought extra work because we could no longer count on Sylvia's modest salary as a secretary. I got an evening job editing a six-page newsletter for the Central YMCA in Chicago. The previous editor had taken all week to do it. I proceeded to clean it up and do a faster job of reporting and writing. I got all kinds of compliments on the improvement. Soon I discovered that, with my City News writing experience, I could do the whole publication in two evenings. Augie Bonhivert, the executive secretary and my boss, called me in one day and fired me. "Why?" I asked. "I thought you liked it." He explained that I had improved the publication but I didn't take enough time doing it. Augie later came to me for a job when I was running our PR agency. He didn't get hired.

*   *   *

I lost my way driving alone in a car on my way to our Rochester, N.Y. office. No gas stations on the small road I had blundered onto. And no people to ask except for one man on a ladder painting a part of his house. I shouted for directions. "One moment," he said, as he came down the ladder. I told him I didn't want to disturb him and apologized. But he went into his house for a map, which he then spread on my car. "A guy once gave me wrong route instructions," he explained when he returned. " I drove 100 miles out of my way. Know what I did? I went back, found him and beat the s— out of him."

*   *   *

Jerome (Jerry) Stone is former chairman of Stone Container Corp., and fundraiser extraordinaire for many causes. Jerry has an insouciant way of extracting big sums from people for worthy causes, and can also carry the crown of Punster ad Nauseum. Jerry's late wife was afflicted with Alzheimer's at an early age and, after she died, he founded the Alzheimer's Association. At one time Jerry was chairman of Roosevelt University in Chicago. The university, situated in what was formerly a hotel, decided to remodel and downsize former hotel suites. One dean came to Jerry to ask if he would be losing his private toilet. Jerry said, "We'll try not to discommode you."

*   *   *

Lawyer Don Reuben, now living in Rancho Mirage, Ca., who has an unusual kinship with his dogs, was told he couldn't bring his dog, Portia, with him into a condo apartment he was buying on Chicago's Magnificent Mile. Don avoided the rule by registering the ownership deed in the name of his dog. How can you ban a lawful owner? Others in the building followed suit when they heard what Reuben had done. The developers weren't happy about Don.

*   *   *

Earle Ferris, our New York affiliate in the early days of our PR firm, had a service through which he would wire short anecdotes to be reprinted in newspaper columns in the name of performers. He hired a nerdy looking guy to freelance the gags. The latter would show up every Saturday morning and drop off a sheaf of material. I saw him do this once. He would make his delivery and depart without a word. He was paid $200 a month. We should have signed him to a long-term contract. His name was Woody Allen.

*   *   *

Granddaughter Betsy to grandmother Sylvia: "Grandma, were you ever so angry at grandpa that you wanted to hit him?"

Grandma Sylvia: "No, but several times I wanted to kill him."

*   *   *

He churned the water in the lap pool every morning for his daily exercise. He then stepped into the nearby hot Jacuzzi to relax and warm his body. He was resting with his eyes closed when he heard a voice: "May I join you?" A lovely young lady with long black hair stood at the edge of the Jacuzzi. He looked up and invited her to join him and, at that, she shed her white robe, standing completely nude before him. She stepped into the water as he wondered whether his wife unexpectedly would show up and what would the neighbors think. They had a brief conversation during which he learned she was from Scandinavia visiting relatives in the same development. Soon as she departed, guess what he did? Wrong! He rushed to a phone and called the chairman of the house rules committee to inquire about the dress code at the jacuzzis.

In Retrospect

I had one of the best careers you could possibly imagine. I could identify with Ben Bradley, the former executive editor of the *Washington Post*, who entitled his book," A Good Life," because a friend said, "Ben, you had a good life." And so did I. I started with nothing. No family background, not enough education and built one of the most significant public relations organizations in the U.S. if not the world.

I was also fortunate I developed an aptitude for journalism early as high school and rose rapidly to positions of responsibility as a reporter, rewrite man and editor before moving on to public relations. I must admit I had the time of my life in journalism with many exciting experiences but soon realized my eyes were on a career in public relations.

As I finish this book, I can count my blessings, and there are many, not the least of which is a wonderful wife still at my side after 58 years of marriage despite a six-week courtship. We survived against the odds that our short relationship would not prove to be permanent and fruitful, producing three devoted children and four equally devoted grandchildren plus two step grandchildren through Richard's marriage to Gloria.

My blessings include that I survived a near fatal infection, which incapacitated me for several years, at one time confining me to a wheelchair for a year. There were dire predictions about death and amputation but I couldn't let that happen to me and survived with the nurturing assistance of a live-in nurse, Sylvia.

I walk well now, no longer using a cane, after an hour every morning working out at a gym with weekly ministrations from professional trainers. When I started my workouts six years ago, I came to the gym with the assistance of a walker and couldn't walk unassisted.

The unexpected vicissitude threw my life into a tailspin. No more tennis, which I loved, and no more three games a week with my golf buddies. And no more teaching at the college. The positive part is that I had to think through my life and values. It forced me to "repot" myself, as the expression goes, and I had to seek new rewards including the writing of this book, the adventures provided by the fathomless world of the computer, and the opportunity to spend more time enjoying the companionship of Sylvia.

I give thanks to my daughter Betty for having the wisdom to urge her father to forego his incapacitating depression and start writing again. This book is the result. Like the sorcerer's apprentice, I just kept writing. There wasn't much more I could do.

It's been said a man is lucky if he has one good friend. I had a handful. I've written about them in this book. One of the closest, Bob Dickerman, unfortunately did not survive. Also, most recently, Mike Mater, a very special man.

Along the way, I was fortunate a number of people helped me acquire presence, polish and poise sufficient to be able to function in the competitive arena of the business world. Bill Stuart gave me the first hint of my personal obligation when he speculated whether I could function in the New York arena and at his marketing conventions.

When I was involved in covering the news, I doubt I owned a suit. I did my work in slacks, a shirt and occasionally a sweater. When the Community and War Fund hired me, I visited Bond Clothes and bought a herringbone suit, which came with two pairs of pants. When Sylvia and I were about to married, she urged me to get rid of the ill-fitting garment and paid for my first bespoke suit, a handsome gray flannel.

A wonderful couple I met while publicizing the Bismarck hotel was Pat and Charles Reader. She was a singer appearing in the Walnut Room, an attractive lady with great style and voice and an ample wardrobe to match. Charles was the entertainment director of the Pierre hotel in New York. As our friendship flourished, they took me in hand. . One day they escorted me to a shirt maker on Madison Avenue in New York. Charles said it didn't matter whether I owned only one suit but it was very important for me to have good ties and shirts with cufflink sleeves. In our business, behind my back, I became known as "Cufflink Morry," as I passed on this trait to our staff.

Another person who became a strong influence in my life was Barry Levinson, agent and television producer, who taught me something with his engaging charm and infectious sense of humor. He also taught me about lightness of spirit and generosity. Liv Ulman once told me that she talked to Barry every day of her life. Susannah York told me Barry always seemed to be part of her life. As he was mine. Unfortunately he succumbed while on a business trip to the Middle East.

I find myself inadequate to express sufficiently my gratitude to my two sons for continuing to encourage and assist me when the going was rough during the past six years.

The mosaic of my life has a big piece in it with the name Isaac Gershman, my former boss at the City News Bureau, who gave me by big break in journalism, and then became a surrogate father, advising Sylvia and me every step of the way.

My blessings should include the fact, despite only a year and a half in a junior college, I was able to become an adjunct professor, teaching communications at the College of the Desert in Palm Desert; that my advice and counsel was sought by the heads of many of America's leading corporations, and that I number among my friends musicians, writers, actors, politicians, scientists, business leaders, artists and others in all walks of life in many parts of the world.

I have always believed that I should serve my community, nation, and faith. I gave ten percent of my time over 20 years to the Rehabilitation Institute of Chicago; received the Prime Minister's Medal from Israel for my efforts in selling Israel Bonds;

served as a trustee of Roosevelt university; a director of Alzheimer's Association, and the National Association for the Prevention of Child Abuse. I am now a Life Director of the Rehabilitation Institute and an honorary trustee of Roosevelt. When Sam Wanamaker launched his effort to build a replica of the original Shakespeare Globe Theater on the Thames in London, I did what I could to help him. Sylvia and I have our names on a flagstone in the theater's courtyard.

My membership in the Young Presidents organization and its successor senior organizations brought many blessings to Sylvia and me and our children—friendships throughout the world, an extraordinary opportunity for all of us to participate in the learning experience provided by YPO, an opportunity to travel the world, and learn many things, including business procedures. In effect, to me YPO provided a post graduate education in business which was crucial to me as I began to develop my public relations firm. .

It was a good life indeed and I have many blessings to reflect upon.

Collected Letters

UNITED STATES DELEGATION TO THE
GENERAL ASSEMBLY OF THE UNITED NATIONS

October 31, 1947

Dear Bill:

Thanks for your letter of October 29. I have just
told Mrs. Wright, by telephone, that General Marshall has
tentatively agreed to come to Chicago to speak on the 18th
of November, the day after Congress convenes and two days
before he leaves for England. However he has to clear the
date in Washington and it is not yet firm. I have advised
Mrs. Wright and suggested that the sponsors be the Council
and the Association of Commerce, jointly. The radio arrangements will be worked out from Washington.

I will collaborate with Bill Stoneman in connection
with the visit of the students and will arrange for Mrs.
Mrs. Roosevelt and Senator Austin or someone to meet them
but I cannot guarantee a Russian. Unhappily General Marshall
will be spending his time in Washington now and I am afraid
there is little chance of his being here while the students
are here.

I note what you say about looking after the Secretary's
press arrangements during the few hours he is in Chicago and
I will mention that to his staff, but I doubt if he will care
to have any press conference before the speech and will
fly back to Washington at dawn the following morning.

Forgive this hastily written letter. I am, as always,
on the run.

Sincerely yours,

Adlai E. Stevenson

Mr. William R. Harshe,

8 South Dearborn Street,

Chicago 3, Illinois.

ART BUCHWALD

2000 PENNSYLVANIA AVENUE, N.W.
SUITE 3804
WASHINGTON, D.C. 20006

TELEPHONE
393-6680

January 28, 1986

This is to testify that I have known
Morry Rotman for 60 years. We first met
when he was a left tackle and I was quarter-
back for the old Chicago Bears. Morry blocked
for me and I doubt if I could have achieved
the NFL record of 2,000 yards in one season
if it hadn't been for, what we liked to call
in those days, "The Icebox."

Morry was a most generous man and shared
all his women with me. And then there was
that time in Las Vegas--but why go on?

Let's say that if it had not been for
Morry Rotman, I would have never put my life's
savings in the Penn Square Bank.

Sincerely,

Art Buchwald

Art Buchwald

ISAMU NOGUCHI   33-38 10TH ST   LONG ISLAND CITY   NEW YORK   TEL LR5-0042

March 31, 1968

Mr. Morris B. Rotman, Chairman
Harshe-Rotman & Druck Inc.
108 North State Street
Chicago, Illinois   60602

Dear Mr. Rotman:

Forgive me for my delay in answering your letter of March 5th.

Your telling me about so interesting a client as you describe
is intriguing. I would like to know more about him.

However, to give any breakdown of costs would be very difficult
even that of average costs since this all depends upon the
complexity of the problem, the size and where it is done.
However, gardens are necessarily expensive though not in the
same class as a building. Generally speaking, I have worked
with architects and I think this is probably the best approach
so that the creative design would be mine but the execution
could be handled by an architect or a architectural firm..

Please let me know further what you have in mind.

Sincerely,

Isamu Noguchi

IN:j

State of West Virginia
Governor's Mansion
Charleston 25311

February 16, 1981

Dear Mory:

Thank you very much for your recent letter.

I appreciate Mrs. Mirisch's interest in Jay, but I must quickly disabuse her of any plans that Jay would have for running for president. The proposed Reagan budget cuts will hurt West Virginia very deeply, and Jay will have his hands full just being a good Governor for the next four years. He really has no intentions whatsoever of seeking higher national office in the near future.

I appreciate your contacting me and conveying this message back to Mrs. Mirisch. Jay was flattered by her interest and hopes that she understands that mere survival is the name of the game for Democrats now!

Sincerely,

Sharon

Sharon P. Rockefeller

Mr. Morris B. Rotman
Harshe-Rotman & Druck, Inc.
444 N. Michigan Avenue
Chicago, Illinois 60611

EMERGENCY COMMITTEE *of* ATOMIC SCIENTISTS
INCORPORATED
ROOM 28, 90 NASSAU STREET
PRINCETON, NEW JERSEY

January 18, 1947

Dear Rabbi Weinstein:

A group of our friends in Chicago have arranged for a luncheon and afternoon meeting for Saturday, February 8th, at which the issues which made necessary the organization of this Committee will be discussed. I, myself, shall be unable to attend but Dr. Harold C. Urey and my other colleagues will be present to speak together with our good friend, John Hersey.

I have regretted that you were unable to attend our meeting in Princeton at which our campaign for public support was initiated and I have, therefore, suggested to our Chicago friends that they invite you.

You will no doubt receive an invitation from the Chicago group within the next few days. I hope that you will be able to attend.

Faithfully yours,

A. Einstein.

Rabbi Jacob J. Weinstein
920 East 50th Street
Chicago, Illinois

AE:eh

3 P on "Dilemma of Liberals"

A Letter Found While Doing PR For KAM Temple.

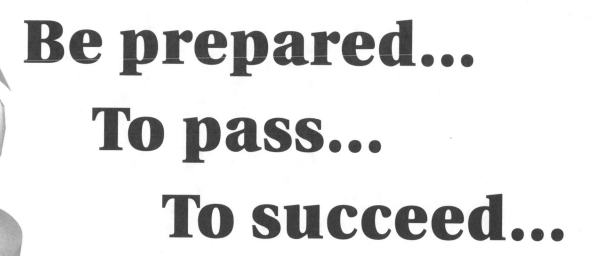